Radical Economics

Recent Economic Thought Series

Editor:

Warren G. Samuels
Michigan State University
East Lansing, Michigan, U.S.A.

Other books in the series:

Feiwel, G., *Samuelson and Neoclassical Economics*
Wade, L., *Political Economy: Modern Views*
Zimbalist, A., *Comparative Economic Systems: Recent Views*
Darity, W., *Labor Economics: Modern Views*
Jarsulic, M., *Money and Macro Policy*
Samuelson, L., *Microeconomic Theory*
Bromley, D., *Natural Resource Economics: Policy Problems and Contemporary Analysis*
Mirowski, P., *The Reconstruction of Economic Theory*
Field, A., *The Future of Economic History*
Lowry, S., *Pre-Classical Economic Thought*
Officer, L., *International Economics*
Asimakopulos, A., *Theories of Income Distribution*
Earl, P., *Psychological Economics; Development, Tensions, Prospects*
Thweatt, W., *Classical Political Economy*
Peterson, W., Market Power and the Economy
DeGregori, T., *Development Economics*
Nowotny, K., *Public Utility Regulation*
Horowitz, I., *Decision Theory*
Mercuro, N., *Law and Economics*
Hennings, K. and Samuels, W., *Neoclassical Economic Theory, 1870 to 1930*
Samuels, W., *Economics as Discourse*
Lutz, M., *Social Economics*
Weimer, D., *Policy Analysis and Economics*

This series is devoted to works that present divergent views on the development, prospects, and tensions within some important research areas of international economic thought. Among the fields covered are macromonetary policy, public finance, labor and political economy. The emphasis of the series is on providing a critical, constructive view of each of these fields, as well as a forum through which leading scholars of international reputation may voice their perspectives on important related issues. Each volume in the series will be self-contained; together these volumes will provide dramatic evidence of the variety of economic thought within the scholarly community.

Radical Economics

edited by

Bruce Roberts
College of William & Mary

and

Susan Feiner
Hampton University

Kluwer Academic Publishers
Boston / Dordrecht / London

Distributors for North America:
Kluwer Academic Publishers
101 Philip Drive
Assinippi Park
Norwell, Massachusetts 02061 USA

Distributors for all other countries:
Kluwer Academic Publishers Group
Distribution Centre
Post Office Box 322
3300 AH Dordrecht, THE NETHERLANDS

Library of Congress Cataloging-in-Publication Data

Radical economics / edited by Bruce Roberts and Susan Feiner.
p. cm. — (Recent economic thought series)
Includes bibliographical references and index.
ISBN 0-7923-9178-0
1. Radical economics. I. Roberts, Bruce, 1948- . II. Feiner, Susan. III. Series.
HB97.7.R32 1991
330.15—dc20 91-31511
CIP

Printed on acid-free paper.

Printed in the United States of America

CONTENTS

Radical Economics

INTRODUCTION: CURRENT CONTROVERSIES IN RADICAL ECONOMICS

Bruce Roberts and Susan Feiner

Radical economics is a long and vibrant tradition, at once both analytical and, explicitly or implicitly, moral and political. It is home to Marxism in its many variant forms, but also to perspectives thoroughly critical of virtually every tenet of Marxian method and analysis. Radicals typically share a commitment to a broadly socialist critique of capitalism, yet more often than not they are unable to agree on the precise nature of the problems associated with capitalism, the core aspects of capitalism which give rise to these problems, or the form which a socialist society should take in order to present an alternative which is both viable and desirable. Radical economics opposes the orthodox tradition in economics in many ways, on many levels—indeed, radicals have presented devastating analytical, methodological and empirical critiques of neoclassical orthodoxy—yet radical economics continues to be shaped in part by that orthodox tradition and its canons of scientificity, responding to its criticisms, policies and interpretations, and borrowing from its intellectual trends. As a result, while radical economics is today more alive with new developments and approaches than at any time since the 1960s, the radical tradition now faces a number of serious challenges, due in part to recent world events but even more to the widespread perception of those events as a validation of the inherent superiority of capitalism and the "common sense" of traditional theory.

The goal of this volume is to present varying assessments of the current state of radical economic research. Inevitably that means confronting controversy, and while of course not every radical perspective is represented among the contributors, the pairs of essays and commentaries presented here certainly touch on—and exemplify—issues of controversy. Of course, where there is controversy there is necessarily a dispersion of viewpoints, and radical economics at present is clearly marked by fragmentation and experimentation. In part, the causes of this are internal to the discipline, a reflection of the multitude of different theoretical and political influences at work, and the different choices concerning priorities for analysis made by radicals in response. But in part, the causes are external and dispersion the result produced within a discipline which both is and feels challenged. And after a decade of references to the "crisis of Marxism," with conservative political forces seemingly ascendant worldwide, at a time when a leading spokesman for the right-wing of the orthodox economics profession can refer to the coming "post-socialist century,"[1] the challenge is clear.

Defining what is meant by radical economics is no easy task. At the most general level, the term "radical" is a political label defined as counterpoint to equally amorphous terms like "liberal" and "conservative." When applied to economics, the result cuts across the grain of normal academic parlance. Radical economics is not a "field" defined by particular subject matter in the traditional academic sense—radicals work in all fields within economics and typically trespass freely across the boundaries between them and between economics and other academic disciplines. Equally, radical economics is not an "approach," at least not in any singular sense—the differences among radicals in terms of analytical style and method are at least as great as the similarities.

What, then, are the unifying features of radical economics? First, as befits a group which as often as not refers to its labors as "political economy," radicals share certain general political commitments and allegiances. Radicals are critical of capitalism as an economic system and its consequences and conditions in other social sites outside the narrowly economic sphere—household, state, academia, and so on. They are typically proponents of socialism in some form, though as a result often critical as well of socialist institutions like those of the former Soviet system. The specific political allegiances of radicals are, however, as diverse as the many political movements which have been influential in defining the tradition. Since the 1960s and the impact of the New Left, civil rights and anti-war movements, currents from feminism, ecology, and various national liberation struggles have mixed with those from labor and (at least outside the U.S.) left political parties to shape the agenda for economic analysis. And while there is hardly anything like a common political platform, there are shared, broadly normative values: radical economists favor social and particularly economic change, by the subtraction of structures and institutions promoting exploitation, oppression, domination, alienation, and militarism, and by the addition of those engendering empowerment, autonomy, fairness, participation, and ecological balance.

Second, radical economists share certain theoretical commitments, though these are in practice difficult to specify except in general terms. The theoretical assumptions, strategies and priorities of the mainstream neoclassical/Keynesian tradition are to at least some degree targets of criticism for all radical economists, just as all express some degree of indebtedness to Marx and various Marxian traditions. Thus, for example, radical economists stress the social differentiations and distinctions which unite as well as divide us—class, race, and gender, in particular—rather than the universal symmetry of individuals as choosers. Radical analyses are frequently historical, meaning by that not only chronological or concrete conjunctural studies but a more general stress on *process*, on conflict and qualitative change, as opposed to a totalizing focus on stability or equilibrium. And radicals generally display a keen sensitivity to the roles played by ideology, interests and power, both within society and within economic theory, thus rejecting the positivist belief in a value-free economic science as itself supportive of the social and intellectual status quo.[2]

Third, in part implied by the previous points, radical economists are united by the oppositional nature of their project. To be a radical is to be an "outsider" in the economics profession and thus, almost automatically, to be a critic—of society and of the common sense of received economic theory. As is often the case, the discourse which is on the outside is compelled to defend its existence and legitimacy in the face of orthodoxy's asserted monopoly on the "real" questions and answers. This helps to explain why interest in the history of economic thought and issues of epistemology and methodology is so common among radicals (and so unusual among mainstream economists). True, methodological discussions are viewed by some, inside as well as outside the radical tradition, as peripheral to the important tasks of social analysis and prescription, but this is arguably a shortsighted view. Judged in a broader context, issues of methodology, of scientificity, are central because they go to the heart of struggles over the identity of radical economics as a critical discourse.

If these are among the features uniting radical economists, they are also often precisely the issues of contention among them. Political values, basic theoretical concepts and tools, and the methodology of critical analysis are perennial subjects of explicit or implicit debate. For example, the major transformations in eastern Europe and the Soviet Union occurred too recently to be incorporated into the plan for this volume, but it is already possible to see in the spate of analytic and sometimes confessional discussions of "democracy" the beginnings of a transformed debate over the political values of core importance to radicals.

As an example of a more well-developed theme of radical controversy, consider an interesting methodological convergence. In recent years, one of the most striking points of agreement among radicals of almost every stripe is the importance of rejecting reductionist, and particularly economistic, modes of reasoning. A number of different trends seem to have reinforced each other in producing this consensus, among them the analytic and predictive failures of past varieties of totalizing theory, a greater awareness of critical philosophical literatures on science and method, and the tactical need for theories capable of appealing to groups with diverse interests and priorities. Yet beneath the superficial agreement, what is most apparent is a thoroughgoing lack of consensus as to just what a non-reductionist analysis should seek to accomplish and how it should proceed. In the name of avoiding simplistic reductionism, some reaffirm the critical epistemology of Marxism, while others dismiss Marxist reductionism as the source of the problem; some celebrate the richness and rigor of econometric studies, while others criticize the very foundations of empiricism; some seek to further broaden economic analysis by explicitly incorporating political and cultural processes, while others stress the virtue of specifically economic concepts and tools in confronting economic questions. This lack of methodological consensus is apparent in the dialogue between several of the essayists and commentators in this volume.

Related controversies appear as well, particularly those involving the long-simmering tension between Marxian and non-Marxian radical traditions. The reported "death" of Marxism has been greatly exaggerated, but the role of basic Marxian concepts—value, exploitation, imperialism, and so on—their form, and for some their continued meaningfulness in any form, is very much at issue. Should one work within a perhaps revised but still avowedly Marxian problematic, or should one instead pick and choose among Marxian concepts and propositions, keeping only those which appeal on grounds of "rigor," empirical support, or consistency with other frameworks? Both approaches have active supporters.

Curiously, a similar if almost inverse debate has developed over the role, if any, for certain characteristic traits of neoclassical thinking, particularly the premise of rationality and models of constrained optimization. While no one advocates wholesale acceptance of the logic of the traditional enemy, many are increasingly unwilling to settle for ritual denouncements of all things neoclassical as ideological and thus worthless. But to what extent are neoclassical modes of analysis portable "tools" which can be selectively carried over into a radical framework? How is that framework itself transformed in the process? The virtues of such importation, to proponents, are analytical rigor and an expanded "microfoundational" scope; the danger stressed by critics lies in an eclecticism that adds up to less rather than more and remains radical only in its normative commitments. Still, interest in mathematizing and scientizing radical theory has made experiments of this sort more and more common, and several of the essays and comments deal with the resulting challenges and dilemmas.

In the first of the essays that follow, the diversity of basic radical approaches is surveyed by Stephen Resnick and Richard Wolff. They present a two-dimensional taxonomic scheme in which theories can be distinguished and classified according to their respective "entry points" and "logics." The choice of entry point is a choice as to the theory's organizational "focus": out of the welter of mutually interacting social activities, every theorist must pick one or perhaps several of the many aspects as the means to impose "a particular order or coherence." The aspects of society designated as the chosen entry point provide a perspective from which other dimensions of society can be theorized, with different entry points producing ultimately different knowledges of the world. Resnick and Wolff identify and distinguish six different common radical entry points: ownership, authority, consciousness, accumulation, technology, and class.

Alongside these differences in the object of analysis are further differences in "the way in which theorists connect together their ideas about their objects"—different types of logic for conceiving causal relations. Determinist theories seek to construct an ordered causal hierarchy, with the chosen entry point functioning as the determining essence of all other aspects of society; the alternative "overdeterminist" logic eschews such reductionism, viewing all aspects of society, including the entry point, as products of "mutual dependence in causation."

This taxonomy of entry points and logics allows further distinctions. Determinist logic combined with an entry point focus on human characteristics (rationality, a will to power, etc.) defines the approach of *humanism*, the traditional opposite and counterpart to *structuralism*, which essentializes organizational features of the social structure. Despite the now almost universal ritual of condemning reductionist theorizing, Resnick and Wolff view the radical tradition as overwhelmingly dominated by various competing humanist and/or structuralist essentialisms. Indeed, they argue provocatively that, while humanism and structuralism are in one sense opposites, they are also curiously complementary; "composite" entry points may straddle the divide, justifying structuralist concerns through appeals to universal properties of human nature, or vice versa.

Resnick and Wolff pose their own Marxist approach as a break from both humanist and structuralist traditions. Insistently overdeterminist and thus opposed to all structuralist causal hierarchies, their own favored approach is at least structural, in that the class process of surplus labor extraction, appropriation and distribution occupies center stage. But the various non-class dimensions of society employed as entry points in other radical theories—property endowments, power relations, accumulation pressures, forces of production, and states of consciousness—then can be understood to provide conditions necessary for class exploitation, overdetermining the changing forms of class processes while themselves changing in response to evolving class dynamics. For Resnick and Wolff, this approach allows the recognition of a variegated list of radical social concerns, without reducing one to another, and this sort of openness is, for them, a prerequisite for both theoretical progress and the practical dialogue crucial in forging political coalitions.

In his comment, Howard Sherman supports their goals but not the consequences of their unconventional rhetoric. Sherman defends the more traditional term "dialectics" as preferable to overdetermination in describing and prescribing for the process of radical analysis. But dialectics is not a "logic" in any meaningful formal sense; it is instead a method suggestive of *questions* which are "useful in a limited manner to a radical economist." Similarly, while a focus on class is "at the heart" of historical materialism, the latter is "broader" in its concern with the interactions between the economic system or mode of production and the political/ideological system. Historical materialism is, for Sherman, the preferred term, since, properly understood, it precludes any "one-way determinism" by underlining the need for "an interactive model with two-way determinism." Determinism in Sherman's sense is thus not identical to essentialism in Resnick and Wolff's; indeed, as Sherman employs the term, Marxism *is* determinist, which is precisely what distinguishes it from both the political fatalism of "predeterminist" theories and the voluntarism of a "free will" approach. The "scientific determinism" of Marx asserts only that behavior and events are lawful, a premise without which prediction, and more generally science itself, is impossible. So, for Sherman, one can affirm the thrust of Resnick and Wolff's overdeterminist class approach without departing from either the terminology or the traditional tasks of Marxian social analysis.

In the 1990s, as discussion and debate over the "transformation problem" enters its second century, the theory of value and distribution remains one of the most contentious areas in the radical literature, and the one where the heritage of Marx and the future role of Marxism in radical analysis is most overtly contested. For some, "the labor theory of value" in any of its possible forms is internally inconsistent, redundant in price analysis, and therefore obsolete; for others, value categories, properly interpreted or reinterpreted, remain central for theoretical and/or empirical analyses of capitalism. Makoto Itoh reviews "the value controversy," stressing the importance of the Sraffian critique of neoclassical capital theory in shaping the context for the debate within radical political economy concerning Marxian value categories. Itoh affirms the continuing relevance of a value analysis based on the relations and distinctions between the forms and the substance of value.

Itoh's own proposed solution to the transformation problem involves constructing a measure of "the substance of value acquired" through exchange, a measure which, while different from both values and prices of production, in the aggregate equals the total value produced. Then, so long as profit is similarly measured by the substance of value acquired in the form of the surplus product, Marx's other aggregate equality between profit and surplus value holds simultaneously, a result which Itoh feels corresponds to the spirit if not the letter of Marx's own transformation procedure. In Itoh's view, this broad approach offers solutions to other long-standing problems in the Marxian theory of value, including anomalies associated with joint production (indeterminate commodity values and "negative surplus value"), and the formal specification of abstract labor in the presence of heterogeneous worker skills or job classifications. This latter is sure to be controversial, since Itoh argues on political as well as theoretical grounds that skill differences, and more generally all dimensions of distinction among heterogeneous concrete labors, can and should be ignored in aggregating labor times for purposes of value calculation. Thus, for Itoh, the analysis of physically embodied quantities of human labor remains a "fundamental task" if economics is itself to remain a *social* science.

Anwar Shaikh shares Itoh's commitment to the importance of value analysis, but in a different form and for different reasons. He presents a detailed examination of

Itoh's transformation procedure, noting an asymmetry in the treatment of expanded as distinct from simple reproduction. For Shaikh, the task of transformation is precisely to comprehend the *difference* between aggregate surplus value and profit, rather than to seek a way to demonstrate their identity, and that difference can be seen as a necessary consequence of the presence of a "circuit of capitalist revenue" distinct from the "circuit of productive capital." Reproduction of the aggregates on which Itoh focuses is accomplished in general by means of "transfers" of value among these circuits representing "regions" within the overall circulation process. Building on an analysis of international trade flows, Shaikh argues that, in any self-reproducing state, the aggregate difference between profit and surplus value is precisely the positive or negative transfer from "capital" (the transactions which perpetuate the labor process) to "capitalists-as-consumers." This, combined with empirical support which Shaikh cites, validates the usefulness of what he calls "a Ricardian-Marxian structural approach to the determination of prices."

For many contemporary radicals, one of the troubling perspectives associated with traditional orthodox Marxism views individuals as "bearers" of their class (or race or gender) roles; individual actions and choices are thus reduced to expressions of abstract "interests" given by a social structure external to the individual. In reaction, some have explored the literatures on post-modernism and psychoanalysis in an effort to reconceive individual subjectivity as complexly constituted, "decentered" rather than possessed of a unitary nature given by either external or internal conditions. Others, in search of a more traditionally "rigorous" alternative, have borrowed from the rational choice models of the neoclassical tradition. Within this latter group, clearly the most visible and influential theorists have been those loosely grouped under the banner of "analytical Marxism." E. K. Hunt surveys and criticizes the analytical Marxist literature, taking John Roemer and Jon Elster as the exemplars of the school.

For Hunt, the pivotal defining characteristic of analytical Marxism is its acceptance of methodological individualism, the view that since collective entities ("capital" and "labor") do not choose or act, all explanations of social outcomes must proceed from an explicit posing of the goals and conditions of individual agency. This premise easily lends itself to a thoroughly neoclassical conception of individual behavior as rational optimization subject to constraints, with the result that these constraints, the given "data" of the agency problem, end up subsuming and ultimately removing from analysis "the concrete historical set of social relations." In effect, then, the problem with analytical Marxism is that it exogenizes precisely that which Hunt's preferred brand of Marxism seeks to explain—not merely property endowments, but the values, aims, choice strategies, in short, the very social identities of individuals which are, for Hunt, historically inseparable from the class collectivities present in society.

In contrast, the "methodological collectivist" alternative favored by Hunt presupposes an "interactive process" in which social preconditions shape individuals, particularly through the cultural symbolism constitutive of one's "symbolic self," while individuals reciprocally react to and, under some conditions, reconstitute their social circumstances. From this perspective Hunt examines the analytical Marxist reconstruction of Marxian exploitation theory. For Roemer, the concept of exploitation, to the extent that it remains meaningful at all, is simply shorthand for the rationally chosen consequences of initially unequal property endowments; Hunt points out that, with this approach, the conclusion as to "who exploits whom" may vary with every arbitrarily different choice of numeraire commodity. But despite the mathematical symmetry between sellers of labor-power and sellers of any other commodity, the concept of exploitation evolved in the first place to confront the unique experience of *performers* of labor. In its effort to transform the historically concrete problems of class analysis into a universal formalism of choice, analytical Marxism is, to Hunt, "merely the most egalitarian wing of the neoclassical approach," and as such part of "the long tradition of anti-Marxism."

In his comment, Herbert Gintis favors a different response to the problem of agency, in large part because that problem itself is differently conceived. The issue is one of consistency: "economic theory must have logically consistent microfoundations." In this light, methodological individualism is untenable--macro structure does not follow from micro conditions—but methodological collectivism, at least in its traditional Marxist forms, is equally problematic in its inability to incorporate the strategic behavior of individuals. To Gintis, both neoclassical economics and traditional Marxism are guilty of "microfoundational inconsistency" and as a result both are increasingly obsolete. Gintis instead envisions the outlines of a new economics, an alternative to both, one which melds a familiar radical appreciation of the powerful effects of "the structure of social life" with a game-theoretic approach to the strategic behavior of socially constituted individuals. He is at pains to differentiate this approach from an uncritical acceptance of, for example, the exogenous rationality of neoclassical choice models, but at the same time he allows that "the optimization-subject-to-constraints model is often the best model to apply to economic affairs." "We need new theories for new times," he concludes, and the "defunct tradition" of Marxism no longer contributes to the development of "new egalitarian and democratic instruments for the control of economic life."

One of the most active areas of recent radical research concerns issues of gender and the links between gender processes and other social sites. Julie Matthaei surveys this burgeoning literature and the active debates within it, including those concerning domestic labor, the family wage, and patriarchy, with the goal of assessing the contributions of Marxist-feminist thought, broadly conceived. Marxist-feminists have succeeded in stretching the boundaries of radical economics, opening up new problems, questions, and fields of inquiry—though not without resistance from male radicals. In the process, this very enlargement of the scope of the discipline has created a dilemma: is it possible to give adequate weight and attention to patriarchal oppression and gender inequality within a Marxist tradition preoccupied historically with class issues? "Dual systems" theories—those jointly focused on parallel systems of class and patriarchal oppression—tend inherently, she feels, toward imbalance, either slighting gender issues in favor of an enlarged view of capitalism or else stressing them at the cost of separating gender and its special sphere from the rest of society. Moreover, the much-needed effort to incorporate race and other dimensions of oppression within this approach leads merely to an unwieldy and ultimately unworkable proliferation of theoretical "systems."

Matthaei's solution is a "unitary systems approach" which analyzes race, class and gender differentiation as "integral parts" of a single "economic system." This approach, however, requires a "transformation of Marxist methodology," on two fronts. First, Marxism must reaffirm the explicitly historical nature of its inquiries, avoiding abstract theorizing in favor of analyses carefully located in time and space. Second, and more controversial, Marxists must abandon philosophical materialism with its privileging of material over ideal or superstructural processes, particularly the family-oriented realm of consciousness and identity. For Matthaei, materialism is "a central barrier" to the project of incorporating insights on patriarchy and white supremacy into a unitary Marxist theory of capitalism and its historically evolving institutions. Such a transformed approach to radical theory would additionally promote a more promising brand of political practice, since "the only clearly progressive action is action which takes all dimensions of oppression into account simultaneously." To further this project, Matthaei sketches the outline of a research agenda designed to flesh out Marxist-feminist insights into, for example, the links between gendered family relations and the structure of firms and labor markets.

Jane Humphries, in her comment, is less impressed with the transformative potential of much Marxist-feminist work. Any transformation of radical economics has so far been limited, largely *because* of the form of the Marxist-feminist critique posing patriarchy as a separate system of oppression. Patriarchy models have contributed to the "ghettoization" of women's issues by, on the one hand, allowing male radicals to view gender processes as a "field" rather than incorporating women's experiences into all dimensions of theory, and, on the other, allowing feminist critics to perpetuate a simplistic functionalism identifying (male) gender with interests defining behavior. Matthaei's unitary approach rightly rejects patriarchy as a separate system, but her justification for it relies in part on a similar reduction of materialism to the crude claim that only material economic interests matter, a caricature which contributes to the vulgarization of Marxist economics. To Humphries, the unitary approach, "falls short of a useful framework" for future research; what is needed is a variant of dual systems theory in which the relevant dualism is not capitalism/patriarchy but precisely the materialist pairing of production/reproduction. An "expanded concept of the material," rather than its rejection, allows analysis of the interactions between class and gender without falling into biological essentialism; moreover, she cites examples to suggest that such a materialist approach can provide fruitful insights into race and the ideology as well as the reality of racial oppression.

With the possible exception of "exploitation," the two terms most frequently employed in radical analyses are probably "accumulation" and "crisis." Bruce Norton reviews the recent literature on accumulation and crisis theory and again, contrasts of approach and method are at the heart of debate. To simplify presentation of the "fault lines" of an enormous literature, Norton divides radical theories into schools representing what are, in effect, "contending visions of capitalist economies." "Productionist" or falling-rate-of-profit theories typically employ an explicit interpretation of Marx's method to argue that the dynamics of accumulation and crisis reflect the ultimately determinate production sphere. Crises, whether cyclical, secular, or long-wave phenomena, are inevitable expressions of the "laws of motion" of capital, laws deducible from the nature of the contradictions between relations and forces of production. Stagnation models in the monopoly capital tradition elaborate similar assumptions but in a different direction—here it is the circulation sphere which is the immediate site of contradictions inherent in accumulation's inner dynamic. Production is predictable for oligopoly firms, but problematic demand conditions and excess capacity periodically emerge as the endogenous effects of the "inner logic" of accumulation in mature capitalism. Profit squeeze theories, with their conjunctural and empirical focus on the postwar specifics of wages and productivity, do depart somewhat from the pattern of presenting overt theses about capitalism's inner nature, but the related social structures of accumulation approach of at least some theorists reasserts an essentialist conception of the accumulation process. Here the conflicts of interests inherent in capitalist social relations produce periodic modulations in profit, where profit itself is simply the visible expression and measure of capitalist power.

Norton is sensitive to the specific differences, large and small, among the theorists he surveys within each of these groups, yet despite these differences he sees a shared "general theoretical strategy" underlying the diversity of approaches. The defining characteristic of the project of much of accumulation and crisis theory is its premise that crises must be understood as expressions of a given, "abstractly determinate inner logic" of accumulation or of capitalism itself. Whether manifested in arguments based on value theory, macro models or econometric estimation, the form of the conclusions drawn and the scope of the variables admitted for discussion have been constrained by this widespread conception of what an accumulation theory must accomplish. It is this common "mode of reasoning" which Norton seeks to question, if only because of "the plausible suspicion that the world does not work in this fashion." And while he has no doubts that all the various frameworks are sufficiently resilient to persist in future research, Norton suggests that issues often slighted in accumulation theory—race, gender, finance, space, and culture, for example—could well be more readily incorporated if radicals were to reexamine the "totalizing vision" of an inner logic to accumulation.

David Levine's response confronts Norton's critique head-on. Like Norton, Levine regards productionist theories and, to a lesser extent, stagnation theories as reductionist. But he stresses a different methodological tactic uniting them: the assumption of a fixed composition of output. Dynamic analyses built on this premise preclude a "compelling vision" of the role of the market in transforming the lives of those within it, a vision necessary for a meaningful accumulation theory. Levine shares Norton's skepticism about the abstract determinacy of those theories which privilege model-building but feels that Norton goes too far in questioning "the very effort to think abstractly," thus "misconstru[ing] the nature of theoretical work. Restating what Norton had referred to as a "rationalist approach to theory construction," Levine argues that theory moves beyond appearances to "the way [things] really are." To grasp a "structure with a determinate form," one must find an "integrating theme or principle" that gives meaning to the system as a whole. In questioning this, Norton is, in effect, attacking "the possibility or meaningfulness of economic theory," and it is precisely an *economic* theory of accumulation processes to which Levine is committed. The methodological differences separating Norton and Levine thus carry over and affect their priorities for the content of accumulation theory as well.

David Ruccio examines another enormous literature, that concerning economic development and especially the problem of exploding Third World indebtedness. Orthodox economics presents a development theory in which virtually every market-driven interaction that occurs is, by the very fact of the market's involvement, beneficial to all participants. Much of the radical tradition, on the other hand, has been devoted to sustaining the opposite thesis, that capitalism in the "core" and the unequal power relations among nations necessarily impose underdevelopment or distorted development on the "periphery." But new forms of capitalism in the Third World and the "unexpected" success of some developing countries have underlined the need for greater sensitivity to the variety of links within world capitalism, and Ruccio sees an emerging consensus in favor of a more focused and more flexible analysis of class. To that end, he presents the outlines of a novel sort of class analysis of the particular problem of external debt.

Ruccio distinguishes the "fundamental class" process of extraction of surplus value from both the "subsumed class" process of distribution of the appropriated gains and the various "non-class" processes including, for example, exchange. The resulting taxonomy is then applied to principal and interest revenue flows. Traditional balance of payments accounts, with their focus on net exports and an undifferentiated concept of investment, direct attention to non-class revenue flows, obscuring the underlying exploitative class process through which surplus is generated in the first place. But contrary to some radical views, interest payments on external debt are not in themselves "exploitation" in any meaningful sense—nations do not exploit other nations. Still, by altering the terms on which Third World capitalists confront their workers and their markets, debt contracts may impact on every dimension of society, from wages and the labor process to political democratization and state policy. Carefully distinguishing state activities from those of (productive and unproductive) private capital, Ruccio examines several of these interactions, including government agency borrowing and the consequences of bailouts, loan guarantees, IMF-imposed "adjustment" policies, wage reductions and capital flight.

In each case, he stresses that the social effects of change and particularly the class content of those effects are never automatic or inevitable; the class analysis he favors is deliberate in refusing to presume the necessity of either beneficial or detrimental effects. In this, Ruccio anticipates what he views as "a different concept of development itself," one which shifts our focus from the good or bad effects of capitalism, from debates over "more" or "less" development, indeed, from a preoccupation with the level of wealth itself, to "the various class-specific *forms* of development." Such a shift is, he thinks, already under way.

The general direction of Ruccio's approach is supported by Anthony Brewer, who in his comment describes the analysis of classes, class structures and state policy as the "main strength" of radical development theory. In some particulars, though, he is less supportive; Brewer is skeptical of Ruccio's use of value theory, in part because his value-based analysis gives little explicit attention to the incentive to invest and additionally because Ruccio's focus on the formal classification of different types of revenue lacks the complementary concrete analysis needed to avoid "falling into ahistorical formalism." Still, the shift away from the influence of structuralism is to be applauded; Brewer is dismissive of the "false" analytics of dependency theory, pointing to its "denial of the obvious facts" of capitalist development and the inability of the center/periphery model to capture the variety of conditions in Third World countries. Diversity among nations in the rate and form of development can be traced to both individual market choices and varying state policies. The former can be analyzed with neoclassical methods, but only radical approaches treat state policy as itself to be explained in light of "the interests of the dominant classes and the alliances between them." Brewer cites examples of what he sees as useful and provocative concrete analyses of class and policy interactions during Third World transitions, but suggests a need for a more explicit focus on the determinants of profitability and perceived investment opportunities. With this redirection of economic analysis, radicals can then pursue the "urgent task" of examining "political power" in a class-analytic context.

What can we expect in the future for radical economics? There are no received ideas exempt from current rethinking, but of course "rethinking" is a process with many possible outcomes, ranging from reaffirmation to revision to outright rejection. Thus the safest bet is for continued fragmentation of different radical approaches, combined with a process of "normal science" within each—elaborating, testing, concretizing. Certainly there will be no coalescing of opinion on a single object or focus for radical thinking, nor should there be—no single "entry point" has a monopoly on all the interesting questions. In contrast, one can at least hope for greater clarity in the debates over method, but no resolution is likely here either;

fundamentally different views of what constitutes a non-reductionist radical theory are likely to continue to prevail.

At least one common task will be on all radical agendas, though, however differently it may be tackled in each, since all of us, in and out of academia, face a frequent question, of the form: "Well, if you don't want capitalism and you don't stand simply for state ownership and central planning, what is it you *do* want to see instead?" The response will involve greater attention to practical, tactical problems of defining and building institutions consistent with radical values, in the process figuring out the concrete institutional meaning of terms like "economic democracy" and "collective appropriation." And in this, there is an enormous amount to be learned, in both positive and negative senses, from experiences in eastern Europe and beyond. But as always, and as even conservatives are occasionally forced to admit (though only in times of recession), there is also much to learn from the ways America continually reproduces its own multicultural population of the poor and dispossessed, the frustrated and the angry.

All radical approaches expect continuing social changes in the years ahead. But if political and economic institutions in eastern Europe have proven to be inadequate, they are surely only the first of such post-Depression, postwar structures and conventions, seemingly so natural to many in the West, to face a similar fate. And in that process, there will be radical economic analyses, in the plural, to encourage and interpret change.

NOTES

1. The quotation is from Buchanan (1991), one of several essays contained in the provocative (and, for a radical, in many ways frustrating) centennial issue of *The Economic Journal* devoted to predictions of trends in economics over the next century.

2. For an extended discussion of these broad distinctions between radical and orthodox approaches, with particular attention to their consequences for economic education, see Feiner and Roberts (1990).

REFERENCES

Buchanan, J. M. 1991. "Economics in the Post-Socialist Century." *Economic Journal* 101 (January): 15–21.

Feiner, S. F., and Roberts, B. B. 1990. "Hidden by the Invisible Hand: Neoclassical Economic Theory and the Textbook Treatment of Race and Gender." *Gender & Society* 4 (2): 159–81.

1 RADICAL ECONOMICS: A TRADITION OF THEORETICAL DIFFERENCES

Stephen Resnick and Richard Wolff

The tradition of radical economics is a long one, rich in insight, passion, and conflict. Motivated by different forms of a common opposition to capitalism and the economic theories which celebrate it, radicals have offered a variety of analyses of economic and more broadly social interactions, problems, and trends. Our task in this paper is to make sense of the varieties of radical theory: we present a taxonomy, a catalog of some of the major contemporary radical positions, locating both the shared principles which unite theorists within the various schools of thought and the issues of struggle and debate defining boundaries between them. Of course, there are probably as many ways to organize and classify radical economic theories as there are theories to classify; any taxonomic scheme is also inherently an evaluation of the theories considered, and our own perspective is obviously at work in shaping the distinctions we draw. Because of this, we will also explicitly locate our own views in relation to other trends in the field, in the process clarifying the reasons for our allegiance to one particular radical approach.

But before considering particular radical economic theories, we need to ask a prior question: how in general do we establish differences among theories? What exactly would we look for in these theories that would stamp them as uniquely different from one another? Any answer to these questions involves some discussion of epistemological issues. We will take up these issues first, explaining how we think about these theoretical differences, and then use our method to construct indexes of difference that can be used to distinguish different radical economic theories. As we shall see, there are two ways to distinguish theories: establishing their respective "entry points" into social analysis and identifying their "logics."

DISTINGUISHING THEORIES: ENTRY POINTS AND LOGICS

Let us begin with what seems to be a simple problem. Suppose we were asked to make some kind of sense of the relationship among individuals in a household. Now to "make sense" of a household is to theorize what it is, and this theorizing invariably shapes a definition of its object. Thus the objects we think and talk about are always the results of theorizing; they always represent in part the knowledges in which they are defined. Past experience living in a household suggests a first step in theorizing it. We might begin merely by listing the things we think go on there: cooking, cleaning, laughing, loving, educating, ordering, crying, arguing, caring, fighting, borrowing, gifting, repairing, and so forth.

The diversity of the activities which any one person might list as well as the likely differences between the lists of different people suggest that even seemingly simple problems of definition and demarcation are actually quite complex. Moreover, each aspect catalogued on such a list not only exerts its influence on the household relationship, but each one shapes all the others as well. Aspects interact with one another. So, for example, the relationships we have in households are shaped in diverse ways by how we talk to, work with, exert authority over, and love one another there. But our work experience there is also shaped by the different ways we love, talk, and exert authority over one another.

This story about theorizing household relationships can be extended to relationships among individuals in any location or site in society (factory, state, church, union, school) and to society as a whole. The latter becomes the totality of such relationships including all aspects at all sites. As in our household example, each of these social sites (and their collection into a society) also is composed of an enormous list of interacting aspects. Taken together, the sheer number of aspects and their mutual interaction define the central task of social theory: to bring a kind of order, a systematic understanding, to this chaos of interacting aspects. The key question then becomes *how* theory does this. Or, more relevant for our purposes, how do different theories do this differently?

In our view, every theorist picks one (or perhaps several) of the many aspects and uses it (them) as a focus, a means to bring a particular order or coherence to the initial chaos of mutually interacting social activities. In other words, this focus permits a particular understanding of all the aspects from the perspective of the chosen one. This choice assigns great importance to this particular aspect, for it now serves as a guide to the theorist pointing the way to an orderly path out of initial disorder. In a sense, a door has been opened into the analysis of relationships, and thus we refer to this as the choice of an "entry point" concept.

Choosing a particular concept as an entry point implies a commitment to a singular organizational principle or taxonomy in one's theorizing. It means that the theorist has adopted a unique way to approach and classify the complex of interacting aspects with which he or she is initially confronted. Dividing the world into entry point and non-entry point aspects is the necessary first step in making sense of the chaos of aspects—otherwise no sense is possible at all. However, different conceptual divisions produce different kinds of senses; theories with different entry points produce different taxonomies of aspects and ultimately different knowledges of the world.

In the household, for example, a theorist could choose as the organizing idea the aspect of exerting authority, or more specifically, the power wielded by men over women in the relationships within households. That theorist would relate all the non-power aspects of those relationships to this power aspect. The result is a particular kind of theoretical taxonomy: relationships in households, no matter what their complexity, now can be understood initially in terms of their power and related non-power aspects. Such an analysis produces a broadly "political" theory of the household. Alternatively, choosing as entry point the aspects connected to the production and dissemination of meanings (for example, talking, arguing, story-telling, and dressing) results in a "cultural" theory. Choosing cooking, cleaning, repairing, or, in general, working to produce and distribute household goods and services generates an "economic" theory of that entity.

The choice of any one of these alternatives is itself a complex act affected by events and relationships in society and in one's own personal experience. Whether one's entry point is socially conventional or, as happens at least occasionally, entirely novel, the choice need not be wholly or even largely a conscious decision. Thus, to understand any theory it is always pertinent to ask why its entry point concept was chosen or invented at this time and place, a question particularly relevant to the history of thought, including in that history the psychological factors that may shape an individual's choice.

For example, the choice of power as the discursive entry point may flow from an individual's personal and family participations, political practices in society's rule making and enforcing institutions, and his or her experiences with the various theories that exist in society. Indeed, many Americans use power as their organizing idea in part because of the theoretical and political importance given to this concept in both the historic and current American experience. Concern with the idea of power—who wields it and for what purpose—has been a primary American focus from colonial days to the present.

Whatever the complex reasons for our choices, different chosen entry points signal the different priorities we as theorists impose on our unique understandings of the relationships among human beings. We thus have one index of difference among theories: the different political, cultural, and economic entry points they use. Theories are different in part because of their different entry points.

A second index involves the way in which theorists connect together their ideas about their objects. Different theories deploy different connections among ideas—they use different logics in the process of linking their chosen entry point aspect(s) to all the other aspects of society.

One prevalent approach assigns the chosen entry point a dual role in the theory:

it not only focuses the analysis, but it alone is presumed to create or cause the behavior of all other aspects. In a fundamental sense, the destiny of all other aspects can be traced back to the autonomous behavior of the entry point, which is immune from the effects of those other aspects. When an entry point additionally takes on this sort of causal priority, we call it the essence of the analysis, since it plays the role not only of a guide *to* analysis (its entry point role), but also a sovereign *of* analysis (its essentialist or determinist role). We will use the words essentialism and determinism as synonyms in our argument.

The distinctive logic of determinism follows from its approach to the various aspects of economy or society as a field of potential causes and effects. For determinist logic, aspects are inherently distinguishable and separable, and the form of the question asked is, usually implicitly, "'Here' is *X* and 'there' is *Y*—how are they related? Which is causally primary? Which is the independent variable and which is the dependent?" The subsequent argument that *X* is the determining essence of *Y* thus relies on a prior premise that *X* and *Y* can be held up to study as independent entities—potentially related, of course, but nonetheless at least isolable and definable independent of that relationship. A presumption of the *discursive* independence of aspects is implicit in the determinist effort to order them according to their *causal* dependence or independence.

Such an ordering is a determinist theory's principal goal: analysis becomes in practice the demonstration of how the theory's chosen essence actually causes and thus explains whatever object is selected for theoretical scrutiny. Determinist theories need not worry initially about mutual or two-way interactions. Once the entry point concept has been chosen, the structure of theoretical explanation is already defined, for the essential causal core has been discovered. All other aspects play a secondary role, still important to the story then told about relationships, but only in the sense that they provide a surface description of what is going on. Below this, on a deeper, more fundamental level, is the powerful determining role of the essence, creating surface appearances as a reflection of its governing, explanatory power. To discover the ultimate cause of behavior, one must discover the ultimate essence. At that point the truth will be known.

An alternative logic rejects any essentialist priority for the entry point. Here, while the chosen entry point still guides the theorist and imposes a particular taxonomy on the object of study, it does *not* determine the behavior of any other aspect. Instead, the logic is one of mutual dependence in causation: the behavior of the entry point both is itself shaped by other non-entry point aspects and in turn acts to shape the behavior of the rest. Following others, we use the term overdetermination for this approach in which each aspect is simultaneously determining and determined by all the others.[1]

In contrast to a determinist approach, the overdeterminist logic implies that no aspect of society can ever be approached or defined in isolation from its context; its concrete existence is the product of the influences of all the other aspects which literally create its very being and thus form its conditions of existence. The separateness and distinctiveness of aspects which determinism presumes is here explicitly rejected with the premise that for *any* aspect to exist, its conditions must be present, and these by definition must be located in all the *other* aspects. It follows that an entry point concept, such as power, has no meaning, no social role to play at all, except through its relations to all the other non-power aspects. Power must be related to non-power for the former even to begin its assumed role as a guide to analysis.

This overdeterminist logic precludes the very goal of a determinist analysis: an ordered hierarchy of causal importance. In our example of the household, if the concept of power is the chosen entry point, then a knowledge of the household requires the depiction of the mutually constitutive interaction of power and non-power aspects. But this is a task that can never be completed; theory is forever open-ended and partial, since there is no end to the exploration of further dimensions of household behavior, each of which has its power and non-power aspects. Each successive addition to the range of household behaviors considered extends the story about the influence of power but also, because of the multiplication of interactions, changes the shape of the power aspect previously theorized. Every explanation is thus only a partial knowledge reflecting the particular mutual interaction of the power and non-power aspects recognized and examined up to that point.

These alternative forms of causal methodology or logic provide us with our second index of theoretical difference. We may now compare and contrast different theories along two dimensions: their different points of entry and/or different logics. Moreover, these two indexes suggest radically different ways of conceiving of things and their interrelationships. Different entry points and logics produce, then, different conceptual objects, whether they be knowledges of the household, factory, state, or economy.

Not surprisingly, people who deploy different points of entry and/or different logics have basic disagreements; they will argue and perhaps even struggle, with greater or lesser degrees of self-consciousness, over precisely these two dimensions of their theoretical differences. As we shall show, radical economists have been doing precisely that for almost one hundred years.

DISTINGUISHING RADICAL THEORIES

One of the prominent concerns of radical economics has always been the interpretation of the relationship between capitalists and workers. That relationship, as well as the interactions between both groups and other social actors (landlords, money lenders, merchants, managers, state officials, etc.), can be approached from a variety of different conceptual points of entry. In Figure 1 we illustrate the capitalist-worker relationship together with some of the most famous entry points used to organize radical analyses. The list is diverse; each of these different entry points, and sometimes complex combinations of them, provides an interpretive taxonomy which can be used to impose a distinctive order on initially chaotic social interactions.

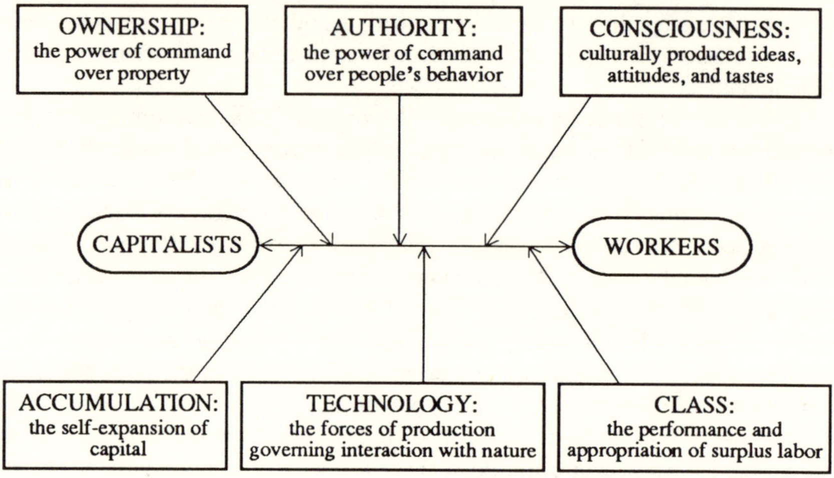

Figure 1: Alternative radical entry points

Some of the entry points direct our attention to aspects of society which are themselves basically economic; others alternatively stress political or cultural dimensions. The broad differences between economic and non-economic points of entry have played a crucial role in the evolution of radical thought at least since Marx's famous distinction between the economic base or mode of production (conceived as a combination of the relations and forces of production) and the non-economic superstructure (the combination of the remaining political and cultural aspects of society). Thus the entry points of class, technology, and accumulation are distinctively economic, whereas consciousness and authority over people's behavior are respectively cultural and political. Property ownership, though, can be conceived in different ways. We prefer to treat ownership as a political entry point, since it is the *power* that ownership confers which gives it significance. However, virtually all property theorists place their stress on the economic *assets* over which control is exercised, so we follow that tradition in classifying ownership as yet another economic entry point.[2]

Since this distinction between economic and non-economic aspects, base and superstructure, is recognized, albeit in different ways, by all radical theorists, all must confront an obvious question: how are these different social aspects related? The answer is given by what we have termed the logic of each theory, and by and large throughout the history of radical economics the chosen logic has generally been that of determinism. Each of the various entry points has been presented by proponents as the essence of events and changes within society. Indeed, many of the pivotal debates within the radical tradition have been struggles between competing economic and non-economic determinisms, each embracing the same essentialist reasoning, the same ultimate sense of the form and meaning of causal interactions, yet posing different and incompatible essences.

The prevalence of determinist explanations in radical economics is to us striking, but it is by no means inherent in the entry points radicals have stressed; a commitment to the alternative logic of overdetermination is possible, at least in principle, irrespective of one's entry point. Historically, though, the lure of determinism has proven difficult to avoid, even for theorists who have consciously stressed the complexity of the interactions of base and superstructure. For example, in a famous comment Engels argued that while "the *ultimately* determining factor in history is the production and reproduction of real life," this economic factor is not "the *only* determining one": "[t]he economic situation is the basis, but the various elements of the superstructure . . . also exercise their influence . . . and in many cases determine the *form* in particular" (Engels 1975, 394–95). Despite the obvious effort to find a kind of middle ground in which the powerful influence of culture and politics is admitted, Engels still expresses a form of economic determinism in which the economic mode of production causes and explains "in the last instance" all other aspects of social relationships. Several recent theorists (Hindess and Hirst 1975; Cohen 1978; Roemer 1988) strike a similar theme: although in non-capitalist societies politics or culture may "dominate" over the influence of economic factors, it is ultimately the economic aspects of society (relations and/or forces of production) which *determine* whether it is politics, culture or economics which assumes the dominant role.[3] While radicals who embrace this sort of argument avoid the obvious criticisms which can be directed at a coarser kind of economic determinism, they nonetheless affirm an ultimately essentialist logic which, at least by this criterion, places them in the same camp as their theoretical opponents who defend the essential priority of some non-economic entry point.[4]

There is yet another dimension of difference among determinist theories with their various alternative points of entry. Do the concepts definitive of the entry point designate *human* characteristics, properties or capacities of some or all individual persons, or do they instead refer to *structural* characteristics of society, organizational features of the social environment encompassing all individuals? These two contrasting approaches, humanism and structuralism, have been in conflict throughout the modern history of social theory, and within the realm of radical economics the struggle has been particularly intense.[5]

Radical structuralists give priority to some structural feature of social organization (one which, in principle, may be economic, political, or cultural), and when this premise is allied, as is typically the case, with determinist logic, that structure becomes the governing essence both of other structures and of the behavior of individuals in their various interactions. Individual choices and actions are viewed as ultimately reflecting the imperatives of a social structure which transcends the individual's role(s) within it. It is just this sense of the individual as role-bearer, obeying the dictates of an underlying all-determining structure, that motivates the humanist alternative. Radical humanists give center stage to the human subject and the traits seen as central to individual subjectivity (traits which again may in principle be economic, political, or cultural) and then typically employ determinist logic to reduce social structures and changes to the status of effects of human striving. Neither approach to the choice of entry point necessarily requires the use of determinist logic,[6] but the prevalence of determinist theories within the radical tradition leads us to reserve the terms humanism and structuralism for opposed varieties of essentialist thinking.

The contentious relationship between humanism and structuralism has helped to shape radical debates between rival economic and non-economic determinisms. Within the radical tradition, economic determinism is most often a form of structuralism, while non-economic determinism is correlated with humanism.[7] Thus, while the language of base and superstructure remains part of contemporary radical discussions, disagreements over the relative importance of economic and non-economic aspects of society also simultaneously concern the relative stress to be placed on social structures versus individual agency. And of course, even within the rival traditions of structuralism and humanism, debate continues over which structures (class or technology or accumulation or property ownership) and which human characteristics (the capacity to wield power or to choose rationally or to communicate) are the most essential for theory to grasp.

WHY USE THE TERM "RADICAL"?

The stark differences between humanist and structuralist approaches, as well as the gulf separating both from the alternative logic of overdetermination, point up an obvious question: what do these theories have in common to make them part of a singular "radical" tradition? Given their differences in entry points and logics, the common thread uniting radical economic theorists seems to be their shared dislike for capitalism as an economic system and for those neoclassical and Keynesian theories which support and celebrate capitalism. Radicals are grouped together more by their common desire for radical alternatives in both the economic and theoretical status quo than by any particular common analytical feature. Thus agreement among radicals often quickly disappears when it comes to detailing the precise flaws in capitalism or the strategies needed to confront them, since the choice of a particular conceptual entry point gives those designated aspects of society an inherent priority in describing or prescribing for capitalism. Yet all radicals can join in castigating orthodox economics for denying an explanatory role to variables of radical concern (class, power, etc.) or for celebrating as causes of wealth and happiness those institutional features which radicals associate with inequality and injustice (e.g., private property, market competition) (see Resnick and Wolff 1987).

We must be careful here though, for despite the real differences between radical and non-radical economic theories, they do have some surprising similarities. The theoretical humanism underlying the neoclassical premise of rational individuals similarly animates those radical theories that posit an autonomous human subject with an inherent capacity to wield power or transform nature (Elster 1985). Similarly, Keynesian macromodels, with their structural interactions based on predetermined parameters summarizing aggregate behavior (consumption, money demand, etc.) are remarkably similar in form if not entry point to radical theories specifying given structures of productive forces or property ownership or mode of production. And with humanist and structuralist camps within both radical and non-radical traditions, the evolution of theoretical debates has sometimes followed a distinctly parallel path. For example, Roemer (1986, 192) argues:

> Marxian analysis requires microfoundations. . . . What Marxists must provide are explanations of *mechanisms*, at the micro level, for the phenomena they claim come about for teleological reasons. In a sense, the problem is parallel to the one bourgeois economics faces in providing microfoundations for macroeconomics.

Thus, the humanist reaction to structuralism clearly transcends the boundaries between traditions; humanists of every stripe are partners in a common search for the essential (micro level) role of the individual human being in determining the behavior of society and the structural relationships visible at its macro level.[8]

There is at least one further characteristic which all radicals, whatever their other differences, have in common: all owe an intellectual debt to Marx. Even those radicals who are avowedly non-Marxist represent positions shaped by a reaction to Marx's prominent place in the tradition of radical analysis and social criticism. Marx was preeminently a proponent of *class* analysis, and the vocabulary of class (surplus labor, exploitation, etc.) has had a special place within radical economic theory for over one hundred years. For many radicals and non-radicals alike, the category of class more than any other has established a conceptual boundary between radical and non-radical theories. Certainly most radical theorists have viewed the class dimensions of social life as one of those key aspects requiring fundamental change. Equally, that goal is not shared by non-radicals, whose entry point concepts devalue or deny the existence of this class aspect.

But the common radical tendency to invoke Marx masks a world of difference in the interpretations offered. In the radical literature, frequently the structuralist Marx who posits the determining role of the economic base confronts the humanist Marx stressing the autonomously acting human subject. Each position finds ample support for its project in Marx's own writings and struggles with difficult questions, and thus different Marxes appear at different times as each part of the tradition uses its own interpretation of Marx to support its position. And since that interpretation of Marx and that position both derive from the same approach, it is not surprising that each variant of radical theory is enormously successful in showing the correspondence between the two.

We too have our own interpretation of Marx and our own related radical theory. A review of Marx as we read him provides the final groundwork needed for our survey of prominent positions in contemporary radical economics. In our view Marxism is distinctive in combining two commitments: the entry point of class and the logic of overdetermination.

MARXISM AS A RADICAL THEORY

For Marx, class designates the economic process through which surplus labor is performed and appropriated. Surplus labor in turn refers to the amount of labor time worked by individuals above and beyond that socially and historically normal and necessary for their survival and reproduction as workers. Marx's revolutionary idea was that appropriators receive this surplus without giving anything in return, thus exploiting the producers of surplus. A society takes on its defining class characteristics according to the different forms in which this surplus labor is performed and appropriated. The famous adjectives used to describe different societies —capitalist, feudal, slave—refer to the different ways appropriators can receive the produced surplus, through distinctively different forms of exploitation (Wolff and Resnick 1987). To argue that capitalism is exploitative in this sense is clearly radically unconventional in a world dominated by orthodox economics, with its powerful and soothing claim that incomes are equated to productive contributions through the invisible hand of market allocation.

But Marx's class entry point is radical in other ways as well, for it conveys one of the most important ethical and moral messages ever developed in social theory. To be an appropriator of surplus is to take from workers some of their labor, their surplus portion. For the worker, the result is no different than if a thief had stolen some of the worker's goods. Irrespective of the intent of individual capitalists, the economic process through which they gain something for nothing is the equivalent of theft; modern capitalists, in their role as surplus labor receivers, are not fundamentally different from the overthrown tyrants of the past, the slavemasters and feudal lords whose exploitation differed in form but not substance. The moral, ethical, and political aim of Marxism becomes then the elimination of this economic crime against workers, with its many complex effects on the rest of society, by changing the relationships among people to make them non-exploitative.

Equally important as the class entry point, though, is the antiessentialist logic of overdetermination. The class relationships within capitalist societies are Marx's primary focus, analytically and politically, but class is conceived neither as the essential determinant of social events nor as a phenomenon of some other singular cause. Instead, any particular form of class relations exists only as the combined effect of all the other non-class aspects of society which provide its necessary conditions of existence. All are jointly necessary because all aspects of society are mutually constitutive; none can be treated as conceptually independent of the others or as "the" cause of some event, action or relationship.

A radical theory based on this reading of Marx is different in specific ways from other radical approaches, and the nature of the difference provides a useful perspective on the array of competing radical positions. Why is it that neither class nor overdetermination commonly receives this sort of stress? One obvious problem in accepting the central status of surplus labor appropriation is explaining why workers would stand for such exploitation. What would cause workers to allow exploitation to continue? Various answers have been offered. Perhaps workers produce something for nothing because they are not conscious of their own exploitation. Perhaps they are forced to produce this surplus because of the capitalists' domination of them or because of their inability to reproduce themselves as workers independently of property owned by capitalists. Alternatively, they may be caught in this exploitation trap because of the ubiquitous technology adopted by modern industrial corporations or the sheer momentum of capitalist expansion and accumulation. For our purposes, what is most interesting about this list is that each of these reasons why workers are exploited represents one of the major radical entry points already mentioned. There is a reason for this.

In the history of radical economic theory, the theoretical status of some answers as to why exploitation exists have been so persuasive to some that these answers have evolved into new conceptual entry points. Typically, for these individuals the original discovery of Marx—class as the performance and appropriation of surplus labor—has become a subsidiary effect of some other more basic cause which has become the new entry point. But if there is to be a singular ultimate cause for workers' exploitation rather than a variety of mutually constitutive conditions for its existence, then overdetermination has been dispensed with in the very act of positing a new (essentialized) point of entry.

From the perspective of overdetermination, each of the reasons listed for exploitation—consciousness, power, property, technology, accumulation—represents an influence on the form of exploitation and thus a condition for its existence and perpetuation. But the humanist and structuralist theories which choose one or another of these reasons as an entry point effectively turn a condition of existence of class exploitation into its essence, thus not only denying the special theoretical location of Marx's class idea *in* the logic of his theory but also in the process rejecting that logic as well. In the resulting determinist theories, class exploitation remains an important but clearly secondary concept to that of the new and different entry point. In some cases, its meaning has been so radically altered by its new subordinate place in radical theory that it takes on an entirely different meaning from that originally formulated by Marx.

We may now examine more closely how each of these various conditions of existence of class exploitation operates as an essentialized entry point, citing authors who exemplify each perspective. We stress, though, that there is no automatic one-to-one correspondence between some of the authors cited and a single theoretical position within our taxonomic system. Many radicals could be cited under more than one heading, for reasons as diverse as simple inconsistency, change and development of ideas over time, or the deliberate use of a composite entry point fusing otherwise incompatible organizing principles. This latter option is particularly interesting, as we will discuss.

PROPERTY THEORIES

Historically, one of the most prevalent radical arguments explains class exploitation as the effect of an unequal distribution of ownership rights to the means of production. The initial thesis here is that in capitalism workers are those who have been dispossessed from the means of production, while capitalists have concentrated such means in their hands. To survive, dispossessed workers must enter into a wage contract, selling the only commodity they have left, their labor power. In Marxian economic theory, labor power is the one commodity capable of producing more value than its own worth (the wage paid to the worker to reproduce his existence in that class role). The capitalist buyer of labor power thus acquires its unique ability to produce that extra or surplus value precisely because sellers of labor power have no choice in the matter. The distribution of property ownership is the ultimate explanation of classes and class exploitation.

Consider the following example of this kind of reasoning:

> The nature of classes in a given social formation . . . is determined by the distribution of the means of production, "the direct relationship of the owners of the conditions of production to the direct producers." It is this "internal distribution" . . . which determines the mode of appropriation of surplus-labor . . . and thereby the nature of class relations in that society. This interpretation implies acceptance of the traditional marxist definition of class as depending essentially on the individual's relation to the means of production. (Callinicos 1982, 149)

Callinicos follows in a proud tradition of radical thinkers (Dobb 1963; Sweezy 1964; Laclau 1977; Cutler, et al. 1977) who bestow on effective possession of property the role of an essential entry point. One recent contribution to this tradition illustrates the overriding dominance radicals may attribute to this single aspect. Roemer (1988) attempts to derive the very concept of class from the choice-constraining effects of unequal ownership of property. However, unlike many others in this property school, Roemer (1988, 131) views the concept of exploitation as clearly unnecessary to Marxian class analysis:

> Exploitation is a misleading concept if one's true interest is in inequality in the distribution of wealth. There appears to be no reason for an interest in the technical measure of exploitation, calculated in the classical Marxist way.

Although few radicals likely would follow him in expunging the concept of exploitation, Roemer exemplifies the results of taking this organizing idea of unequal property ownership and pursuing determinist logic to its ultimate conclusion.

POWER THEORIES

Theories essentializing command over property have been challenged over the years by a different theory of command, one stressing command over people. Authority or power vested in the hands of some individuals or groups can be used to order the behavior of others, the powerless. It follows that the reason for workers' exploitation is, in the last instance, that force or the threat of force compels them to labor for capitalists. The relations of production are thus interpreted as relations of authority: capitalists have power over workers and use force in different forms to perpetuate exploitation.[9]

Many recent works employ variants of this approach (Poulantzas 1973; 1978; Giddens 1975; Dahrendorf 1959; Wright 1979a; 1979b; Braverman 1974; Marglin 1974; Noble 1977; 1984), but Bowles and Gintis are perhaps most explicit in their avowal of power as entry point:

> Unlike the dominant tendency for the past two centuries, which has seen the infusion of political thinking with economic metaphor, we propose the converse: a political critique of economic thinking and the importation of genuinely political concepts concerning power and human development into the analysis of economic systems. (Bowles and Gintis 1986, ix)

Power and related "political concepts" shape the conclusions of their analysis in part because they are present from the beginning in the goal which motivates it: empowering individuals to order their own behavior by abolishing the institutions of the capitalist economy which constrain the generalization of democracy into economic as well as formally political spheres of life.

Power is, however, the essence as well as the organizing principle of the analyses offered by Bowles and Gintis and the other power theorists. The wielding of power by capitalists over workers is seen not merely as *a* condition of existence of capitalist profit (a thesis with which most radical thinkers likely would agree), but rather as *the* essential condition: "Profits are . . . made possible by the power of the capitalist class over other economic actors with which it deals" (Bowles et al. 1986, 137). In this determinist logic, it is only through the successful exercise of power that capitalists can turn the purchase of labor power into an economic gain:

> Labor must be *extracted* from labor power because workers will not willingly pursue the type and intensity of labor which maximizes profits. . . . But how is labor to be extracted? As capital's only formal power is the threat of firing, the extraction must be induced, in the last instance, by enhancing this threat. (Bowles and Gintis 1985, 37)

The threat is made real through various strategies which enhance domination;

investing in supervisory techniques, promoting hierarchy and discrimination within the labor force, and paying higher wages (to enhance the cost of losing one's job) are among these fundamentally political strategies stressed by power theorists as essential to the economic extraction of labor from labor power.

This distinction between labor power and labor effort is all that remains of the Marxian vocabulary defining class as surplus labor appropriation,[10] so it is hardly surprising that the meaning of class has been transformed by viewing social relations through the lens of power. For Bowles and Gintis, classes are now defined in terms of command over people versus lack thereof, the powerful and the powerless. The concept of exploitation remains meaningful only as one of the various effects of domination, rather than as the very definition of class as the object of analysis.

PROPERTY VERSUS POWER THEORISTS

Dialogue and debate between these two different notions of command are as old as the radical tradition itself. Elements of both are present in Marx, who in *Capital* linked workers' exploitation to both their separation from the means of production ("the so-called primitive accumulation of capital") and their relative powerlessness in the face of coercion by capitalists. Still, one could hardly credit Marx with the invention of either of these power concepts. The division of society into classes of the powerful and powerless, propertied and propertyless, clearly predated Marx, and in our view it was Marx's reaction against these senses of class that led him to the distinctive definition of class as a *process* of surplus labor appropriation rather than as a characteristic or property either of individuals or of social structures. Instead, the celebration of power in either form has more to do with the writings of Max Weber than of Marx.[11] But the ongoing battles between essentialist proponents of ownership and authority provide a concrete illustration of the larger tensions between structuralist and humanist tendencies.

Years ago, Engels foreshadowed the contemporary structuralist reaction to domination theories:

> The institution of private property must be already in existence before the robber can appropriate another person's property, and . . . therefore force may be able to change the possessor but cannot create private property itself. (Engels 1976, 180)

For the structuralist, the notion of power is an empty one without an appreciation of the essential priority of the institutional setting which literally creates positions of differential power. Callinicos (1982, 155) states:

> It is . . . a serious error to seek to *reduce* the relations of production to relations of power. The position of authority enjoyed by capital is not somehow [a] primordial fact. . . . On the contrary . . . [t]he fact that capital is dominant within the process of production rises from the capitalists' effective possession of the means of production and workers' resulting need to sell their labor-power to capital.

The same sense that power is inherently a derivative effect of prior social conditions comes through in Roemer's position that "the essential injustice of capitalism is located not in [domination] at the point of production, but, prior to that, in the property relations that determine class, income, and welfare" (Roemer 1988, 107). This view of power relations as logically derivative from prior structural conditions denies the very essence of the power theorists, the inherent struggle of individuals to extract or resist extraction of labor from labor power.

For power theorists, on the other hand, the attempt to read the behavior of capitalists and workers from the given structure of property ownership is itself a flawed project. Such a structuralism ignores the inescapable subjectivity of human agents, in particular making of labor an object rather than a subject in society (Bowles and Gintis 1985, 35–38). If social agents act the way they do because of some external structural imperative, then their struggles reside not *in* them but rather are given *to* them, a premise unacceptable to a humanism of power. Bowles and Gintis (1985, 36) bluntly reject the economic essence they see as inherent in the Marxian tradition: "The treatment of labor as an object thus achieves a radical partition in economic thought: politics is banished from economic thought." For them, the realm of individual human action is by definition "political," a quest for command over oneself and others, and thus to "banish" politics is equivalent to affirming the life of the structure at the cost of the death of individual human will and choice. The logic of determinism then leaves no choice but to invert the causal hierarchy of structuralist property theory by affirming an essential power within each individual to determine his or her own destiny in any social setting.

ACCUMULATION THEORIES

Different from power and property theorists is another school of radicals who conceive the relationship between capitalists and workers as relentlessly driven by capital accumulation. Workers are exploited, propertyless, and powerless because of the inexorable capitalist drive to accumulate, which recreates at every moment the prison of relationships in which laborers are trapped.

Marx is again a key figure for these accumulation-radicals because he is seen as the first economic theorist to define and elaborate the idea of capital as the self-expansion of value. Productive capital initiates a process in which a sum of value expands quantitatively by setting in motion the production and appropriation of surplus value. Successful appropriation then renews this process on an expanded scale as more value is deployed in pursuit of ever greater profit and growth. Capitalism's inherent nature finds expression in the process: its "law of motion" is the limitless pressure for expansion of value.

This nature of capital leaves its mark on every aspect of capitalist society. Because productive capitalists personify productive capital, it must be in their nature to seek to expand value without limit. Similarly capitalist firms bear the stamp of their location within the structural logic of capitalism's law of motion. Capitalist firms and capitalists become, then, bearers of a drive to expand value, given to them by the nature of capital. Sweezy specifies this structuralism nicely:

> The circulation form M-C-M′, in which the capitalist occupies a key position, is *objectively* a value-creation process. This fact is reflected in the *subjective* aim of the capitalist. It is not at all a question of innate human propensities or instincts; the desire . . . (to accumulate capital) springs from [the capitalist's] special position in a particular form of organization of social production. (Sweezy 1966, 80)

For members of this school, the accumulation process is the very mechanism of economic reproduction, and as such it is the ultimate explanation for the entry point aspects of other radical theories. Capital accumulation reproduces the relations of production between capitalist and worker through which surplus appropriation and class exploitation take place. Accumulation by capitalists reproduces as well the uneven structure of property ownership, for it is the capitalists, and not workers, who use the surplus to purchase and thus control the means of production. It also reproduces relations of power enabling the capitalist to boss the worker. Viewed in this determinist fashion, capital accumulation becomes the essence of every dimension of the relationship between worker and capitalist.

Among the authors identified with this approach are Harvey (1982), Levine (1975; 1977; 1978; 1981), Steindl (1976) and Sweezy (1966; 1972); Baran and Sweezy's analysis (1966) remains a classic exemplar.[12] They deploy a two-pronged essentialist strategy: relationships in society are first reduced to the workings of giant monopoly corporations and then the complex actions of these corporations are interpreted as manifestations of their inherent drive to expand:

> The heart and core of the capitalist function is accumulation: accumulation has always been the prime mover of the system, the locus of its conflicts, the source of both its triumphs and its disasters. (1966, 44)

There are, of course, differences among the proponents of specific accumulation theories,[13] but all share a commitment to the notion of productive capital accumulation as the "prime mover" in determining all else, including power over workers and property, receipt of the workers' surplus labor, cultural phenomena, political laws and regulations, and so forth. Like some fundamental law of the natural world, the law of accumulating productive capital embodies within it the secret cause of the expansions and declines of capitalism.

FORCES OF PRODUCTION THEORIES

Another kind of radical theory takes as its entry point the technical ways and means of physically producing goods and services, called traditionally the forces of production. Every sort of economic theory gives a role to technological change, but forces of production theories give technology and its autonomous development the essential place in a strict hierarchy of causal importance. The forces of production constrain and ultimately determine the shape of viable social relations of production; social relations which fail to correspond to ongoing developments in the productive forces must change under the influence of contradictory and sometimes revolutionary pressures. The unity of forces and relations of production (the mode of production or economic base) then governs the political and cultural aspects of the superstructure. The approach thus embodies a thoroughly determinist economic structuralism, in which even economic relations and their dynamics are reflections of the almost pre-economic level of the technological structure.

As is so often the case, proponents of the forces of production as essentialist entry point find ample support for their views in Marx's writings, as in the statement that "The first premise of all human existence, and therefore of all history [is] that men must be in a position to live in order to be able to 'make history.' . . . The first historical act is thus . . . the production of material life itself" (Marx and Engels 1968, 16). The act of laboring to produce "material life" is itself one of the developing forces of production, and this "first premise" is wedded to determinist logic in a long tradition of so-called "orthodox" Marxism (Stalin 1940, Lange 1963, Cornforth 1954, Dobb 1963). Perhaps the leading contemporary advocate is Cohen, who self-consciously stresses his intellectual roots:

> For it is an old-fashioned historical materialism which I defend, a traditional conception, in which history is, fundamentally, the growth of human productive power, and the forms of society rise and fall according as they enable or impede that growth. The focus is on the more basic concepts of the theory, those of forces and relations of production, [with] unusually little discussion . . . of class conflict, ideology, and the state. (Cohen 1978, x)

Little discussion of these topics is needed because, for Cohen, such political and cultural phenomena are merely effects rather than causes, and are far removed from the technological interaction with nature which is to him so basic.

The entry points of other radical theories share a similarly derived status, since for Cohen the existence of a surplus, as well as the social relations affecting its size, form and disposition, depends logically and historically on the prior development of the productive forces. So long as productive forces are very much underdeveloped, labor productivity (the ratio of total wealth produced to the direct labor required to produce it) is insufficient to permit any kind of surplus. Only with the growth and development of the forces of production is it possible to produce the surplus which permits some individuals to live off the efforts of others.

Exploitative class relations thus have an essential precondition: Cohen reduces control over property and power over people to the emergence of a surplus, and then reduces that surplus to the development of the forces of production. He understands the relations of production to be "relations of effective power over persons and productive forces" (Cohen 1978, 63). As aspects of capitalist relations of production, power over physical means of production and power over workers act together to ensure the production of a surplus for capitalists. But their impact on the production of a surplus is itself explained by the development of the forces. Thus relations of production—whether in regard to the class aspect, i.e., the appropriation of surplus labor, or the power wielded by capitalists over laborers and property—are finally grounded in the forces of production: "relations are as the are *because* they are appropriate to productive development" (Cohen 1978, 136). Were they inappropriate, they could not persist, since their role is to facilitate but not prevent the development of the forces (Cutler et al. 1977, 135–53).

With regard to capital accumulation, here again the pattern of cause and effect is inverted. Whereas for accumulation theorists, it is the inherent capitalist drive to accumulate that produces development of productive forces, for Cohen the latter is causally prior. Capitalist firms do indeed seek to expand value, but what makes this inevitable is the fact that competition will bankrupt and eliminate any firm which fails to develop the productive forces in the most efficient manner possible (Cohen 1978, 197). Competition thus enforces accumulation, rather than vice versa, but the competitive relations between capitalist producers are themselves derived from the underlying materialist imperative for qualitative change in the forces of production. No matter how the argument turns, whether dealing with exploitation of labor, power over physical property or people, or with capital accumulation and competition, productive forces remain the essence of the story.

COMPOSITE ENTRY-POINTS: STRUCTURALISM AND HUMANISM COMBINED

From our discussion so far it may appear that structuralism and humanism are simple alternative positions, utterly antithetical and opposed. In fact, the relationship between them is often more complex, with elements of both positions affirmed simultaneously within a single discourse, in a more or less conscious effort to overcome the limits of any single form of determinist logic.

An excellent example of the use of a consciously composite entry point is the approach now known as the "social structures of accumulation" school (Gordon et al. 1982; Bowles et al. 1983).[14] Here, as the name would indicate, it is society's evolving institutional structures which define the different distinguishable phases of capitalist growth, through their conditioning effects on the form and pace of accumulation. These complexly given structures thus have a central role in explaining the profitability of capital and, through that, the crises which periodically erupt in the course of social development. But despite the deliberate bow to structuralist concerns, these authors are simultaneously engaged in a humanist examination of power, especially the power exercised by individual capitalists in dealing with workers, or foreign capitalists, or citizens in general.

The presence of both structuralist and humanist elements raises the question of their relation, and for Bowles, Gordon and Weisskopf, the ultimate weight is given to power and the individual wills of capitalist agents of power. On the one hand, institutional structures are understood to influence or regulate the relative power wielded by capitalists over workers. But on the other hand, the very mediating role of these structures is itself explainable in terms of the deployment of power by capitalists. The composite entry point of power and social structures collapses in the last instance into a singular humanist essence, capitalist power.[15]

A different sort of composite is present, seemingly unconsciously, in the work of Cohen. As already discussed, his project is structuralist: to present a rigorous defense of the essential determining role played by the development of the technical forces of production. And yet, when he confronts in passing the problem of justifying the inevitability of development of the productive forces, Cohen the structuralist slips into a thoroughgoing humanism. Evolution in the structure of technology is a consequence of the inexorable drive of human beings to master their environment, a drive ultimately rooted in three "enduring facts of human nature": people are rational, they always confront scarcity, and they always seek to do better (Cohen 1978, 152). Given these attributes of human nature, he concludes that it would be "irrational" for humans not to develop the forces (1978, 153). Once rationality is stamped on the human species, development logically follows, and Cohen is off and running on his determinist horse.[16]

Cohen is hardly alone in employing this tactic, which is common both inside and outside the radical tradition. When an essentialist argument of one form or another is confronted with questions about the essence it champions, it tends to offer a determinist explanation in terms of a different essence. Structuralism seeks its ultimate justification in humanism, and vice versa.

Roemer's work is perhaps the best example of the tensions created by a consciously composite entry point. As already discussed, Roemer regularly stresses the centrality of the structure of property ownership, but at the same time he is a vigorous proponent of the microfoundations approach, reducing social outcomes to choices made by individual human agents. Both tendencies are visible when he states. "A person acquires membership in a certain class by virtue of rational activity on her part, by virtue of choosing the best option available subject to the constraints she faces, which are determined by the value of property she owns" (Roemer 1988, 10). The resulting composite entry point melds elements of structuralism (the pattern of property endowments) and humanism (individuals with personal preferences and an innate rationality). But this mix is an uneasy one; pushed to defend the central place of either, he tends to retreat to the other in an effort to affirm both.

Property ownership plays an essential role ultimately *because* of the universal rationality of human choosers. Property is not merely *a* constraint on human choice, but the *binding* constraint, only when the criteria for optimal decision-making are identical in every other respect. It is because all choosers are similarly motivated by rational self-interest that their unequal property holdings assume the essential place in explaining different class positions. Conversely though, when challenged to justify the humanist premise of a universal pattern for individual choices, Roemer returns to the structural significance of property ownership. To maintain any link with the Marxian tradition, the preferences on which rational choices are based cannot be treated as exogenous properties of the individual. Roemer deals with this by arguing that "preferences of individuals are to a large extent determined by the property forms that exist in the societies in which they live" (1988, 13). Thus at least this key dimension of the nature of individual action has structural determinants located in the social "environment" (1986, 191–201), although rationality itself seems to remain untouched by anything else. At times the disjuncture between the two entry points takes a discursive form, with his analytical models embodying the pure choice-theoretic approach (with exogenous preferences) while the accompanying prose stresses the significance of the social context. This sort of tension is, we think, almost unavoidable when determinist logic seeks to confront the limitations of any singular essence.

THEORIES OF CONSCIOUSNESS

Other radical social theories begin with an entry point of consciousness. That is, they make the ideas in some or all people's minds the focus and usually also the essence of their explanations of social and economic change. They articulate a cultural essentialism which reverses the usual pattern of linkage between base and superstructure: the culture of a time and place, as expressed in its pattern of consciousness, determines the political and economic relations present.

In the logic of these theories, cultural conditions ultimately govern whether reproduction occurs. Social structures survive only to the extent that people accept them as necessary, desirable, or both; naked power and economic pressure alone cannot long maintain structures which contradict socially prevalent ideas of rights, justice, goodness, etc. Thus, for example, in certain radical theories the existence and persistence of capitalist exploitation ultimately requires the dominance of particular conceptions of the worker-capitalist relation. Workers who view capitalist income as the just reward for saving or risk-bearing will neither resist direction nor protest against the capitalist system. Indeed, they will likely accept the political and economic institutions of capitalism as valid or even inevitable. On this basis, fundamental economic and social change can emerge only given a prior change in the consciousness of the mass of exploited people. Consciousness must break from the pattern of acceptance to one of militant rejection of the ideas that justified previous social roles and relations, a rejection based on allegiance to concepts and beliefs appropriate to an alternative social system. Thus the existence, extent, and outcomes of struggles for social change depend ultimately on the patterns of consciousness of those on all sides of such struggles.

Lukács (1976) exemplifies this approach by treating the consciousness of the industrial proletariat as the key to the possibilities for socialist revolution. So long as the capitalist class succeeds in convincing the mass of people to see the world through its concepts of social life (its notions of fairness, productivity, markets, democracy, human nature, and so on), the masses can only play roles appropriate to ongoing capitalist reproduction. Only when those concepts are supplanted by Marxian alternatives (exploitation, class, equality, democracy, and so on) can the masses find the organization, determination, and vision needed for successful social change.

Thompson's (1963) famous history of the English working class goes further in making the meaning of the term "class" dependent on ideas self-consciously present in people's minds. Only when English workers finally came to see themselves as a distinct, exploited class within and also against the particular structure of capitalist England were they really a class at all:

> Class happens when some men, as a result of common experiences (inherited or shared), feel and articulate the identity of their interests as between themselves, and as against other men who interests are different from (and usually opposed to) theirs. (Thompson 1963, 9)

In effect, class exists here only through the self-consciousness of those who see themselves as class actors.

Another kind of culturally determinist economic theory (present, for example, in Bowles and Gintis 1986) holds that basic ideas of social justice, freedom, and democracy are more or less universal. What varies is the degree to which alternative economic systems support and embody these ideas. If a system does measure up to these ideas, social stability reigns, but if not, struggles ensue as people become "alienated" from economic institutions and from one another. Social consensus disintegrates until institutional change restores conformity with the basic ideas of a good society.

While cultural determinist approaches are common in radical social theory, they figure less prominently within radical economics. By making economic outcomes the effects of non-economic aspects of society, theories of consciousness tend to demote economics from the center of theoretical attention, with the uncomfortable implication that economic theory is somehow less central than cultural theory in understanding society. So radical economists generally shy away from giving major stress to cultural developments, although consciousness is often invoked as a secondary point or theme.

THEORIES OF CLASS AND OVERDETERMINATION

There is wide variation in the entry points chosen by the theories so far catalogued, but all are varieties of essentialism. As suggested, each chooses some aspect(s) of the economic, political, or cultural context for class exploitation and interprets class, and indeed the rest of society, as shaped and ultimately determined by the chosen aspect(s). In the process, the concept of class takes on different meanings in each, as class is understood as a phenomenon of each successive essence. A radical alternative within the radical tradition thus involves not simply shifting the focus to surplus labor appropriation, in place of the various aspects of the context said by others to cause it, but also rejecting the causal conceptions of determinist logic in favor of the mutual interaction and constitutivity of overdetermination. The final radical theory we consider does just that: our own position within the spectrum of radical economics affirms the entry point of class and the logic of overdetermination.

Our emphasis on the class aspect of society deserves explanation. We take class as our entry point because the story of class exploitation is the one we are most interested in telling since, in turn, it is the one we are most interested in changing. As already suggested, we regard Marx's invention of the vocabulary of class analysis as his original contribution to social theory. But the class dimension of social life is as little recognized, as much repressed, today as it was in Marx's time, and not only by theorists in the neoclassical tradition. To view class exploitation as a derivative effect of underlying structural conditions or human traits is to strip it of the central place which we, as both Marxists and antiessentialists, wish to preserve.

By placing the concept of class at the center of our analysis, we do indeed wish to say that class is "most important" *to us*, but only in a very specific sense. The distinction made at the beginning of this paper is relevant here: a theory expresses its priorities through both its entry point and its logic, but the implications of these two theoretical choices are quite distinct. There is a fundamental difference between, on the one hand, the "importance" attributed to some aspect chosen as the focus, the organizing principle of analysis, the means by which one's political and moral goals are expressed and given priority in discourse and, on the other, the "importance," in the causal sense, of an aspect elevated to a privileged place within the logic of theory. Perhaps the most radically unconventional characteristic of our approach is that we affirm the importance class has to us, as the focus of analysis and efforts for change, precisely by denying, to it or any other aspect of society, the sort of causal importance which determinist theories forever seek to assign. Both the theory and the politics of class are, we think, better off without the seductive simplicity of "the last instance."

The problem then is how to make sense of class as one aspect within a totality of aspects, each conceived as the site of influences emanating from all the rest, each therefore existing in a state of ongoing contradiction and change. Our answer is that for any distinctive sort of class process to exist, it must have its conditions of existence secured, conditions which include the very aspects taken as entry points in alternative radical theories.

For example, surplus value is produced for and appropriated by capitalists due in part to the complex consciousness of workers and capitalists about themselves, their relationship to each other, and to the work process. Here we recognize the focus of the consciousness theories just discussed. From the perspective of overdetermination, though, consciousness is only a partial rather than an essential determinant of class exploitation. Clearly, without appropriate and sustaining attitudes, ideas, and feelings within and between workers and capitalists, class exploitation is problematic, but even a radical change in consciousness will not necessarily alter the class process in a way that automatically fulfills the aim of the radical theorist. For example, workers who understand that they are exploited cannot be assumed to respond with a struggle to eliminate or even change that class status. The awakening to exploitation will certainly push workers in a new direction, since their altered consciousness represents a new and contradictory influence on every aspect of behavior, but it is also possible for other cultural processes with their own different and complex meanings to undermine the impact of that very class consciousness. For instance, workers may come to understand their exploitation but because of patriotic feelings generated by a nationalistic message, work even harder to produce surplus for the capitalists.

In like fashion, each of the other aspects already catalogued as the essentialized entry point of a different radical theory can be similarly understood as a *partial* determinant of the existence and form of class exploitation. Each has its own effects: power, since capitalists use a variety of different institutional mechanisms to coerce surplus labor from workers; property, in that workers are dispossessed from effective control over the means of reproducing their social existence; accumulation, because capitalists continually reproduce the relations of exploitation by reproducing productive capital on an expanded scale; technology, through the pressure on capitalists to innovate or risk going out of business and thus losing their surplus value. Each non-class entry point makes its own valid contribution to the story of why class exploitation exists. Consequently, from the overdeterminist perspective, the notion of class exploitation takes on a rich meaning as the locus of all these different and unique effects propelling workers to produce and capitalists to receive surplus value. Class exploitation cannot be reduced to any one of them, as its essence. It follows that for class exploitation to continue, each of its conditions of existence must be reproduced. But, as suggested above, since there are many different configurations of consciousness (power, property, etc.) capable of sustaining capitalist class relations, no particular state of consciousness (power, property, etc.) can ever be considered an essential condition for class exploitation.

The logic of a theory of course affects its agenda for change. The chief goal of a class theory is change in the performance and appropriation of surplus labor, but given overdetermination, we recognize that that aim itself cannot be achieved without changing one or more of the non-class aspects supportive of exploitation. The agenda for this sort of class theory must include the altering of both class and various non-class processes, in the hope that those changes will produce contradictions threatening the survival of the class structure.

But even though overdetermination argues the importance of these non-class aspects to the survival of the class aspect, the constitutive effects are inherently two-way. It is the generation, appropriation, and subsequent *distribution* of the surplus in particular ways that allows for the perpetuation of power differentials, inequalities of ownership, and so on. Capitalists use parts of their appropriated surplus, for example, to pay managers to maintain a hierarchical structure of authority and to accumulate productive capital, sometimes embodying new production techniques. They use parts to pay owners of capital to gain or maintain access to physical or financial property. And they pay taxes out of their surplus to the state to produce an educational system which, among its other effects, reinforces in each generation the attitudes, beliefs, and allegiances "natural" to participants in an exploitative economy. The reproduction of a capitalist surplus requires these distributions, but equally it is the class process of surplus generation which provides the revenues available to reproduce these non-class aspects.

Systematic interdependence of this sort can be incorporated into the vocabulary of class itself. Some individuals may occupy what we have called "fundamental" class positions if they participate directly in the class process either as performers or appropriators of surplus labor. But since many activities beyond these are intimately linked to the reproduction of the class structure, we use the term "subsumed classes" to designate individuals whose non-class activities (necessary for the existence of fundamental classes) allow them to receive a share of the surplus (Resnick and Wolff 1987). Capitalist society is thus composed of its fundamental and subsumed classes: each is necessary for the other, and both, in the richness of their varied forms, represent the meaning of class as a developed entry point.

As already noted, other radical theories understand classes in their own very different ways. Capitalists, for example, may be defined as "accumulators" or "innovators" or "owners" and so on, or perhaps composites of these. In the effort to cut through to what is "really" causally important, determinist theories seem invariably to end up reducing some dimensions of class to others, in the process losing both the separation and the interdependence of fundamental and subsumed classes. Our approach directly seeks to avoid this. In the end, it is not that we consider property, power, accumulation, technology, or consciousness to be unimportant. It is that the web of interconnections among them is so elaborate, so conditional, and so changeable that any sort of "ultimate" causal hierarchy subtracts from rather than adds to our ability to comprehend the changes needed for the end of exploitative social relations.

A FINAL WORD

Our critical examination of alternative radical economic theories and the grounds on which we distinguish them are, of course, much influenced by the particular radical theory we embrace, the overdeterminist class theory (Resnick and Wolff 1987). For us, it avoids the constraints imposed by essentialist logic, while affirming the relative importance of diverse aspects of life in (over)determining that life. It thus recognizes the attempts of both structuralists and humanists to affirm the importance of their respective positions, but refuses to allow the essentialist claims of either position. Our approach offers class as the entry point of analysis but denies to class the status of hidden essence of non-class parts of life. It is class which we choose to stress because, like many Marxists before us, we view its existence in society as an outrage. The strength of this feeling shapes in part our commitment to class as an entry point.

Nonetheless, we recognize the key contributions of those other radical theories to our own, for they underscore the importance of struggles over property, power, consciousness, accumulation, and technology to the struggles over class. We would only hope that other radical theorists would likewise recognize the importance of struggles over class to the various struggles they see as crucial. It seems to us that such mutual recognition is possible without reducing the importance of one struggle to the other. Anti-essentialism can be an important principle in rebuilding the unity that has eluded radical forces for some time.

NOTES

1. We prefer this term to the alternative, "dialectics," because the latter is loaded historically with diverse meanings from Greek and especially Hegelian philosophy. Marxian dialectics, although influenced by both philosophies, still differs from them. See Althusser (1969); Resnick and Wolff (1987).

2. Our discussion of these economic and non-economic entry points problematizes our use of the term "economic," since for us there is no discernible field strictly definable as "radical economic theory." All theories considered in this paper are *social* theories: they employ different social aspects—economic, political, and cultural ones—as their respective entry points, and examine social, and not just economic or political or cultural, changes. We use the term "economic" rather than "social" merely because currently it represents a labeling with which most radicals feel reasonably comfortable.

3. In practice, this distinction is often less clearcut than it may seem here. In defining "relations" and "forces" of production, many authors allow *non*-economic aspects—dimensions of power or cultural abilities—to creep into the meaning of what were supposedly sovereign *economic* categories. This breakdown of boundaries between categories suggests the difficulty of specifying aspects of life independently of one another. The very terms "relations" and "forces" of production seem to deconstruct themselves when some radicals put them to use in social analysis.

4. To their credit, Hindess and Hirst recognized in their *Mode of Production and Social Formation* (1977) the slip into economic determinism of their first book on modes of production (1975). Their work on the methodological issues since then has been exemplary for its antiessentialist stance, although they are not always so successful in their social analyses.

5. For a thorough and interesting discussion of the differences and similarities between radical structuralists and humanists, see Cullenberg (1988).

6. For example, the work of some members of the Frankfurt School, particularly

Horkheimer (1972), employs an entry point of human consciousness and culture, and yet the stress on "dialectical" interactions is thoroughly in tune with overdetermination.

7. We stress only correlation since there is no necessity for the pairing always to hold, particularly for non-radical theories. For example, a theory whose essentialized point of entry is the given international distribution of power among nation states represents a *political* determinism which is nonetheless thoroughly structuralist. And neoclassical economics, with its stress on individual choice, is clearly a theoretical humanism, and yet by viewing each human as "homo economicus," neoclassicals employ an essentialist logic in which equilibrium outcomes reflect the bedrock *economic* traits of human nature.

8. Radical and neoclassical humanists obviously do differ, in that the former underscore the inevitability of conflict between capitalists and workers while the latter emphasize the harmony that emerges from their superficially antagonistic interests. The radical humanist sees an inexorable drive by capitalists to take advantage of workers, while the workers' inherent interest is in resisting those pressures. In direct contrast, the non-radical humanist stresses the process by and through which the different desires of capitalists and workers are brought into harmony with one another in the market. While Adam Smith's work helps to provide the solution for the non-radical humanist, Thomas Hobbes's thought problematizes that very solution and gives support to the radical humanist's notion of inevitable conflict and struggle.

9. Two excellent surveys of power theorists can be found in Olson (1985) and Hillard (1988). The use of power as an essence is also discussed in Resnick and Wolff (1987, 113–15, 242–45).

10. It is interesting to note that Bowles and Gintis have no need for the Marxian notion of the extraction of surplus labor. Their discarding of the latter idea is premised on their rejection of the labor theory of value and its dependence on the distinction between necessary and surplus labor (Bowles and Gintis 1985). In effect they have collapsed together the notions of necessary and surplus labor to equal merely labor. Consequently, they abstract from the very definition of class exploitation established by Marx. According to the latter, class exploitation involves capitalist extraction not of labor but rather of surplus labor.

11. The influence of Weberian ideas on Marxian thought can be found in Wiley (1987). See also Wolff's review (1988) of this book for further discussion of the importation of some of Weber's ideas into the modern Marxian discourse.

12. Norton in several articles (1983; 1984; 1986; 1988a; 1988b) provides a superb analysis of how this drive to accumulate is at the heart of the work of each of these authors.

13. Indeed, there are economistic and humanist variants, and the internal debates between them concerning the nature of the drive to expand have much in common with those between structuralist property and humanist power theories. See Cullenberg (1988) for an excellent survey.

14. For an insightful critique of the social structures of accumulation approach and, in particular, of its power reductionism, see Norton (1988c). A reaction to Norton is in Bowles, Gordon, and Weisskopf (1988).

15. This rendition of the social structures of accumulation (SSA) is more closely identified with the work of Bowles, Gordon and Weisskopf (1983; 1986) than with Gordon, Edwards and Reich (1982). In the latter approach, the SSA is not reducible to capitalist power in the forms specified by Bowles et al., especially in their more recent work (1986).

16. Cutler et al. present an analysis of this collapse of economism into humanism in their

critical examination of the relationship between forces and relations of production within the writings of Marx. See Cutler et al. (1977, 139–43).

REFERENCES

Althusser, L. 1969. "Contradiction and Overdetermination" and "On the Materialist Dialectic." In L. Althusser, *For Marx*, trans. B. Brewster, 89–128; 163–218. New York: Pantheon Books.

Baran, P., and Sweezy, P. 1966. *Monopoly Capital: An Essay on the American Economic and Social Order*. New York: Monthly Review Press.

Bowles, S.; Gordon, D.; and Weisskopf, T. 1983. *Beyond the Waste Land: A Democratic Alternative to Economic Decline*. Garden City: Anchor Press/ Doubleday.

———. 1986. "Power and Profits: The Social Structure of Accumulation and the Profitability of the Postwar U.S. Economy." *Review of Radical Political Economics* 18 (Spring/Summer): 132–67.

———. 1988. "Social Institutions, Interests and the Empirical Analysis of Accumulation: A Reply to Bruce Norton." *Rethinking Marxism* 1 (3): 44–58.

Bowles, S., and Gintis, H. 1985. "The Labor Theory of Value and the Specificity of Marxian Economics." In *Rethinking Marxism: Essays for Harry Magdoff and Paul Sweezy*, ed. S. Resnick and R. Wolff, 31-44. Brooklyn: Autonomedia.

———. 1986. *Democracy and Capitalism: Property, Community and the Contradictions of Modern Social Thought*. New York: Basic Books.

Braverman, H. 1974. *Labor and Monopoly Capital: The Degradation of Work in the Twentieth Century*. New York: Monthly Review Press.

Callinicos, A. 1982. *Is There a Future for Marxism*? Atlantic Highlands, NJ: Humanities Press.

Cohen, G. A. 1978. *Karl Marx's Theory of History: A Defense*. Princeton: Princeton University Press.

Cornforth, M. 1954. *Historical Materialism*. New York: International Publishers.

Cullenberg, S. 1988. "Theories of Social Totality, the Okishio Theorem and the Marxian Theory of the Tendency for the Rate of Profit to Fall." Ph.D. diss., University of Massachusetts, Amherst.

Cutler, A.; Hindess, B.; Hirst, P.; and Hussain, A. 1977. *Marx's Capital and Capitalism Today*. Vol. 1. London and Boston: Routledge and Kegan Paul.

Dahrendorf, R. 1959. *Class and Class Conflict in an Industrial Society*. London and Boston: Routledge and Kegan Paul.

Dobb, M. 1963. *Studies in the Development of Capitalism*. New York: International Publishers.

Elster, J. 1985. *Making Sense of Marx*. Cambridge: Cambridge University Press.

Engels, F. 1975. "Engels to Joseph Bloch," Sept. 21, 1890. In *K. Marx and F. Engels Selected Correspondence*. Moscow: Progress Publishers.

Engels, F. 1976. *Anti-Duhring*. New York: International Publishers.
Giddens, A. 1975. *The Class Structure of Advanced Society*. New York: Harper and Row.
Gordon, D.; Edwards, R.; and Reich, M. 1982. *Segmented Work, Divided Workers*. New York: Cambridge University Press.
Harvey, D. 1982. *The Limits to Capital*. Chicago: University of Chicago Press.
Hillard, M. 1988. "The Political Economy of Invention, R&D Engineers and the Industrial Enterprise." Ph.D. diss., University of Massahusetts, Amherst.
Hindess, B., and Hirst, P. 1975. *Pre-Capitalist Modes of Production*. London and Boston: Routledge and Kegan Paul.
———. 1977. *Mode of Production and Social Formation*. London: Macmillan.
Horkheimer, M. 1972. "Traditional and Critical Theory." In *Critical Theory: Selected Essays*, trans. M. J. O'Connell, 188_243. New York: Seabury Press.
Laclau, E. 1977. "Feudalism and Capitalism in Latin America." In E. Laclau, *Politics and Ideology in Marxist Theory*, 15–50. London: New Left Books.
Lange, O. 1963. *Political Economy*. Vol. 1. Trans. A. H. Walker. New York: Macmillan.
Levine, D. 1975. "The Theory of the Growth of the Capitalist Economy." *Economic Development and Cultural Change* 23 (October): 47–74.
———. 1977. *Economic Studies: Contributions to the Critique of Economic Theory*. London and Boston: Routledge and Kegan Paul.
———. 1978. *Economic Theory, Vol. One: The Elementary Relations of Economic Life*. Boston and London: Routledge and Kegan Paul.
———. 1981. *Economic Theory, Vol. Two: The System of Economic Relations as a Whole*. Boston and London: Routledge and Kegan Paul.
Lukács, G. 1976. *History and Class Consciousness*. Trans. R. Livingston. Cambridge: M.I.T. Press.
Marglin, S. 1974. "What Do Bosses Do: The Origins and Functions of Hierarchy in Capitalist Production." *Review of Radical Political Economics* 6 (2): 60–112.
Marx, K., and Engels, F. 1968. *The German Ideology*. New York: International Publishers.
Noble, D. 1977. *America by Design*. New York: Alfred Knopf.
———. 1984. *Forces of Production*. New York: Alfred Knopf.
Norton, B. 1983. "The Accumulation of Capital as Historical Essence: A Critique of the Theory of Monopoly Capitalism." Discussion Paper Series, Association for Economic and Social Analysis, Amherst, MA.
———. 1984. "Marxian Stagnation and Long Wave Theories: A Review." Paper presented at the Amercian Economic Association meetings, December.
———. 1986. "Steindl, Levine, and the Inner Logic of Accumulation: A Marxian Critique." *Social Concept* 3 (Dec): 43–66.

———. 1988a. "Epochs and Essences: A Review of Marxist Long Wave and Stagnation Theories." *Cambridge Journal of Economics* 12 (June).

———. 1988b. "The Marxian New Classicism: Accumulation and Society in Marx and the Theory of Monopoly Capitalism." Paper presented at the History of Economics Society meetings, June.

———. 1988c. "The Power Axis: Bowles, Gordon, and Weisskopf's Theory of Postwar U.S. Accumulation." *Rethinking Marxism* 1 (3): 6–43.

Olson, W. 1985. "Concepts of Class in Economic Theory: A Critique and Reformulation." Ph.D. diss., University of Massachusetts, Amherst.

Poulantzas, N. 1978. *Classes in Contemporary Capitalism.* Trans. D. Fernbach. London: New Left Books.

Resnick, S., and Wolff, R. 1986. "What are Class Analyses?" In *Research in Political Economy* 9, ed. P. Zarembka, 1–32. Greenwich and London: JAI Press.

———. 1987. *Knowledge and Class: A Marxian Critique of Political Economy.* Chicago: University of Chicago Press.

Roemer, J. 1986. "'Rational Choice' Marxism: Some Issues of Method and Substance." In *Analytical Marxism,* ed. J. Roemer, 191–201. Cambridge: Cambridge University Press.

Stalin, J. 1940. *Dialectical and Historical Materialism.* New York: Monthly Review Press.

Sweezy, P. 1966. *The Theory of Capitalist Development.* New York: Monthly Review Press.

———. 1972. "On the Theory of Monopoly Capitalism." In P. Sweezy, *Monopoly Capitalism and Other Essays.* New York: Monthly Review Press.

Thompson, E. P. 1963. *The Making of the English Working Class.* New York: Vintage Books.

Wiley, N., ed. 1987. *The Marx-Weber Debate.* Beverly Hills: Sage.

Wolff, R. 1988. "The Marx-Weber Debate." *Rethinking Marxism* 1 (1): 169–73.

Wolff, R., and Resnick, S. 1987. *Economics: Marxian Versus Neoclassical.* Baltimore: Johns Hopkins University Press.

Wright, E. O. 1979a. *Class, Crisis and the State.* London: New Left Books.

———. 1979b. *Class Structure and Income Distribution.* New York: Academic Press.

RHETORIC AND RADICAL ECONOMICS: A COMMENT ON RESNICK AND WOLFF

Howard J. Sherman

In their paper on "A Tradition of Theoretical Differences," Stephen Resnick and Richard Wolff sharply criticize the methods or approaches of many Marxists. I agree with the essence (if I may use that much-abused term) of their criticisms and the essence of their own approach. I disagree, however, with their terminology or rhetoric. If one is convinced that a traditional term, such as dialectics, has often been used in an incorrect fashion, there are two possible ways to deal with this problem. One way, used by Resnick and Wolff, is to invent a brand new name for the concept. The concept is then completely reinterpreted under its new name, as when, for example, they substitute "overdeterminism" for "dialectics." The advantage is that everyone is clear that they are doing something new. The disadvantages include a proliferation of new terminology, loss of continuity with traditional Marxist concepts, a more difficult task when explaining the concept from scratch, and a more difficult job in persuading other Marxists.

A second way to deal with popular but mistaken concepts, which this author has often adopted, is to use the traditional name, such as dialectics, but to make it explicit that this is a complete reinterpretation of the concept under the old name. The advantage here is that most Marxists find the name to be familiar, so the new concept is more easily accepted; the disadvantage is that some people may confuse the new interpretation of the concept with the old. This paper demonstrates the second way by (1) substituting my interpretation of dialectics for Resnick and Wolff's concept of overdeterminism; (2) substituting my interpretation of historical materialism for their concept of class; and (3) substituting my interpretation of determinism for their view that it means the same as essentialism.

DIALECTICS AND OVERDETERMINISM

Resnick and Wolff have introduced a useful new concept called an "entry point," meaning the point where an analysis should be started (but not the sole essential factor). For example, one can use class analysis as an entry point in social science. They give a good description of a dialectic process when they say "the behavior of the entry point both is itself shaped by non-entry point aspects and in turn acts to shape the behavior of the rest." They choose to call such an approach "overdeterminism" and, in a footnote, they reject the use of the term "dialectics" because in the history of thought it has been loaded with many other connotations. It might be noted that one reason for rejecting the term "overdeterminism" is that is has a very different meaning and connotation in mathematics.

Hegel conceived of dialectics as an absolute idea which provides a true ontological picture of the laws of movement of the universe (he also used the term to designate a logic and a methodology). Stalin similarly described dialectics as the true, essential laws of movement of the material world. Stalin's concept, not to mention Hegel's, was unscientific in the sense that one cannot state absolute laws for all times and places with no constraints, especially when such laws are merely speculative rather than the result of the experimental process.

As a formal logic, dialectics also makes no sense, since the term "logic" refers to a consistent way of thinking. A logic based on contradiction is a contradiction in terms. Its first axiom would be that every proposition is both true and false. While there is an interesting and titillating bit of insight in that statement, it cannot be the basis of a logic as that term is used in the modern world.

The insight contained in the vague notion that "things are contradictory" comes into play in the use of dialectics as a method or approach to problems in the social sciences (for a detailed discussion of dialectics as a method, see Sherman 1976). When dialectics is treated as a method, the usual criticisms of it—that its laws are overgeneralizations from casual knowledge and are not scientifically testable—are not relevant. A *method* is not tested by checking it against the facts, because it does not assert any facts. A method or approach grows out of our empirical knowledge and experience of the way that social scientists behave. But it does not consist of statements about their behavior; that is the job of the history of science. It rather tries to tell social scientists—or anyone else—the best ways to approach social problems. It suggests what questions to ask; it does not give any answers.

The test of a method is not whether it is true to the facts, but whether it is useful or not useful. A useful method helps produce fruitful hypotheses and directs the attention of researchers to questions that help to expand our research in productive directions. If it is useful for radical social scientists, the dialectic method is a good method; if not, it should be discarded. This paper attempts to present, very briefly in outline fashion, its most important questions.

Interconnection. It is suggested that it is wrong to treat each issue in isolation, as does neoclassical economics; rather the approach to a problem should be relational. Always ask the question: what are the interconnections of this problem to all of society? Thus racism or sexism or drug-pushing cannot be treated as simple matters of individual preferences; one must ask their interconnections with the structure of society, including the relations of production. At the very least, one may ask how the individual preferences are formed, what social structures have determined their evolution, and so forth. More generally, economic problems may not be seen as separate from political or sociological aspects of society because they are all aspects of one society.

Change. Unlike the ahistorical approach of neoclassical economics, radical economics should always ask questions about the historical dimension. Is the social system changing? From where have its present institutions evolved? Where is it going? For example, price is a phenomenon which occurs in a particular stage of society; it did not exist in primitive collective societies and may not exist in its present form in some future societies.

Conflict and Harmony of Opposites. Neoclassical economics, in its version of welfare economics, assumes that there can be harmonious change in a manner which helps everyone while hurting no one. Radical economists should ask: do the different classes have opposing interests? What holds the opposing classes together in a tenuous unity in the present system? Do any tensions exist between the dominant ideology and the actual reality of a society?

Incremental and Revolutionary Changes. Neoclassical economics considers only incremental changes that are quantitatively measurable. Radical economists should not only measure incremental changes but also ask whether there have been or may be revolutionary changes in a given system. We may ask in what direction are incremental changes leading and at what point may a crisis occur, in a given part of a system or the whole system. On the other hand, if we are investigating a revolutionary change, then we should ask what incremental changes have led up to it.

These few suggestions for questions to ask are far from the exciting mysticism of Hegel, but they are useful in a limited manner to a radical economist. The initial questions about interconnection are obviously similar in purpose to Resnick and Wolff's emphasis on viewing the interaction between class and other aspects of society as an ongoing process. The dialectic emphasis on interconnection is exactly opposite to theories of one-way causation by one "essential" factor.

THE TERMINOLOGY OF CLASS OR HISTORICAL MATERIALISM?

Resnick and Wolff state: "In our view, Marxism is distinctive in combining two commitments: the entry point of class and the logic of overdetermination." Translated into traditional Marxist terminology, this means that Marx's most important contributions to methodology are historical materialism and dialectics. Obviously, Resnick and Wolff dislike and thus reject the essentialist connotations of the term "historical materialism," as applied by some Marxists.

In my view, class analysis is the heart of historical materialism (see Sherman 1979). No Marxist can forget that "the history of all hitherto existing society" (except primitive ones) "is the history of class struggles." Yet one should not reduce historical materialism to class because it is broader than that "essential" core. Historical materialism is mainly concerned with the interaction between the economic system and the political-ideological system. The economic system—or mode of production, in traditional Marxist terminology—includes both the forces of production and human relations in production. These relations of production have been class relations except in primitive societies.

As Resnick and Wolff note, there are economic determinists among Marxists for whom the forces of production determine class conflict, while class conflict determines everything else, including political institutions and ideas. On the other side, there are those Marxists who focus their attention on changes in consciousness. A class is defined by these latter Marxist as a group of people with a particular consciousness. Ideas determine class and all the rest of the social-economic structure, as well as historical change.

The economic determinists are wrong because class conflict is influenced by many factors beside the forces of production. Among other things, changes in ideas and consciousness have obviously influenced the course of class conflict. For example, once the ideas of Liberty, Equality, and Fraternity spread widely among the people, they helped shape the class conflicts leading up to the French Revolution.

On the other hand, those Marxists who go to the opposite extreme, explaining everything on the basis of consciousness alone, are equally incorrect or incomplete in their analyses. How is consciousness shaped? It is determined by all of our experiences in a given environment of political and social institutions, class relations, and the forces of production. For example, one can argue that ideology of racism greatly influenced class conflict in the U.S. South before the Civil War. That is true, but the ideology of racism did not come from outer space. It was a convenient rationalization and propaganda tool for slavery; racism or some equivalent ideological distinction between groups has appeared throughout history wherever there has been slavery. Systems need justifications and always find some way, however indirect and complex, to produce them.

My conclusion is broadly the same as Resnick and Wolff's: neither economic determinism nor psychological determinism is an adequate analytic framework. Instead of any one-way determinism, we must use an interactive model with two-way determinism. We must investigate how economic structure and class relations affect ideas and political institutions, but we must also understand how ideas and institutions influence class relations and the forces of production.

One of the best statements of the interactive interpretation of Marx is provided by Schumpter's evaluation of Marx:

> The economic interpretation of history does not mean that men are, consciously or unconsciously, wholly or primarily, actuated by economic motives.... Marx did not hold that religions, metaphysics, schools of art, ethical ideas and political violations were either reducible to economic motives or of no importance. He only tried to unveil the economic *conditions* which shape them and which account for their rise and fall. . . . of course men "choose" their course of action, which is not directly

> enforced by the objective data of their environments; but they choose from standpoints . . . that do not form another set of independent data, but are themselves molded by the objective set. (Schumpeter 1950, 10–12)

Marx's theory of historical materialism is not merely a theory of interaction at a given time, but is also a dynamic theory of evolution over time through conflict. As Marx put it:

> At a certain stage of development, the material forces of society come in conflict with the existing relations of production, or—what is but a legal expression for the same thing—with the property relations within which they have been at work hitherto. From forms of development of the productive forces these relations turn into fetters. Then begins an epoch of social revolution. (1970, 52)

In this quote, Marx identifies two parts into which he sees the entire economic structure divided. One part is the material forces or productive forces of society, in other words, land, labor, capital, and technology. But Marx always emphasizes the other part, the human relations of production, which he notes are reflected in the laws of property relations. In a class-divided society, the relations of production are then the relations between classes. So class does play the entry point role that Resnick and Wolff assign to it.

In terms of dynamics, Marx argues that, in each type of economic system, the new class relationships at the beginning of the life of that system promote the rapid advancement of the material forces of production. Thus, as Marx described, the advent of capitalism led to miracles of technological growth and capital accumulation. No one has ever described the virtues of early capitalism promoting the growth of the economy with more glowing adjectives than did Marx. His point is that during that period the class structure and the material forces of production worked in harmony to bring about the maximum growth possible in that system.

As the material forces of production develop, however, the class relationships freeze into a rigid and strongly defended form, as those in power defend their wealth. Thus, one does not see slaveowners all agreeing that slavery should be ended. One does not see capitalists all agreeing that private property should be abolished. Instead, each group with economic power uses that power to attempt to control the policies of the state in order to preserve the existing class relationships.

Problems arise, then, because the material forces of production outgrow the old, frozen class relationships of production. For further growth, a different form of class relationship is necessary. For example, although the Roman empire made major advances in the efficient use of government and other administrative procedures, it failed to create much in the way of technological advance during its long history. Finally, it could not cope at all with economic conditions and was replaced by feudalism in Western Europe. Similarly, under capitalism every now and then the strange disease of recession and mass unemployment breaks out in epidemic form. Because the class relations are no longer adjusted to the progress of the forces of production (including technology and capital accumulation), excess output piles up and the production process is scaled back, resulting in increasing unemployment.

Thus Marx has stated a very general dynamic law which helps us to understand evolution, stagnation, and revolution. For Marx, revolution occurs because the increasing tension between productive forces and production relations causes an increase of class conflict. And the conflict that occurs is not only economic. At the level of ideology, there are battles between points of view favoring the capitalist class and points of view favoring the working class. At the level of economics, there are clashes, such as strikes under capitalism. At the level of politics, one class (or class coalition) attempts to replace another. If the ruling class gives in peacefully, then there is evolution. Normally, however, the ruling class defends its "inalienable rights" with the use of violence—resulting in eventual revolution. Notice that the revolution does not come in spite of a given consciousness, but because of a changing consciousness among the rising class or classes.

After a political revolution which empowers a new class, there are revolutionary changes in the dominant ideological views within society. There are also revolutionary changes in class relationships. The new class relations, plus the new political and social institutions, plus the new dominant ideology and new consciousness—all resulting from the revolution—together lead to a new expansion of the productive forces (such as Marx described after the bourgeois revolution). At this point, we have come full circle because the new relations, institutions, and ideas are congruent with the expanding forces of production, so there is little or no tension between them.

DETERMINISM AND PREDETERMINISM

Resnick and Wolff state: "We will use the words 'essentialism' and 'determinism' as synonyms in our argument." Their meaning of essentialism was discussed above. But, in my view, it is useful to use the term determinism in a completely different fashion (see Sherman 1981).

Among economists, it is often assumed that there are only two logically possible positions on this issue. One view is that everything is rigidly predetermined, people are puppets, and the only reasonable political view is fatalism. The opposite view is that everyone has free will, that humans are at liberty to do whatever they will, and that the only reasonable political view is voluntarism. Resnick and Wolff seem to equate "essentialism" with the former view, which can be called "predeterminism," though they do not seem to subscribe to the opposite view stressing free will. However, it appears that Marx criticized both the predeterminist and the free will positions, taking an alternative stance that might be called scientific determinism. Let us examine these three views in detail.

Many religions have considered the path of history to be predetermined by God or Fate, forcing believers to accept their destiny with fatalist resignation. The only pie is in the sky after death. Hegelian philosophy is similar, though not explicitly religious. Hegel spoke of the "world spirit" requiring or predetermining a particular development, such as the rise of Napoleon. In the same way, some historians have explained the rise of American imperialism as "manifest destiny." As late as 1927, one well-known American historian stated: "These great changes seem to have come about with a certain inevitability, there seems to have been an independent trend of events, some inexorable necessity controlling the progress of human affairs. . . . History . . . has not been the result of voluntary efforts on the part of individuals or groups of individuals, much less chance; but has been subject to law" (Cheney 1927, 7). This statement thoroughly confuses predeterminism with laws. If the term law is used in its scientific sense (which only asserts that *A* regularly follows *B*), then events can certainly be subject to laws without being in any sense predetermined.

Some so-called Marxists such as Stalin have interpreted Marx as having a predeterminist theory of the inevitable march of history. They presume general laws of history which operate independently of the actions of individuals. These laws are supposed to be economic in nature, so economic changes control the path of history, regardless of human psychologies or actions. It is this economic predeterminist view that Resnick and Wolff correctly equate with essentialism.

The distinction between this predeterminism (fatalism) and a scientific form of determinism has been clarified:

> *Fatalism* is the view that everything is predetermined, that what happens is not affected by what we do. . . . Everything . . . just happens to us, for nothing is the result of our own decisions. *Determinism* is the view that everything occurs lawfully. That is, for any event there is a set of laws or regularities connecting it with other events. With respect to human conduct, this implies . . . that there are circumstances—in our constitutions, background, environment, and character—that are jointly sufficient conditions for our behavior, including the choices we make. It implies that our choices have causal consequences . . . that our choices sometimes make a difference. (Brodbeck 1968, 671)

John Stuart Mill pointed out the error in thinking that, because about the same number of people are lost at sea every year, it is useless to attempt to save your own life if your ship sinks. On the contrary, he notes that our predictions of deaths at sea assume that people do try to save their lives.

There are those who deny any determinism in history. They can point out that men and women make any decisions they wish to make. One can choose to vote for candidate *X* or candidate *Y*. Yet one can predict to an extent how many people will vote for *X* and how many for *Y* using information on their religious, racial, gender, and class backgrounds. These predictions are based on the average behavior of each group of people. Obviously, an individual who is black, Jewish, female, and working-class may choose to vote for George Bush, but our knowledge of behavioral regularities allows—within limits discussed below—a contrary prediction for the average member of her group because circumstances and background do affect human decisions. A simple example of this ability to predict for large groups of people on the basis of behavioral regularities or "laws" is the yearly estimates of suicides or divorces.

The voluntarist view, that people can make any choice regardless of their circumstances, is widespread in modern American social science:

> Voluntarism has historically been a liberal concept to justify the status quo. When asked why there are rich and poor, liberalism argues that rich and poor exist because many choose to attend school or not, to work hard or not . . . to save or not, etc. . . . [In neoclassical] economic theory each consumer is treated as sovereign, as an autonomous being whose preferences are responsible for all economic behavior, and, consequently, for the entire capitalist system. In bourgeois political theory the voter . . . is likewise treated as [a] sovereign . . . whose political choice determines the course of the political system. (Szymanski 1973, 59)

The entry point of neoclassical economics, which views every action as a result of individual choice and preferences, obscures the functioning of the socio-economic institutions and environment within which we live.

After World War II, in response to the predeterminist views of Stalinist Marxism, the "free will" argument was revived by the existentialist school of Marxism. One existentialist-oriented historian says: "Existentialist-Marxist thought . . . emphasizes . . . the freedom of man to act. . . . many philosophers and historians have rebelled at the idea that men are ruled by 'laws' or 'patterns' of historical development" (Zinn 1970, 279). An existentialist-Marxist philosopher goes further to argue: "Given a scientific interpretation of the world . . . the potential for human liberation is stifled since man has given up responsibility and control of his life to an external force. . . . If we were to follow the argument that Marx is a determinist, we would find no political task for human actors" (Pozzuto 1973, 53–55). Note that these writers not only attack what they call determinism, but also any scientific interpretation, and any scientific laws or patterns — clearly this is not what Resnick and Wolff argue. The confusion lies in their notion that determinism and scientific laws mean just the same as predeterminism and fatalism.

The mess was sorted out to a large extent by Jean Paul Sartre, one of the founders of existentialism who realized that a synthesis with the correct features of Marxism was necessary to have a sensible method. For example, Sartre attacks the vulgar Marxist notion that an artistic work can be explained by the class background of the artist. Sartre argues that, in addition to class, one must consider the gender, race, religion, family background, and personal experiences of the artist to understand the work fully (see Sartre 1968). Sartre's position here is clearly determinist and scientific, but not essentialist, and so it is similar to Marx's own position.

Marx's scientific determinism opposes both predeterminism (fatalism) and free will (voluntarism), while recognizing the grain of truth in each of them. A scientific determinist position simply asserts that all social events are explainable on the basis of observed relationships, *including the existing psychology and behavior of human beings*. In this view, human beings make their own history; that is, human beings can make their own decisions on the basis of their own ideas and psychologies, but these ideas are shaped by the given natural and social constraints in their experience. Without an initial premise that we can explain ideas or dominant ideologies in terms of the social situations that shape them, there can be no science. This type of determinism falls well within Resnick and Wolff's concept of overdeterminism.

Of course, scientific explanation and determinism do not guarantee correct prediction. The success of our predictions is always constrained by (1) the extent of known facts, (2) the analytical theories available (including the available level of mathematics), (3) our imperfect reasoning power, (4) the time available to research a problem, and (5) the fact that we are part of the social process and therefore have limited or biased views of it.

Scientific Marxist determinism emphasizes that humans are "free" to make any decision they care to make, so political struggles may change human decisions, which are a vital part of the social matrix. Humans are "determined" in the sense that their decisions are predictable as a statistical probability for an entire group—within the limits of prediction given above. This is analogous to the prediction of the weather as a statistical probability within the same kind of predictive limitations. Thus, it is perfectly possible for Marx to predict a socialist revolution as a statistical probability within the limits of the knowledge of his period.

CONCLUSION

In my view, Resnick and Wolff are correct in advocating a class entry point and an overdeterminist methodology. But it is better terminology to speak of dialectics, historical materialism, and scientific determinism.

REFERENCES

Brodbeck, M. 1968. "Introduction to Part Eight." In *Readings in the Philosophy of the Social Sciences*, ed. M. Brodbeck. New York: Macmillan.
Cheney, E. 1927. *Law in History and Other Essays*. New York: Harper and Row.
Marx, K. 1970. "Preface to *A Contribution to the Critique of Political Economy*." In *Dynamics of Social Change*, ed. H. Selsam et al. New York: International Publishers.
Pozzuto, R. 1973. "Pre-Marxian Marxism." *Insurgent Sociologist* 3 (Summer).
Sartre, J. P. 1968. *Search For A Method*. New York: Vintage.
Schumpeter, J. 1950. *Capitalism, Socialism, and Democracy*. 3d ed. New York: Harper Torchbooks.
Sherman, H. J. 1976. "Dialectics as a Method." *Insurgent Sociologist* 4 (Summer).
———. 1979. "Technology vis-à-vis Institutions: A Marxist Commentary." *Journal of Economic Issues* 13 (March).
———. 1981. "Marx and Determinism." *Journal of Economic Issues* 15 (March).
Szymanski, A. 1973. "Marxism or Liberalism?" *Insurgent Sociologist* 3 (Summer).
Zinn, H. 1970. *Politics of History*. Boston: Beacon.

2 THE VALUE CONTROVERSY RECONSIDERED

Makoto Itoh

Since the 1970s the ongoing value controversy has focused on the viability and relevance of the Marxian labor theory of value. The number and variety of participants as well as the scope of the theoretical problems considered make this controversy conspicuous even in the long history of economic theories.[1] Along with the need for analyses of the contemporary economic crisis, value-theoretic issues were a driving force behind the recent renaissance of Occidental Marxian political economy. But why does abstract value theory suddenly become so attractive and so central in this period? What are the main issues of the recent value controversy, the background for those issues, and their methodological implications? I shall consider these points briefly in this essay and present my own contributions to some of them, mostly by underlining the importance of the structural relations between the forms and the substance of value.

There are three characteristics of the controversy worth noting as general background. First, the controversy has not developed merely as an internal debate among Marxians: the three-way theoretical confrontation among neoclassical, neo-Ricardian and Marxian schools forms the framework for current debates. Participation of the neo-Ricardian approach in particular characterizes the contemporary value controversy as a "triangular" one. The presence of these fundamentally different methodologies is important, since different attitudes among Marxian value theorists often come from their reactions to other perspectives within the triangle.

Second, the development of value theory is generally regarded among Marxians as relevant to current actual political economic issues, not simply as an abstract theoretical project. Value theory provides an essential frame of reference in the actual analyses of, for example, the social functions of the differentiated wage rates of segmented workers, the social role of women and domestic work, and the feasibility and effects of extending market principles in existing socialist countries. Contemporary Marxian theoretical research is generally motivated to at least some degree by these sorts of actual issues.

Third, in the world economic crisis since 1973 we are witnessing a great historical reversal of certain trends in capitalist development over a century: capitalist investment has become both lighter and more flexible with the development of micro-electronics technologies, eroding both the social position of workers and trade unions and the economic role of the state.[2] This paradoxical restoration of a freer capitalist economy based on market principles has naturally stimulated theoretical interest in the relevance of the basic theory of capitalism, and in value theory especially. At the same time, the deep crisis of Soviet-type societies seems to require Marxians to reflect on their theoretical foundations. Is it too much of an exaggeration to see a reflection of the fundamental nature of the global historical crisis of our age in the fervent controversies over basic value theory?

THE SRAFFIAN THEORY AND CRITIQUES OF THE NEOCLASSICAL SCHOOL

Piero Sraffa's *Production of Commodities by Means of Commodities* (1960) gave a shock to Western academic economists by reaffirming the classical tradition of an objective theory of value and challenging the long dominant neoclassical approach based on psychological preferences. Sraffa mathematically showed that the relative prices of commodities and the general rate of profit are simultaneously and consistently determined by physical data: the viable methods of production of commodities and the real wage rate in physical terms (i.e., physical quantities of wage goods obtainable by workers' wages). Neoclassical price theory, which analyzes the determinants of both exchange values and the distribution of income on the basis of subjective preferences and the equilibrium relations between demand and supply in all markets, is then unnecessary and can be rejected. In addition, Sraffa's analysis of technical choice showed that the selection of favorable technical methods of production turns out quite different from that asserted by neoclassical theory. In the marginalist "parables" based on the aggregate production function, a more labour-intensive method of production must be chosen as most profitable when the wage rate is low, but it will be superseded by successively less labour-intensive methods as the wage rate rises. In contrast, Sraffa proved that reswitching of technologies backward to or forward from a labour-intensive method can occur in a continuous process of rising wages combined with a falling profit rate, depending on the composition of means of production used in each technological method.

The proof of reswitching demonstrated the internal inconsistency of the neoclassical aggregate production function, but it further implied a deeper critique of the neoclassical notion of the value of capital. Neoclassical marginal productivity theory can assert that profit is determined by the marginal contribution of capital to production only by assuming that the quantity of capital can be defined independent of the rate of profit or interest. But the case for reswitching showed anew that if capital is realistically composed of heterogeneous means of production, then its value as a magnitude cannot be given prior to the determination of the profit rate, but must instead be determined simultaneously with the profit rate. Neoclassical theory thus faces a theoretical vicious circle in its attempt to determine values of capital consistent with the profit rate. One must tacitly presume some transcendental common substance of value to salvage the neoclassical approach to capital value and profit, an ironic result given the original neoclassical intent to negate any notion of a common (labour) substance of value, as in the classical and Marxian labour theory of value. These implications of Sraffa's critique combined with similar arguments from left Keynesians like J. Robinson to drive the capital controversy since the 1960s.

Another implication of Sraffa's theory is that the proportion of wages in net national income can vary from zero to one while still permitting viable social reproduction at the resulting profit rate and price structure. This negates the neoclassical conservative view that wage struggles simply frustrate the workings of the market and are therefore economically irrational, generating only increased unemployment and inefficiency. Political implications such as this help explain why Sraffa's seemingly quite technical theory has gained popularity among European leftists, and especially among the supporters of the Italian Communist Party, in addition to Sraffa's already well-known intimacy with A. Gramsci.

Sraffa's theory and subsequent extensions of it have powerfully rehabilitated the objective theory of value buried since the marginal revolution by the dominant neoclassical school, particularly in Anglo-American academia. Combined with the Marx Renaissance in Western philosophy, politics, sociology and other fields, it encouraged a younger generation of economists to revive intellectual interest in Marx's labour theory of value as a development and extension of the classical objective theory of value. Dobb (1973) in particular celebrated Sraffa's contribution to the rehabilitation of the Smith-Ricardo-Marx line of descent in the theory of value and distribution, as opposed to the counter-classical character of the Smith-Malthus line leading to marginalism. But although Dobb's work was profound and influential, he was (probably quite intentionally) silent concerning the basic differences between Sraffian theory and the Marxian theory of value. However, more recent developments in the contemporary value controversy have made it more and more important for us to reconsider the methodological differences between those two theories, as well as their common character as objective theories of value.

Above all, unlike the labour theory of value in the tradition of Ricardo and Marx, the Sraffian theory does not need to define any common substance of values behind prices. Sraffa instead took off from Ricardo's early corn theory of wages and profit developed before his generalized labour theory of value. This characteristic of Sraffian theory in fact made its critique of neoclassical value theory even more persuasive for the young western scholars and students trained as professional neoclassicals. Ever since the classic debate between Böhm-Bawerk and Hilferding,[3] dialogue on value theories between marginalism and Marxism had produced mostly external critiques, those which ultimately question and clarify different assumptions and premises. In contrast, the Sraffian critique of marginalist theory was viewed as a penetrating internal critique, decomposing the neoclassical logic like a detergent working on an oil stain. More specifically, for the young western generation trained in the dominant neoclassical mode, Sraffian theory was easy to understand, with its mathematical, functional and analytical approach and its focus on the determination of equilibrium prices in a market setting. Unlike Marxian value theory, with its unfamiliar analyses of the labour substance of values, its dialectics, and its concern with the historical character of a commodity economy and capitalism, Sraffa's theory was more easily accessible because its criticism of the internal inconsistency of neoclassicism emerged from a conception of the tasks of economic theory fundamentally similar to that of the neoclassicals, who took physics as the ideal model of scientific practice.

The critical achievements of Sraffian theory have been largely approved and adopted by the Western Marxian school which has revived in economics since the 1970s. Since most Marxian economists are also initially educated as professional neoclassicals, their critiques of neoclassical orthodoxy have generally been sharpened by an accurate understanding of the debates between neoclassical and Sraffian theories. But by broadening the perspective of the Sraffian analysis, recent Marxian critiques of orthodox economics, including Keynesianism, have made conspicuous and substantial contributions to the long history of the Marxian critique of political economy (see, for example, Hunt and Schwartz 1972; Green and Nore 1977; Schwartz 1977).

From this Marxian perspective, neoclassical theory is not merely internally inconsistent, as pointed out by the Sraffian school. By viewing the market as the ultimate natural order for economic behavior, neoclassical theory is imbued with subjective individualism and naturalism. This in turn obscures the historically specific character of the capitalist economy, the internal relations of production pressing capital to acquire surplus value from the surplus labour of workers, and enforces a vulgar theoretical consciousness which, as Rowthorn (1980, 16) puts it, functions as an "epistemological obstacle" inhibiting the development of an authentic science of social problems. Through general equilibrium theory, which evades the formal thrust of the Sraffian critique of the aggregate production function, neoclassical theory can determine the market prices of commodities, but only by narrowly and arbitrarily assuming that the structure of initial endowments of resources, goods, and services is given to individuals. Thus, irrespective of the personal intentions or motivations of those who learn or teach neoclassical economics, the theory operates to justify the capitalist social order.

In certain respects, these Marxian critiques of neoclassical economics are applicable also to the neo-Ricardian approach. Actually, younger Marxians often do not hesitate to criticize the theoretical limitations of neo-Ricardianism, unlike their forerunners such as Dobb and Meek. For instance, although Sraffian theory can allow for a sort of class confrontation between real wages and profit, it treats them in practice as complementary shares, as if the distribution of the net product were cooperatively determined. The formal Sraffian analysis is silent concerning the internal mechanism of production of surplus value based on the commodity form of labour-power, and the specific historical nature of such a mechanism. Insofar as Sraffian economics concentrates simply on theoretical determination of equilibrium prices and a general rate of profit, it remains on the same theoretical terrain as neoclassical economics and is similarly trapped by the fetishism of commodities, despite its insistence on an objective theory of value against the subjectivism of marginalist theory.

In opposition to such Marxian criticism, the neoclassical and neo-Ricardian schools offered repeated attacks on Marxian value theory. Beginning from the transformation problem concerning Marx's procedure for transforming values into prices of production, those schools have jointly raised more fundamental questions about the labour theory of value, questions to which the Marxian school has been forced to reply in order to preserve and develop its own theoretical position in the debates.

THE TRANSFORMATION CONTROVERSY

The Sraffian critique based on the reswitching issue pointed out the implicit neoclassical assumption of a common substance or quasi-substance of value when heterogeneous capital goods are quantified prior to determination of equilibrium prices and profits. The critique also revealed theoretical inconsistency in the neoclassical treatment of changes or differences in the composition of capital. In this sense, Sraffian theory worked more generally like a double-sided mirror, reflecting the similar problems of both other approaches. Sraffians played prominent roles in both the capital controversy with neoclassical economics and the transformation controversy with Marxian economics. What accounts for such a simultaneous double critique? Is it simply because neo-Ricardian theory rejects any concept of a substance or quasi-substance of value? In any case, the combatants in the capital controversy found common cause in criticizing the similar problems of the Marxian transformation of values into prices of production. The Marxian responses to such criticisms rekindled the transformation controversy and extended it into a second stage qualitatively distinct from the earlier debates within Western academia in the 1940s and 1950s.

As is generally known, Marx defined the quantity of labour embodied in a commodity as its value, and in the first two volumes of *Capital* investigated the inner laws of motion of capitalist production by assuming equal exchange of such labour values as the content of the law of value. Then in volume 3 of *Capital*, commodity values were transformed into prices of production—cost price plus average profit—which are enforced by competition of capitals as the actual standard for fluctuating market prices. If we define the labour value of a commodity as $a_i = c_i + v_i + s_i$, where c_i represents constant capital transferred from means of production, v_i variable capital necessary to purchase labour-power, and s_i surplus value embodied, then, assuming for simplicity only circulating capital with a uniform one year turnover, Marx's definition of price of production p_i can be written as $p_i = (c_i + v_i) + r(c_i + v_i)$, where $r = \Sigma s_i / \Sigma(c_i + v_i)$. In this formulation, the average profit added to cost price is simply redistributed surplus value—each capital gains a portion of total surplus value calculated at the general rate of profit r. As a result, in the aggregate, total profit equals total surplus value ($r\,\Sigma(c_i + v_i) = \Sigma s_i$) and total price equals total value ($\Sigma p_i = \Sigma a_i$).

As Marx himself noted, there remain two problems in this transformation of values into prices of production. First, if the actual standard in the market is prices of production and not values, what special relevance do values have which requires their presentation prior to the notion of prices of production? This is the so-called "contradiction" between the first and third volumes of *Capital*, a theme of continued controversy since Böhm-Bawerk's Marx critique and Hilferding's counter-critique. Second, in Marx's definition of prices of production, the components of cost price are expressed in terms of labour values ($c_i + v_i$) which have not yet been transformed into prices of production. This theoretical incompleteness requires revision.

The first stage of the transformation controversy in the West concentrated on this second problem, setting the first one aside. The debates until the 1950s thus defined the transformation controversy in a narrow sense: all the participants, from Bortkiewicz, a turn of the century Ricardian, through Sweezy, who revived Bortkiewicz's solution and initiated the controversy, followed "the rules of the game" in taking Marx's labour theory of value as a given presupposition. With this as a common premise, the controversy focused on mathematical solutions and the characteristics of those solutions when the elements of cost price are also consistently transformed into prices of production. It was shown that *relative* prices and a general rate of profit can be determined from physical data: input-output coefficients (the technological conditions of reproduction) and real wages; the n simultaneous equations for n industries contain $(n - 1)$ value-price coefficients and the general profit rate as unknowns. In such a solution, labour is assumed to be homogeneous across industries and joint production is excluded. A focal point of controversy concerned Marx's two aggregate equalities—does a correct solution permit simultaneous equality of total profit and surplus value

($r\,\Sigma(c_i + v_i) = \Sigma s_i$) and total price of production and value ($\Sigma p_i = \Sigma a_i$)? It turned out that either of these conditions could be individually used to determine the *absolute* levels of prices of production, but in general both cannot hold simultaneously.

Unlike this first stage of the transformation controversy, in the second stage since the 1970s the previously accepted rules of the game became an issue for debate. The modern transformation controversy merges the earlier transformation problem defined by Bortkiewicz with a broader questioning of the very concept of labour value in the tradition of Böhm-Bawerk. Samuelson, a representative neo-classical, opened the second stage of the controversy in 1971, arguing that Marx's labour theory of value holds as a theory of relative commodity prices only with special assumptions: the absence of means of production (zero constant capital) or profit (zero surplus value), or the presence of a uniform organic composition of capital in all industries. Further, Marx's theory of price of production defining the elements of cost-prices in terms of labour value, is valid only in the case of "equal internal compositions of capital," in which in all industries the proportions among goods used as physical inputs and among goods consumed as means of subsistence by workers are identical to the proportions among goods in total social output. This case surely lacks generality. Furthermore, the procedure which transforms the elements of cost prices into prices of production in line with the Bortkiewicz-Sweezy (B-S) solution simply begs a prior question, in Samuelson's view. Since the result is the same as the solution of a system of price equations directly constructed from technological input-output data in physical terms, Samuelson concludes that the value analysis in volume 1 of *Capital* is nothing but an "un-necessary detour."

Morishima (1973) followed up this line of argument, although he narrows Samuelson's criticism somewhat. Morishima is more sympathetic to Marx's formulation of the relation between the rates of surplus value and profit, as is seen in his use of Okishio's (1963) "Fundamental Marxian Theorem." However, he stresses that Marx's notion of prices of production, with cost-prices defined in terms of value, is valid only when industries are "linearly dependent," a restrictive condition, though less so than Samuelson's "equal internal composition" case which it subsumes. Ultimately, though, Morishima also recommends abandoning Marx's labour theory of value, replacing it instead with a von Neumann type of theoretical model, on grounds of the theoretical difficulties faced in the presence of heterogeneous labour and joint-products or fixed capital.

These criticisms had an unexpected effect among young Western scholars, who now realized that Marxian economic theory, no less than neoclassical or neo-Ricardian economics, might be worthy of mathematical analysis. At the same time, they touched off criticisms by Sraffians along similar lines. For example, Steedman (1977) echoed Samuelson in denouncing the labour theory of value as redundant, since equilibrium prices can be deduced from the physical data of reproduction in a Sraffian way.

A characteristic in common among these recent critics is that all admit the deducibility of embodied labour values from the physical data of reproduction, at least when the problems of heterogeneous labour and joint products are excluded. In this sense, recent critics of the Marxian theory of value do deviate from the older ones like Böhm-Bawerk, who totally rejected the very project of deriving labour values in favor of the marginal utility theory of value. Furthermore, the B-S procedure for transforming values into prices of production is not regarded by recent critics as in itself logically wrong. They have to admit that labour values and prices of production are derivable from the physical data of reproduction, just as equilibrium prices are derivable from the same data in the Sraffian approach. Therefore, the thrust of their criticism is that the labour theory of value lacks general relevance as a direct price theory and is redundant as a means to deduce equilibrium prices in comparison with the more direct Sraffian approach.

In response to this redundancy critique, Marxian theorists almost unanimously stress that Marxian value theory, unlike alternative approaches, is not designed simply to determine equilibrium prices but above all to elucidate the relations of production of surplus value between capital and workers. If, in the classical and Marxian tradition, one views it as a task of economics as a social science to reveal the social relations based upon human labour behind prices, then, far from being redundant, the labour theory of value is essential. Thus, what is at stake is really a question of what the proper tasks of theory are: is the social content of the labour theory of value to be considered a virtue in its own right, apart from the issue of its logical correctness or consistency? This question is not amenable to a formal "scientific" solution, but it is not even admitted as a question within the narrowly limited methodological scope of neoclassical and neo-Ricardian theories.

Contemporary Marxians pondered the transformation problem anew in light of the Sraffian contributions, but with the almost unanimous premise that the principal virtue of Marxian value theory is its focus on capitalist relations of production. For example, Medio (1972) utilized the Sraffian approach for a mathematical analysis of the relation between the rates of surplus value and profit. Desai (1974) emphasized the dimensional difference between the visible price domain and the invisible value domain, and therefore the incommensurability of labour value and price, in assessing the B-S type of transformation procedure. Shaikh (1977) showed that Marx's own transformation procedure was correct as the first step in an iterative process; if Marx's prices of production are used to recalculate the elements of cost price, and the resulting solutions are similarly deployed in subsequent steps, then the process converges to a result identical to the B-S solution. Okishio (1973) made the same point, though the two works were done independently.

As these works gained prominence, other older views ebbed in influence. Hilferding's "historical-logical" interpretation had influenced orthodox Marxians to view transformation from values to prices of production as a process corresponding to the historical development from simple commodity production to full-fledged capitalism. Although Meek (1973) and Becker (1977) made similar arguments, this view is now rather exceptional in contemporary western Marxism. The labour theory of value is generally seen as relevant to the analysis of capitalist relations of production rather than a pre-capitalist simple commodity economy. At the same time, in order to understand the structural relation between values and prices of production in capitalism, the notion of forms of value gained renewed attention. This view is, in particular, associated with the Japanese Uno school, which views the logical distinction as well as the connection between the forms and the substance of value as essential to Marxian theory.

There are some points which now command general agreement among the parties to the recent controversy: the quantities of labour embodied in commodities are consistently determined by given physical data defining the technical conditions of production and the real wage rate, at least when homogeneous labour and single-product industries are assumed, and the social structure of prices of production can be consistently derived from them via the B-S procedure. But there are divergent positions as well, particularly concerning Marx's propositions on the equality of two sets of aggregates. Shaikh (1977), for example, argues that total value or "direct price" must equal total price of production, whereas Laibman (1973–4) maintains that the rate of exploitation must be held invariant in the process of transformation. These two positions are not in general consistent with each other, and neither in general allows for Marx's proposition that total surplus value equals total profit. Desai's dimensional separation between values and prices of production, a position close to some of the Japanese Uno theorists' treatment of prices of production as a form of value dimensionally different from the labour substance of values, can avoid the problem of reconciling Marx's propositions, but does not fully confront the real content of the issue. The equalities represent a continuing theoretical problem, one carried over from the first stage of the transformation controversy.

In my view, this problem can be solved on the basis of a dimensional distinction between the forms and the substance of value, by investigating three interrelated aspects of values. We must inquire how (i) the substance of value produced, or the amounts of labour embodied in commodities given their social and technical conditions of production, determines (ii) prices of production as a form of value expressed in terms of money, but also (iii) the quantities of labour—the substance of value—acquired through those prices of production by each class and industrial branch. If we follow Itoh (1980, 75; 1988, 222)[4] in reformulating the two tables traditionally illustrating the value system and the transformed system of prices of production into three tables showing these three aspects of values, the crucial point can be clarified. If we limit ourselves to comparing produced values and prices of production, (i) and (ii) above, it is hardly surprising that Marx's propositions on the two sets of totals do not directly hold, since the substance of value and surplus value has a quantitative dimension different from that of prices of production and profit. The former is measured by hours of labour and the latter by, for example, pounds or dollars. But the relevant comparison in evaluating Marx's propositions is between (i) and (iii): total value and surplus value produced, and total value and surplus value acquired through prices of production.

These latter magnitudes (iii) can be conceived as follows, assuming stable physical conditions of production, even if these conditions do not last long. First, the substance of value acquired through the transactions involving constant and variable capital is identical to the original value components c_i and v_i. Whatever the set of prices of production, when the elements of cost price within them are used to repurchase means of production and labour-power, the value substance acquired through prices of production must simply replace the labour substance in the constant and variable capital used to produce the products and their values (i). Then, of the components of value, total surplus value (s)—the surplus labour embodied in the social surplus product—remains as the only portion of the substance of value which is partitioned among industries through the average profits incorporated into prices of production. If we assume either a surplus product composed of a single commodity, as in Itoh (1980; 1988), or a uniform composition for the commodities purchased out of profit in an *n*-sector model, each sector's surplus value acquired (s_i') is a share of total surplus value proportional to the industry's profit (p_i) as a share of total profit (p), so that $s_i' = (s)(p_i/p)$. The resulting numbers representing the substance of value acquired ($a_i' = c_i + v_i + s_i'$) and surplus value acquired (s_i') do of course differ from the corresponding entries for value and surplus value produced in each industry, but the totals are the same: total value and surplus value produced are identical to total value and surplus value distributed through prices and profits. Both (i) and (iii) incorporate the elements of cost price ($c_i + v_i$), so it is simply the redistributed surplus value obtained through the receipt of money profits which differentiates the substance of value acquired from the substance of value produced in each industry. Though not fully identical to Marx's handling of the issue, these results are essentially similar and probably well accord with what Marx intended to say in his propositions on the two sets of totals. I think this represents a satisfactory solution to this longstanding problem in the transformation controversy. It is worth noting that the basic logical structure of Itoh's three tables and the main conclusions derived from them remain unchanged even when the model is extended to *n* sectors, and even when market prices are substituted for their gravitational center (prices of production), except for possible cases of destructive price fluctuations.

As discussed, another issue of controversy since Böhm-Bawerk concerns the relevance of the labour theory of value, which poses labour values as theoretically prior to the notion of prices of production. If we reject the historical-logical interpretation and assert the relevance of the law of value in a capitalist commodity economy, can we really maintain that equal exchange of the labour embodied in commodities is the substantial core of the law of value? If this is simply assumed, then the subsequent analysis of capitalist production of surplus value could also be regarded as an assumption without general theoretical validity. My proposal (see

Itoh 1988, 109-48) is to reformulate the content of the law of value by recognizing that, while social reproduction generally requires replacement of the labour time transferred from consumed means of production and that necessary to sustain expended labour-power, no such requirement holds for surplus value. Thus from the beginning the law of value leaves room for unequal exchange of labour, though the deviations are limited by the magnitude of surplus labour embodied in commodities. Distinction of the forms and the substance of value makes such a reformulation possible and permits us to view prices of production as a concrete developed form of the working of the law of value, rather than an exception to it. As discussed in Itoh (1988), this point enriches our understanding of the economic norms common among social formations, and also of the possibilities which can be consciously pursued under socialism as a basic set of social relations.

THE VALUES OF JOINT PRODUCTS

In addition to the question of transformation, the issues of joint production and complex labour have attracted wide attention in the recent value controversy. Many transformation discussions have presumed the absence of joint products and skilled or complex labour. Does dropping this premise entail serious difficulties for Marxian value theory? Morishima recommended abandoning the labour theory of value on just these grounds, and Steedman (1977) caused a turmoil by making the same points in a sensational way in promoting Sraffian theory.

As argued above, in the absence of joint production and complex labour, the values of commodities—the labour substance embodied in them—are fully determined by a simultaneous equation system expressing the physical conditions of production in all industries. Steedman extends this logic to the case of joint production and points out an anomaly in the labour theory of value. Suppose that technical production process *I* jointly produces 6 units of commodity *A* and 1 unit of commodity *B* by means of inputs of 1 unit of labour and 5 units of *A*. The net product of a unit of labour is then one unit of each commodity: (*A* 1, *B* 1). We can define the total labour substance of this net product as $l_a + l_b = 1$, but we cannot determine the division of this labour substance between the two goods. Here the labour values of individual commodities become indeterminate. However, if in addition there is a second technical production process *II* (as must be assumed in Sraffa's theory of the prices of joint products), producing (*A* 3, *B* 12) by means of 1 unit of labour and 10 units of *B*, then l_a and l_b can be determined by solving the following simultaneous equations:

$$5l_a + 1 = 6l_a + l_b$$
$$10l_b + 1 = 3l_a + 12l_b$$

The solutions, however, turn out to be $l_a = -1$, and $l_b = 2$. The labour values of commodities are no longer uniformly positive; they can be negative like the value of A in this case.

Further, if the real wage in physical terms per unit of labour is (A 1/2, B 5/6) on the same technological basis, its labour value must be $(-1)(1/2) + (2)(5/6) = 7/6$. As a result, the surplus value per unit of labour is also negative, since $1 - 7/6 = -1/6$. At the same time, the numeraire prices of commodities expressed in terms of the real wage per unit of labour (P_a and P_b) and the average profit rate r can be determined from the same technological data in the Sraffian fashion, assuming that wages are paid at the end of the year, by the following equations:

$$(1+r)5P_a + (1/2\,P_a + 5/6\,P_b) = 6P_a + P_b$$
$$(1+r)10P_b + (1/2\,P_a + 5/6\,P_b) = 3P_a + 12P_b$$

The solutions, $r = 20\%$, $P_a = 1/3$, $P_b = 1$, are all consistently positive. Therefore, in a viable capitalist economy with fully positive prices and profits, negative value and negative surplus value can emerge in the Marxian labour theory of value. In Steedman's view this reveals a contradiction, an internal inconsistency in the labour theory of value.

The form of Steedman's criticism reveals the limitations of the one-sidedly technological approach of Sraffian theory. When there are joint products, the Sraffian approach cannot determine equilibrium prices and the profit rate without assuming exactly the same number of parallel processes of production as the number of joint products. Realistically, fulfillment of this assumption is hardly guaranteed. Nonetheless, Steedman's critique gave a jolt to a large number of Marxians who had considered the technological determination of labour value to be as solidly grounded as the Sraffian technological price theory. Marxians unanimously objected to Steedman's demand that the rate of surplus value be replaced by the wage-profit ratio as the measure of the rate of exploitation, on grounds that the notion would lose its essential social content if divorced from analysis of the labour time expended by workers. Nevertheless, there remained difficulties and divergent opinions as to how to treat the values of joint products.

Armstrong, Glyn, and Harrison (1978), for example, view the notion of negative values as meaningless, arguing that values cannot be attributed to commodities in the case of joint products; they propose defining the value of labour-power as the total labour required by that group of production processes which is minimally necessary to produce at least the wage bundle with as small as possible a residual of other joint products. A rate of surplus value can be calculated using this definition of the value of labour-power. However, the labour time deemed necessary to reproduce labour-power under this definition will typically produce some of the surplus product as well, and consequently the rate of exploitation will be systematically underestimated. The more prevalent joint production is, and the more interlinked are wage goods with other goods as joint products, the more this definition of the rate of exploitation approaches meaninglessness.

Himmelweit and Mohun (1981) argue from a different angle. According to them, the labour substance of Marx's concept of value depends on the commensuration of different sorts of useful concrete labour as abstract labour through the exchange of commodities, an approach not identical to the Ricardian notion of "embodied labour." The anomalies that cause negative surplus value with positive profit arise from the contradiction between the basic commensuration of labour time through commodity exchange and a secondary commensuration of it via the equalization of profit rates. The anomalies thus reflect a real contradiction in capitalism which, for them, seems to preclude any sort of positive resolution for the theory of value. This attempt to counter Steedman by underlining the role of the market in Marx's notion of the form of value has virtues, but it must be extended in a different direction.

In my view, an original aspect of Marx's theory is his analysis of value not merely as technologically determined embodied labour but as a substance linked with the forms of value in the market. This does not necessarily mean that abstract labour is always qualitatively and quantitatively defined through commodity exchanges, as Himmelweit and Mohun assert in the Rubinite tradition. Qualitatively, both abstract and concrete labour are characteristics of human labour in general, not concepts applicable only in a commodity economy. Quantitatively, the abstract labour embodied in a commodity is generally determinable from the technical conditions of production, independent of fluctuating market prices. However, the theory of market value or market price of production, relevant where different conditions of production are in use within an industrial branch, links the value of output to its representative conditions of production, the technical conditions dominating the adjustments of supply to fluctuations of demand for the product in the market.[5] Therefore, if the more efficient process *II* in Steedman's numerical example above is still in only limited use for a time, while process *I* is the overwhelmingly dominant condition of production, then it is process *I* which defines the market value, since within the social allocation of labour among industries process *I* must be regarded as the standard condition for production of *A* and *B*.

Under these circumstances, the substance of market value, the labour embodied in a unit of *A* and *B* together, must be $l_a + l_b = 1$, since this net product (*A* 1, *B* 1) is produced by a unit of labour in process *I*. But there is no technical rule in common across various social formations to determine the ratio $(l_a/l_b) = \alpha$ within this constraint. In a case like this, we confront a basic freedom, a social "elasticity" in apportioning the labour substance between the joint products, just like the open-ended and elastic possibilities for the disposal of social surplus labour in general. In a communal planned economy without market pricing, the ratio $\alpha = l_a/l_b$ can be lowered if there is a social consensus to foster the direct or indirect consumption of *A* in comparison with *B*, reflecting a particular social ordering of needs in relation to the given technical production processes. The ratio can be elastically adjusted to an appropriate level by observing the effects on consumption and production caused by its alteration. In a capitalist economy though, adjustments of the relation between social consumption and production occur through the price mechanism of the market. Therefore, in theorizing capitalism, a ratio like α above, which allocates the labour substance between jointly produced commodities, can be understood as given by the ratio of the equilibrium prices which express the form of value of such jointly produced commodities. Except for the possible minor repercussions from changes in the labour embodied in other products which use A or B as means of production,[6] the determination of α through the market pricing mechanism would not affect the total labour time embodied in A and B together. And crucially, this approach eliminates the possibility of anomalies such as negative value or surplus value in the theoretical treatment of joint production.

It is interesting to reconsider how the one-sidedly technological approach to value theory which follows from the Sraffian model is not totally effective in comprehending the social relations expressed in amounts of labour and their social disposal. This is an issue fundamentally related to the elastic freedom available in determining and disposing of labour substance generally under various forms of social relations, as in the division of the labour substance embodied in joint products I have proposed. We should recognize the social function of the market pricing mechanism in relation to the forms of value, since this is the mechanism which, in a capitalist economy, determines those aspects of labour relations which are otherwise technologically indeterminate. This recognition fully complements the analysis of the social relations of labour time based on the objective conditions of production and in fact limits the specific aspects of labour substance to be defined through the market mechanism under capitalism. It is thus far from both neoclassical theory and the Rubinite approach,[7] to which we will return below.

COMPLEX (SKILLED) LABOUR IN THE THEORY OF VALUE

The theoretical problems created by complex or skilled labour have been another issue in the contemporary value controversy.[8] If capitalism has an ongoing tendency to deskill and degrade labour, as Braverman (1974) argued, any such problems would be gradually reduced in importance. However, recent studies of the labour process since Braverman have found that systematic segmentation of workers by management is intensifying, along with general degradation of labour. A theoretical frame of reference permitting the critical analysis of segmentation of workers has to be incorporated within the labour theory of value.

For workers performing the same kind of concrete useful labour, the degree of skill is easy to measure by comparing output per unit of labour time. In most productive workplaces capitalist managers typically normalize and rationalize the labour skill involved in each kind of concrete labour by introducing mechanization and automation. Generalization of compulsory and higher education in the capitalist countries also serves the aims of management in promoting such normalization. However, where there are different kinds of useful labour, the skill and intensity of labour cannot be so easily compared. Segmentation of workers actually tends to enhance these sorts of differences among workers. It is a theoretically complicated issue to confront differentiated and complex types of useful labour.

Marx (1976, 135) argued that "complex labour counts only as intensified, or rather multiplied simple labour," claiming that "the various proportions in which different kinds of labour are reduced to simple labour as their unit of measurement are established by a social process that goes on behind the backs of producers," although he never really clarified the nature of this "social process." If it refers to the determination of exchange values in the market, Marx's basic effort to define labour values strictly on the basis of the objective conditions of production seems compromised, as has been charged by non-Marxians since Böhm-Bawerk. On the other hand, Marx also reasoned:

> All labour of a higher, or more complicated, character than average labour is expenditure of labour-power of a more costly kind, labour-power whose production has cost more time and labour than unskilled or simple labour-power, and which therefore has a higher value. This power being of higher value, it expresses itself in labour of a higher sort, and therefore becomes objectified, during an equal amount of time, in proportionally higher values. (1976, 305)

This statement may be interpreted in different ways and does not fully clarify Marx's position on the theoretical relation between the value of complex labour-power and the amount of value produced by it (see Itoh 1988, 152–54). However, an orthodox Marxian interpretation derived from Hilferding's counter-critique of Böhm-Bawerk has argued that complex labour itself represents the embodiment of the labour expended to produce skilled labour-power through a process of special education and training. This position, recently elaborated and mathematically refined by Okishio (1963) and Rowthorn (1980), seems both fully in accord with the technological determination of labour value and rational in proposing that the value created and transferred to output by the labour of skilled workers depends on the labour costs of producing skilled labour-power. I cannot agree with this view, though, as I will explain below.[9]

A different approach to the issue of complex labour is presented by Bowles and Gintis (1977), who oppose the conventional Marxian reduction of complex to simple labour, seeking instead the conceptual tools needed for value theory to encompass the burgeoning phenomenon of labour segmentation. For this purpose they propose an economic model incorporating heterogeneous labour, or multiple types of complex labour; the solution is derived from the (typically different) wage bundles of each type of labour and input-output matrices for both commodity and direct labour inputs. Bowles and Gintis show that, even without any reduction of complex labours, the average rate of profit and prices of production can still be expressed in terms of the structure of value relations, although commodity values, rates of exploitation and organic compositions of capital are all defined as vectors of different kinds of labour. They also show that there is normally an inverse relationship between each wage rate and the rate of profit. For them, these results imply that reduction of complex to simple labour is unnecessary. This approach is, however, quite similar to that of the neo-Ricardians, and indeed Steedman (1977, 87–94) utilizes a similar vector-value analysis of heterogeneous labour in his Sraffian critique of Marx aimed at discrediting the very notion of abstract labour.

Certainly, Bowles and Gintis would not fully accept this critique of Marx, since they underline the necessity of the notion of abstract labour in understanding human social relations and present an account of the rate of surplus value in terms of a unit of "common labour." Common labour in this context signifies that labour hours can be added or compared without any special qualifications or weights allotted to different types of labour. This is an interesting approach, but their exposition fails to examine what makes such a treatment theoretically feasible.

Traditionally in the literature the twin problems of concrete and abstract labour, on the one hand, and complex and simple labour, on the other, have been regarded as theoretically distinct and separate issues. Let us challenge this separation and reconsider the second problem in conjunction with the first. In dealing with the complex labour problem, most have followed Marx's suggestion that complex or skilled labour is intensified simple labour which creates more value in the same working time. However, we should reconsider why various kinds of concrete labour are commensurable as abstract labour even for unskilled workers. The fundamental reason must be the common capacity of human beings, unlike other animals, to perform a wide range of tasks and to work interchangeably at them, a capacity based upon rich mental and linguistic ability, itself the product of the long history of human beings (though one intensified in some ways by the generalized modern system of education). Because of this, even the most unskilled and monotonous work is still the expenditure of this common and extensive power of human beings. The concept of abstract labour should be grounded on this common potential of human beings to perform various kinds of work. Precisely because each worker has such wide potential, "the less he is attracted by the nature of the work and the way in which it has to be accomplished, and the less, therefore, he enjoys it as the free play of his own physical and mental powers, the closer his attention is forced to be" (Marx 1976, 284), and the more tiring that work must be.

In this sense, simple unskilled labour, no matter how monotonous, actualizes this complex human capacity to work, using different combinations of the various human mental and physical abilities depending on the different form of concretely useful labour involved. Hence, even when we consider only different kinds of unskilled work, a comprehensive comparative assessment or measurement of the differential intensity of labour is theoretically problematic, indeed impossible. Of course, in practice these problems of measuring and comparing the intensity or productivity of labour across different varieties of work make it easier for management to justify the introduction of artificially fine distinctions and segmentations among various jobs which workers can basically perform interchangeably without much difficulty. However, the critical theoretical point is that, despite these artificial managerial differentiations, each sort of work is equally an expenditure, albeit in a specific form, of a common human capacity to labour, and thus these different concretely useful labours are reducible to abstract human labour on a common basis: they can be measured directly as abstract labour according to physical hours of labour performed.

From this perspective, complex skilled labour is equally an expenditure of the general human capacity to labour in various special forms. Of course, insofar as complex labour-power needs specific education or training beforehand, simple labour-power cannot instantly be converted to some kind of skilled work, whereas complex labour-power can be used in simple work. Hence, job gradations and wage distinctions are easily applied to skilled workers. However, setting aside the question of wage differentials for a moment, skilled labour and simple labour are fundamentally alike, representing expenditures of the general human capacity to labour. With this property in common with simple labour, skilled workers' own labour must also be reducible to abstract human labour on the same basis as simple labour, being directly commensurable across job categories simply in terms of physical hours worked. In this regard, the differences are less important than the similarities: all labour, whether skilled or simple, is on an equal footing as part of the total human social activity of maintaining material reproduction. Indeed, in comparison with simple labour, which covers a wide range of different human abilities, complex skilled labour need not even be regarded as particularly intensified labour activity. It may in fact often be less intensive and less tiring, since skilled workers have been given special training, experience or education for their jobs and tend to work under relatively less pressure of competition.

My approach does, of course, differ from some of Marx's statements. In the initial theory of commodities in *Capital*, Marx tended to analyze the labour substance of value in a manner too closely linked with the form of value in exchange; thus he was probably inclined to assume that skilled labour operated in an intensified fashion (a rather mystical fashion, in my view) to create greater value than simple labour in the same period of time, just as skilled workers produce goods with relatively higher market exchange values. If we theoretically separate the forms and the substance of value as dimensionally different orders, we can depart from Marx's lead and reach a clearer and non-mystical understanding of their relations. We can conclude that a unit of skilled workers' labour creates the same amount of the labour substance of value as one of simple labour, and that this is quite independent of the relatively higher exchange value of skilled workers' labour-power, or that of their products.

It is on this basis that I reject the reduction of complex to simple labour proposed by Okishio and Rowthorn. It is theoretically confused and ultimately wrong to treat the labour costs of training or education as affecting the labour time embodied in the products of skilled workers; this view treats skilled labour-power as analogous to constant (fixed) capital goods produced by past labour. Apparently more past labour embodied in skills will yield greater value transferred to output by the skilled worker's labour, just as more past labour embodied in a physical input yields a greater transfer of value to output when that input is productively consumed. But the worker using skilled labour-power is a subjective agent, not an objective result of past labour or work. Thus the labour cost of producing skills may affect the value of the skilled labour-*power*, but that, unlike the value of means of production, cannot be a direct component of the value of commodities produced. It is fundamental for Marx that a change in the value of labour-power affects surplus value, but does not change the value the worker creates $(v + s)$ or the value of the total product $(c + v + s)$. The Okishio-Rowthorn approach is a possible interpretation of some of Marx's statements, but it contradicts Marx's fundamental theory of the production of surplus value by mistakenly treating skill training as affecting value creation when the real question is how such training and education affects the value of skilled workers' labour-power.

Let us consider this question of the value of skilled labour-power. Insofar as reproduction of labour-power across generations is a private family matter in a market economy, the supply of those kinds of skilled labour-power which are socially necessary has to be guaranteed by relatively higher wages, which compensate for the private costs of training or education to create complex skills. If, as argued, the expenditure of complex labour-power does not involve transfer of previously incurred labour costs for training or education, if it therefore materializes in output the same amount of labour substance as simple labour in each time period, then the higher wage of skilled workers beyond the ordinary wage rate of unskilled workers simply reduces the social surplus labour and surplus value obtained by capitalist firms. If wages are so high as to preclude the performance of surplus labour by individual skilled workers, then it is not theoretically justified to view theseworkers as members of an exploited class.

In more complex circumstances, the presence of an institutional system of public education or of subsidies for education and training costs would clearly affect the extent to which the special labour costs of reproducing skilled workers are born privately by their families as opposed to publicly by the state. In a case where such costs are entirely publicly funded from taxes in a manner sufficient to produce the number and sorts of complex labour-powers needed to meet the social demand, then, at least in the absence of artificial managerial segmentation of workers, the value of skilled labour-power need not contain any special compensation for private educational or training costs and should theoretically be reduced to the level of the common unskilled worker by capitalist market pressures.

In an ideal communal socialist society where, before the social product is divided among individuals, a portion of output is set aside to cover the labour costs necessary for the common satisfaction of needs, such as schools, health services, administration, and so on, the educational funds which reproduce skilled or complex labour-power would also presumably be dealt with on a social communal rather than an individual basis. Then, after those socially necessary deductions have been made, there is no reason why a skilled worker should get back more from society than an unskilled worker—neither some "contribution" to society made by skilled labour time, nor the costs of maintaining particular necessary skills can justify such a differential in rewards. This argument raises theoretical doubt concerning Marx's proposition that in a lower phase of communist society it will remain a "bourgeois right" for workers to have unequal access to products, in proportion to the different quantities of labour they perform in the same time period and their probably different degrees of skill (see *Critique of the Gotha Program* in MacLellan 1977, 568). We should oppose the use of such a doubtful proposition to legitimate hierarchical privileges and special material rewards for state and party bureaucrats and technocrats in contemporary "socialist" societies. On the one hand, the egalitarian principle expressed in "from each according to his ability, to each according to his needs," which Marx assumed would be realized only in a higher phase of communist society, should not be regarded as a goal too far away to be actually achieved; it should instead be actualized as much as possible from the beginning in constructing socialist society, as well as in the socialist movements under capitalism dedicated to implementing demands such as those for major changes in welfare policies. On the other hand, differentiated incentive wage rates, which seem now to be gaining popularity in current and formerly "socialist" countries, should not be considered an inevitable and permanent part of a socialist economic order, but rather a tentative and temporary conventional means to revive and increase labour efficiency.

Thus in my opinion, even with regard to the complex labour problem, the Marxian labour theory of value can, if properly developed, offer the basis for a fundamentally egalitarian view of social relations, a view which should always be a crucial element of Marxism. This point of view provides a deeper and more critical theoretical frame of reference for considering a host of important current issues, among them the social function and historical meaning of artificially segmented work in modern capitalist corporations, the rationale for hierarchical social structures in contemporary "socialist" countries, and the significance of "unequal exchange" in trade between advanced and third world countries.

THE FORMS OF VALUE AND ABSTRACT LABOUR

In each of the aspects of the value controversy considered above, the theoretical relation between the forms of value and abstract labour has become a basic issue, one central to the differences among Marxian theoretical positions.

In retrospect, Sraffian theory presented a way of determining equilibrium prices based on the objective ground of the physical system of production, but without considering any notion of a common substance of value. Its mathematical techniques, however, proved to be useful in determining the labour substance of value embodied in commodities under certain preconditions, which seemed to strengthen the orthodox technological determinist theory of value among Marxians. Paradoxically, though, a series of anomalies in the technological determinist labour theory of value were then pointed out from the same Sraffian point of view, causing confusion and controversy among Marxians, as discussed above.

In reaction to both the Sraffian criticism and the perceived difficulties of technological determinist Marxism, what has come to be known as the Rubin school has developed since the 1970s among western Marxians.[10] This school argues that the various kinds of useful labour in the physical system of production are reduced to abstract labour only through the prices of commodities as the form of value and the abstracting social effects of money in markets, processes which are relatively independent of the purely technological dimensions of production. This view originated with Rubin (1972), who was purged for his opposition to the orthodox Soviet technological determinist theory of value in the 1920s, and has recently been renewed and extended by Marxians such as Himmelweit and Mohun (1981), Krause (1981), Eldred and Hanlon (1981), and Wolff, Callari and Roberts (1984).

If abstract labour as the substance of value is really assessed only through exchange values in the market or the quantities of money representing them, most of the controversial issues in recent debates from the transformation problem onwards simply evaporate; there is no longer a need for theoretically substantial solutions. The labour theory of value in this approach loses its theoretical status as an objective theory deriving the substance of value from technological conditions of production, becoming instead consonant with other types of price theory. Thus, by opposing the technological determinism of orthodox Marxian value theory, the Rubin school goes to the other extreme and opens a space for the relevance of neo-Ricardian or even neoclassical approaches like general equilibrium theory. Such an intermingling of Marxian and non-Marxian approaches to value may well have serious consequences for Marxism, in particular obstructing the substantive deepening of uniquely Marxian theoretical insights into the forms and substance of value. At the same time, the Rubinite notion of abstract labour is overly narrow in restricting its applicability to commodity economies alone. Neglected in this is the universal need to allocate specific amounts of past and present abstract human labour time to socially necessary kinds of concrete labour, an indispensable aspect of the general economic norms common to any social formation. This fundamental reality makes amounts of labour time commensurable as abstract labour and allows their estimation from the technological conditions of production independent of the presence or absence of the market mechanism.

However, in conventional Marxian orthodoxy, which tends to be just as one-sided in emphasizing the technological determinacy of (the substance of) values,

Marx's original theory of the forms of value has not yet been fully utilized and developed. The forms of value like commodity prices are often treated simply as a formal or unmediated expression of the more basic values, neglecting their relatively independent motion and their impact on the social relations underlying labour time materialized and distributed in a market economy. The structural social relations between the forms and the substance of value must be properly investigated and clarified. But the Rubinite attempt to do this, answering the Sraffian critiques of the technological determinist labour theory of value by defining abstract labour directly through money prices in the market as the form of value, is equally inadequate and one-sided—indeed it basically inverts the approach of its opponents. Despite the sharp rivalry between the orthodox technological determinist labour theory of value and the Rubinite theory, both share a common tendency to view the substance and the forms of value as inseparable and adnate, differing mainly on which is seen as primary.

In order to overcome the theoretical defects resulting from the one-sidedness of each, we should analytically distinguish the relatively independent social mechanisms governing the forms and the substance of value, and investigate more fully and systematically their structural relations under capitalism. This project requires answers to three questions concerning quantitative relations involving abstract human labour: (i) the extent to which they are technologically determined by the objective conditions of reproduction; (ii) where and how they have social determinants relatively independent of technological conditions; and (iii) how they emerge concretely as the developed forms of value, through capitalist pricing mechanisms. Though this project is obviously not complete, in this essay I have attempted to show the importance of studying these problems structurally in order to be systematic in confronting the various issues in the recent value controversy. I believe it is a fundamental task for us to reconsider the essential meaning of human labour and its roles—throughout human history and in future socialism, as well as in elucidating the logic of motion of a capitalist economy. Our economic theory as a social science should not overlook such a substantial social concern.

NOTES

1. See, for example, the works cited in Elson (1975), Steedman et al. (1981), and Mandel and Freeman (1984), as well as those cited below.

2. Itoh (1990) develops this view of contemporary capitalist development on the basis of concrete empirical analysis.

3. This debate, along with an essay by von Bortkiewicz, is encapsulated in translation in Sweezy (1966).

4. This essay as a whole, and particularly the remainder of this section and the following two sections, depends substantially on my previous work (Itoh 1980; 1988).

5. My understanding of the theory of market value, as well as the general distinction between the forms and substance of value, owes much to Uno's works (for example, Uno 1980). See Itoh (1988, 226–35) for more detail on the theory of market value.

6. This effect happens to be ruled out in the numerical example above, in which $(l_a + l_b) = 1$ irrespective of changes in α, but it can occur in the case where A or B is a direct or indirect input into the means of production used in producing A and B.

7. On these grounds, I regard Clark's (1989) argument in his review of Itoh (1988), that my treatment of joint products exemplifies the Rubinite position, as improper.

8. The notions of complex labour and skilled labour are used almost interchangeably in this essay, although the latter is sometimes used in a context of comparison with unskilled work within the same sort of concrete useful labour.

9. Rowthorn (1985) is a more recent essay which is closer to my position in this paper.

10. On the Rubin school, see, for example, Gleicher (1983), although the list of theorists criticized by Gleicher as belonging to the school does not seem to me fully appropriate.

REFERENCES

Armstrong, P.; Glyn, A.; and Harrison, J. 1978. "In Defence of Value." *Capital & Class*, no. 5 (Summer): 1–º31.

Becker, J. 1977. *Marxian Political Economy*. Cambridge: Cambridge University Press.

Bowles, S., and Gintis, H. 1977. "The Marxian Theory of Value and Heterogeneous Labour." *Cambridge Journal of Economics* 1 (2): 173–92.

Braverman, H. 1974. *Labour and Monopoly Capital*. New York: Monthly Review Press.

Clark, S. 1989. "The Basic Theory of Capitalism: A Critical Review of Itoh and the Uno School." *Capital & Class*, no. 37 (Spring): 133–49.

Desai, M. 1974. *Marxian Economic Theory*. London: Basil Blackwell and Mott.

Dobb, M. 1973. *Theories of Value and Distribution Since Adam Smith*. Cambridge: Cambridge University Press.

Eldred, M., and Hanlon, M. 1981. "Reconstructing Value-Form Analysis." *Capital & Class*, no. 13.

Elson, D., ed. 1975. *Value: The Representation of Labour in Capitalism*. London: CSE Books.

Gleicher, D. 1983. "A Historical Approach to the Question of Abstract Labour." *Capital & Class*, no. 21 (Winter): 97–122.

Green, F., and Nore, P., eds. 1977. *Economics: An Anti-Text*. London: Macmillan.

Himmelweit, S., and Mohun, S. 1981. "Real Abstraction and Anomalous Assumptions." In I. Steedman et al., *The Value Controversy*. London: Verso.

Hunt, E. K., and Schwartz, J., eds. 1972. *A Critique of Economic Theory*. Harmondsworth: Penguin Books.

Itoh, M. 1980. *Value and Crisis*. London: Pluto Press; New York: Monthly Review Press.

———. 1988. *The Basic Theory of Capitalism*. London: Macmillan.

———. 1990. *The World Economic Crisis and Japanese Capitalism*. London: Macmillan.

Krause, U. 1981. "Heterogeneous Labour and the Fundamental Marxian Theorem." *Review of Economic Studies* 48 (1): 173–78.

Laibman, D. 1973-74. "Values and Prices of Production: The Political Economy of the Transformation Problem." *Science and Society* 37 (4).

MacLellan, D., ed. 1977. *Karl Marx: Selected Writings*. Oxford: Oxford University Press.

Mandel, E., and Freeman, A., eds. 1984. *Ricardo, Marx, Sraffa*. London: Verso.

Marx, K. 1976. *Capital*. Vol.1. Trans. B. Fowkes. Harmondsworth: Penguin Books.

Medio, A. 1972. "Profits and Surplus Value: Appearance and Reality in Capitalist Production." In *A Critique of Economic Theory*, ed. E. K. Hunt and J. Schwartz. Harmondsworth: Penguin Books.

Meek, R. 1973. *Studies in the Labour Theory of Value*. 2d ed. New York: Monthly Review Press.

Morishima, M. 1973. *Marx's Economics*. Cambridge: Cambridge University Press.

Okishio, N. 1963. "A Mathematical Note on Marxian Theories." *Weltwirtshaftliches Archiv*: 287–99.

———. 1973. "Convergence of Marx's 'Transformation' Procedure" (in Japanese). *Riron Keizaigaku* (August).

Rowthorn, B. 1980. *Capitalism, Conflict and Inflation: Essays in Political Economy*. London: Lawrence and Wishart.

———. 1985. "Notes on Skilled Labour." Mimeo.

Rubin, I. I. 1972. *Essays on Marx's Theory of Value*. Trans. M. Samardzija and F. Perlman. Detroit: Black and Red.

Samuelson, P. 1971. "Understanding the Marxian Notion of Exploitation: A Summary of the So-called Transformation Problem Between Marxian Values and Competitive Prices." *Journal of Economic Literature* 9 (2).

Schwartz, J., ed. 1977. *The Subtle Anatomy of Capitalism*. Santa Monica, CA: Goodyear.

Shaikh, A. 1977. "Marx's Theory of Value and the 'Transformation Problem.'" In *The Subtle Anatomy of Capitalism*, ed. J. Schwartz. Santa Monica: Goodyear.

Sraffa, P. 1960. *Production of Commodities By Means of Commodities*. Cambridge: Cambridge University Press.

Steedman, I. 1977. *Marx After Sraffa*. London: New Left Books.

Steedman, I., et al. 1981. *The Value Controversy*. London: Verso.

Sweezy, P., ed. 1966. *Karl Marx and the Close of His System by E. von Böhm-Bawerk and Böhm-Bawerk's Critique of Marx by R. Hilferding*. New York: M. Kelly.

Uno, K. 1980. *Principles of Political Economy*. Trans. T. Sekine. Brighton: Harvester Press; Atlantic Highlands, NJ: Humanities Press.

Wolff, R.; Callari, A.; and Roberts, B. 1984. "A Marxian Alternative to the Traditional 'Transformation Problem.'" *Review of Radical Political Economics* 16 (2/3): 115–35.

VALUES AND VALUE TRANSFERS: A COMMENT ON ITOH

Anwar Shaikh

Itoh's essay provides a valuable retrospective on recent debates concerning the Marxian theory of value. He points out that the economic crisis enveloping both capitalist and socialist worlds from the 1970s onward challenged economists to rethink and refine their basic approaches. Among other things, this sparked a resurgence of interest in fundamental issues such as the theory of value. Thus, what appears as an abstract discussion is actually rooted in historical events, with political and economic implications for the current period (above, 53–54).

Itoh also emphasizes the importance of Sraffa's work in revitalizing the Marxist discussion of value theory. Sraffa's pathbreaking work provided a new platform for a critique of neoclassical economics, even as it "rehabilitated the objective theory of value" which is characteristic of the classical and Marxian traditions. But his narrow focus and elliptical style left open the question of the relation between his approach and that of more general economic frameworks. Not surprisingly, many of his followers set out to incorporate his unconventional approach into a more orthodox "neo-Ricardian" framework, in which the emphasis was on mathematical and functional analyses of equilibrium prices. Inevitably, this gave rise to a divergence between neo-Ricardian and Marxian writers (54–60). Two issues are highlighted by Itoh: the problems which arise with Marx's procedure for linking labor value and money price magnitudes (the transformation problem), problems which appear to undermine the Marxian claim that value magnitudes are the foundation of price magnitudes; and the claim that value categories are in any case redundant, since market prices actually gravitate around prices of production, not labor values (60).

In his survey of the debates around these two axes, Itoh makes many insightful comments and criticisms. He also presents his own solutions to certain key problems raised in the debates, such as those involved in joint production and heterogeneous labor. Here, though, I focus on the most basic issue: the transformation problem and its implications.

One difficulty with Itoh's presentation is that his survey focuses principally on works written before 1980.[1] This is problematic for two reasons: first, the literature on the subject burgeoned in the 1970s and 1980s; second, his pre-1980 focus presents some difficulties for my own commentary, since most of the arguments upon which I rely were advanced after that date, and are therefore not addressed by Itoh.[2] In what follows, I will begin with points of agreement, move on to the general nature of Itoh's proposed solution to the transformation problem, and then contrast it with my own alternative approach.[3]

One crucial point of agreement is that the transformation problem is an analytical issue, not a historical one. The real process of capitalist competition operates on actual market prices, not on prices proportional to labor values nor even on prices of production. A market price embodying a higher than average profit rate attracts a correspondingly more rapid influx of capital into the industry, until supply expands more rapidly than demand, pushing down the market price and hence the profit rate. As this occurs, the influx of capital begins to slow down until eventually supply grows more slowly than demand, and the price and hence the profit rate begin to rise. The overall process is one of perpetual oscillation, in which the industry's average rate of profit fluctuates around the social average, in what Marx calls "an anarchical movement in which rise is compensated by fall and fall by rise" (Marx 1972, 174–75; Shaikh 1984, 48–49). *There is never any state of equilibrium in which market prices "converge" to prices of production.* Thus prices of production never exist as such.

A second important point of agreement is that labor values are dimensionally distinct from prices of any sort, since the former are in hours of socially necessary labor time, while the latter are the forms of value expressed in money terms. Of course, this merely implies that in order to compare the "sum of values" (hours) with the "sum of prices" ($), or "total surplus value" with "total profit," one must convert one set into the units of the other (Shaikh 1977, secs. IV–V; 1984, 43–44; Itoh 1980, 70–71; above, 61–62). This point is at the heart of our alternative approaches to the the transformation problem. I will return to it shortly.

Prices of production function as the inner regulators of market prices. It is Marx's contention that labor values in turn regulate prices of production, just as surplus value regulates normal profit.[4] To demonstrate this, Marx proposes to show that one can analytically derive prices of production by beginning from a situation in which prices are proportional to labor values and profits proportional to surplus value, and then redistributing profits among industries so as to achieve equal rates of profit. But Marx's procedure involves a well-known incompleteness, in that the prices of production he derives are themselves based on input costs still expressed in (prices proportional to) labor values. This deficiency was eventually remedied by showing that Marx's procedure may be thought of as the first step in an *iterative* process of calculation whose end result is exactly the "fully transformed" prices of production of Bortkiewicz or Sraffa (Itoh above, 60). Thus, in the end, prices of production (and any other prices as well) are simply the expression of some redistribution of values and surplus values.

Completing Marx's transformation procedure demonstrates the link between his initial derivation of prices of production and the subsequent Bortkiewicz "simultaneous solution" method (Sweezy 1964, ch. V). But this does not directly address an apparently more intractable problem: in any full transformation procedure, one cannot maintain both the sum of prices and the sum of profits at their initial levels (i.e., at levels proportional to the sum of values and the sum of surplus values, respectively). Note that the transformation problem involves the comparison of two different sets of relative prices for a given set of products produced with a given set of material inputs, labor hours and consumption bundles for workers. Thus the surplus product is also given. As long as the system is in a self-reproducing state, i.e., in simple or expanded reproduction, the sum of prices represents the purchase price of the total product. Thus keeping the sum of prices constant when considering different sets of relative prices is tantamount to keeping the general purchasing power of money constant. But different sets of relative prices will yield different measures of (constant \$) money profit, even though the surplus product and hence the total amount of surplus value is unchanged. It therefore appears as if the amount of (constant \$) profit is in general independent of both the surplus product and surplus value. This is the central problem raised by the transformation question.

The same result obtains if we keep the general value of money constant instead. A given sum of money prices purchases the total output, in which the sum of labor values is materialized. The general purchasing power of money over labor value is defined by the ratio of the sum of the money prices of total output (\$) to the corresponding sum of labor values (hours). The reciprocal of this is what Marx defines as the value of money. Multiplying any sum of money by the value of money allows us to translate it into the general labor-value-commanded by this quantity of money. In this sense, the "sum of (translated) prices" of the whole product will always equal the sum of values of that product, regardless of what happens across any transformation procedure (i.e., whether or not the sum of money prices or money profits or any other sum is kept constant). But here too, as in the earlier case of a constant use-value purchasing power of money, the "sum of (translated) profits" will vary independently of surplus value, as relative prices change.

Tables 1A-2A in Appendix 1 illustrate the basic problem. Table 1A is identical to Itoh's Table 1 of produced labor values in a schema of simple reproduction (Itoh 1980, 75), while Table 2A is his Table 2 of money price of production translated into general labor-value-commanded by the value of money *m*.[5] Although both tables have the same sum of prices, the sum of profits in Table 2 (175 hours) differs from the sum of surplus values (200 hours) in Table 1. This is solely the effect of different sets of relative prices applied to the same set of inputs and outputs. The question is: what is the import of this result?

On the surface, the above result seems to suggest that circulation can create or destroy value, which contradicts the Marxist claim that value and surplus value are created only in production. For this reason, many Marxists have wrestled with this problem, coming up with a variety of answers (some of which are surveyed by Itoh). Itoh himself claims to have a new solution, which he lays out in his books (1980, 74–76; 1988, 220–26) and summarizes in his survey above.

In effect, Itoh switches the focus of attention away from the discrepancy between produced values and realized values (i.e., between Tables 1A-1B) *to the identity of aggregate physical flows which is implicit in any self-reproducing state.* In simple reproduction, for instance, every department must allocate particular physical quantities of materials and labor-power in order to produce particular physical quantities of products. The required quantities of materials lay claim to one portion of the total product. Given the consumption requirements of workers, the required quantities of labor-power determine a claim to yet another portion of the total product. What remains is by definition the total surplus product, and in simple reproduction this must be absorbed by the aggregate personal consumption of capitalists.[6]

As long as we are holding input-output and labor consumption coefficients constant (which is usually the case in the transformation problem), the structurally determined physical flows outlined above underlie both the value schema and also any corresponding price counterpart. This point is brought out in Tables 1B-2B, which depict the invariant aggregate uses of production under different valuation schemes. From what we have noted about the identity of central physical quantities across the two sets of tables, it follows that any (translated) money expenditure for materials $c_i x$ in Table 2B acquires commodities whose values are c_i in Table 1B; any money expenditure for labor-power $v_i y$ and hence for worker consumption $(C_w^*)_i$ acquires quantities of consumption goods and hence labor-power whose values are v_i; and the aggregate money expenditures for capitalist consumption C_c^* in Table 2B acquires goods whose value is C_c in Table 1B (which in simple reproduction is also the value of the surplus product, i.e., surplus value s).

Table 3 presents the "acquired" value quantities in more detail. The first two columns represent the labor values c_i and v_i of commodities purchased by money expenditures $c_i x$ and $v_i y$ respectively, as discussed above. The column for investment expenditures is blank because there is no investment in simple reproduction. So far this is merely a detailed representation of the mapping between Tables 2B and 1B. But the column for capitalists has a new element in it. As already noted, the physical quantity of capitalist consumption goods is the same regardless of the valuation scheme. Thus total capitalist consumption expenditures of 175 hours in Table 2B purchases goods whose value is 200 hours in Table 1B (which in simple reproduction is also total surplus value s). This is reflected in the column sum of the fourth column of Table 3. But the structural pattern of physical flows tells us nothing about the inter-departmental distribution of capitalist consumption. To derive this, we have (like Itoh) assumed that capitalist consumption in each department is derived from the department's profits. On this basis, each row in Table 3 represents the values of the commodities purchased (acquired) out of the money revenues realized earlier by each department in Table 2A. The correspondence between aggregate sums in Tables 3 and 1 is a consequence of the assumption that the system is in a self-reproducing state.

Since in simple reproduction the whole surplus product is absorbed in capitalist consumption, the total value of capitalist consumption goods C_c = the value of the surplus product = surplus value = s. Then, and only then, the formula for value acquired through individual capitalist consumption $(p_i/p)C_c$ can also be written as $(p_i/p)s$. With this change, Table 3 immediately becomes Table 4—which is Itoh's table of acquired values in simple reproduction (Itoh 1980, 75: Table 3).

Itoh's focus on acquired values provides a valuable reminder that, as long as the system is in a self-reproducing state, different exchange-ratios attach different valuations to a largely unchanged set of physical flows (only the inter-departmental distribution of individual capitalist consumption is affected by relative price changes). However, some of the charm of his presentation fades when one notes, as he himself does (Itoh 1980, 76–77, and above, 62), that his particular mode of deriving the acquired values as the proportion of surplus value represented by each department's profits ($s_i' = (p_i/p)s$) is only generally valid in simple reproduction (see the discussion above and in the notes to Table 3).

Tables 7–9 illustrate this latter problem in the case of expanding reproduction. Tables 7A–B shows the production and the corresponding dispositions of the total product in value terms (scaled to make the mass of surplus value the same as before), while Tables 8A–B show the same physical flows in (translated) prices of production. It will be noted that in each case the use of department I-II's product now encompasses both replacement expenditures and expansion expenditures for constant and variable capital, while the portion of profit devoted to capitalist consumption expenditures is correspondingly restricted. Table 9 puts together all the relevant information to derive the values acquired through the expenditures of the money revenues of each department. As is evident from a comparison of column five (values acquired through the expenditure of profit) and column six (the proportion of surplus value represented by each department's profit, as in Itoh's procedure in Table 4 earlier), the procedure which Itoh uses to construct his simple reproduction tables does not carry over to expanded reproduction. The reason for this is fairly simple. In simple reproduction, each department's capitalist consumption, and thus its share of the value of surplus product acquired, is proportional to its profit. In expanded reproduction, capitalist consumption is still proportional to departmental profit, but now investment expenditures are proportional to the department's (circulating) capital advanced,[7] so that a department's portion of the value of surplus product acquired is not proportional to its profit (except in the very special case in which each department has the same organic composition so that $c_i + v_i$ is proportional to s_i for each i—in which case there is no transformation problem in the first place!).

But the issue of the general formula for acquired values is not the important one.

In his own approach to the problem, Itoh is motivated by Marx's notion that since prices and profits are the money forms taken by value and surplus value materialized in production, "the true meaning and consistency of Marx's propositions" requires us to demonstrate "the equality between total value and total price, and [also] between total surplus value and total profit" (Itoh 1980, 73–74).

It is always correct to say that the money spent to purchase any commodity will purchase the value materialized in that commodity, so that the the money spent to purchase the surplus product (profit) will purchase the value materialized in this surplus product (surplus value). But, however illuminating this focus on acquired values may be, it does not really address the central issue raised by the transformation problem (or by comparison of any two schema with differing relative prices), as illustrated in Tables 1A–2A. Table 1A represents the production of value and surplus value. It also represents the realized value and profit flows when prices are proportional to values. Table 2A represents realized value flows when prices conform to prices of production. We may imagine yet other Tables 2A′, 2A″, etc. in which prices reflect monopoly prices or market prices, etc. All of these tables will reflect the same surplus value, all will command the same physical product and surplus product, yet in each case the realized profit will be different, even though the underlying surplus value is the same. Itoh would be content to say that the varying amounts of aggregate realized profit in Tables 2A, 2A′, 2A″, etc. would all purchase the surplus product and hence acquire an amount of value equal to surplus value. *But this would tell us nothing whatsoever about the determination of the magnitude of aggregate profit, which would be different in each case*!

Marx's claim is that profit is *derived* from surplus value. The analysis of acquired values tells us that (in a self-reproducing state) profit *purchases* the surplus product. These two statements are not the same. The central puzzle remains: given that surplus value is only transferred during circulation, how is it that aggregate profit can vary independently from aggregate surplus value merely because the mode of circulation varies?

In contradistinction to Itoh, I have long argued that it is precisely because prices and profits are the money forms of values and surplus values, respectively, that aggregate profit must generally deviate from surplus value when prices are not proportional to values. This is because Marx's claim that value is conserved in exchange[8] necessarily implies that price-value deviations (with both prices and values expressed in common units) will bring about transfers of value which will cause profits to deviate from surplus value. Indeed, Marx himself remarks on this problem, during his analysis of price-value deviations arising within the theory of rent[9]:

> This phenomenon of the conversion of capital into revenue should be noted, because it creates the *illusion* that the amount of profit grows independently of the amount of surplus-value. (Marx 1971, 347)

Let us first consider the general issue of transfers of value. Suppose region *A* exports commodities having a value of 600 million hours for money having a value of 800 million hours.[10] Region A then gains 200 million hours of value on its exports. If it also pays a quantity of money having a value of 1 billion hours (trade does not have to be balanced) for imports having a produced value of 700 million hours, then it loses 300 million hours of value on its imports. The overall effect is a net loss (negative net transfer) of value of 100 million hours for region A. To this there of course corresponds a equal net gain for the region's trading partners, taken as a whole. Note that, in calculating the net transfer of value, we must take into account transfers on both exports *and* imports.

Transfers of value are fundamental to Marxian analyses of intersectoral, interregional and international trade.[11] For our present purposes, they carry the important implication that the surplus value *realized* in a region is the sum of the surplus value produced there *and* the net (positive or negative) transfer of value brought about by price/value deviations of commodities traded. For region A, this means that its realized surplus value (the labor value of its aggregate profits, other things being equal) will be 100 less than its produced surplus value.

Marxists have generally failed to appreciate that this very same mechanism is the source of the famous discrepancy between produced and realized surplus value (if the sum of prices is held constant) or between produced and realized total value (if the sum of profits is held constant) within the confines of the transformation problem. To see how this works, it is useful to imagine that all sellers and buyers of commodities conduct their business through the mediation of a fictitious trading company which incurs no costs in the performance of its function. All flows will be in value or realized value terms, with the sum of prices held constant, as in the tables analyzed above. We will initially discuss simple reproduction, as in Itoh's own examples (Itoh 1980, 75).

Each department produces commodities worth a_i hours which it sells to the fictitious trading company for P_i dollars. Note that the exports of each productive department consist of its total output. The realized value received by any department will be P_i, the total price of production of its product. For each department, the net transfer of value on exports is therefore $(P_i - a_i)$. For all departments taken together, the net transfer on exports is zero (since $P = a = 875$).

But this does *not* imply that the net transfer of value between the productive sector and its customers (since the trading sector is only a go-between) will be zero. On the side of imports, each productive department imports constant capital of value c_i for which it pays $c_i x$ in value of money. It also imports labor-power of value v_i for which it pays $v_i y$ to workers. Note that in this latter case the transfer is between productive capitalists and workers (who in turn pay $v_i y$ to the trading sector for consumption goods $(C^*_w)_i$ having value v_i, effecting a parallel and opposite transfer between themselves and the trading sector). In simple reproduction, this exhausts the imports of the productive sector. The net transfer of value on each productive sector's imports is therefore $[(c_i + v_i) - (c_i x + v_i y)]$.

The overall net transfer of value to/from each department's circuit of productive capital M_i-C_i-M_i' is simply the transfer on exports $(P_i - a_i)$ plus the net transfer on imports $[(c_i + v_i) - (c_i x + v_i y)]$. Since price $P_i = c_i x + v_i y + p_i$ and value $a_i = c_i + v_i + s_i$, it follows that each sector's overall transfer of value accounts for the difference between its profit and its surplus value, and that the same principle applies to productive capital as a whole:

Net transfer to/from the ith circuit of productive capital
= Transfer on exports + transfer on imports
$= [P_i - a_i] + [(c_i + v_i) - (c_i x + v_i y)] = p_i - s_i$

Net transfer to/from the overall circuit of productive capital
= Total transfer on exports + total transfer on imports
$= [P - a] + [(c + v) - (cx + vy)] = p - s$

The above result tells us that the apparently mysterious difference between the labor value commanded by aggregate profit p and the corresponding produced surplus value s is *none other than the value transferred in/out of the circuit of capital during the circulation process.* The circuit of capital *M-C-M'* is only one "region" in the overall circulation process, and as in all such cases, any transfers of value in or out of this "region" will make its realized surplus value deviate from its produced surplus value. Instead of being mysterious or damning, this result is a perfectly necessary and normal consequence of the fact that value is preserved during circulation under the conditions in question. Table 5 details this process for simple reproduction.

If the circuit of capital is only one "region" in circulation, what are the others? As Marx notes in his analysis of the schemes of reproduction, the overall circulation consists of entwined circuits of capital and circuits of revenue. Outside of the circuit of productive capital, we have the circuit of trading capital, and the circuit of revenue (personal consumption) of workers and of capitalists. We can exclude the trading sector from any net transfers of value, because as long as the whole product is sold (which is the condition of the present problem), its total exports exactly its total imports. We can also exclude the total circuit of revenue of workers, since the value of money $v_i y$ which workers receive as wages is then paid out to the trading sector for consumption goods $(C_w^*)_i$ whose value is $(C_w)_i = v_i$. Workers export their labor-power v_i for value of money $v_i y$, but then import commodities of value v_i for value of money $v_i y$. The net transfer for the class as whole is zero.

This leaves only the circuit of revenue of capitalists themselves. In simple reproduction, each department's capitalists expend funds p_i to purchase capitalist consumption goods $(C_c^*)_i$ whose value is $(C_c)_i$. For capitalist-consumers as a whole the total value of consumption goods C_c = the value of the surplus product = surplus value s. Unlike workers, who must sell their labor-power in order to consume, capitalists can consume by virtue of their ownership of the means of production. They import without having to export, because they draw upon the profits of the production sector for their consumption fund.[12] In this case the net transfer of value = value transferred on exports + value transferred on imports $= 0 + (C_c - p) = (s - p) = -(p - s)$.

This amount is simply the dual of the previously discovered transfer of value of the circuit of productive capital. For the system as a whole, the net transfer is zero. *The deviation of aggregate profit from aggregate surplus value is explained by this transfer between the circuit of productive capital and the revenue circuit of capitalists-as-consumers.* Table 6 illustrates the transfers involving revenue circuits, and Appendix 2 diagrams the overall transfers in simple reproduction.

The above results can easily be extended to the case of expanding reproduction. Table 10 shows that the net transfers to/from the circuit of productive capital account for the differences between profits and surplus value in each department. Table 11 looks at the circuits which are not encompassed by the profit/loss circuit of productive capital. There are now three: two circuits of personal revenue, for workers and capitalists-as-consumers respectively, and the circuit of investment purchases, which in business accounting would show up in *capital* (balance sheet) accounts but not in the profit/loss (income statement) account upon which discussions of the transformation problem are normally predicated. As is evident, the overall sum of the net transfers in the revenue and capital accounts of Table 11 (16.44 hours) is equal but opposite to that in the profit/loss account of Table 10 (–16.44 hours).

The analysis can even be generalized to cover situations in which the economy is not in a self-reproducing state (in which case we must also account for stocks and flows of commodities and money). Moreover, it should be evident from the mode of analysis that the results apply to any type of prices, not just prices of production. The deviation between labor values and (the labor commanded by) market prices gives rise to exactly the same phenomena that have bedeviled the transformation debate, ones resolvable in the same manner. But the issue is even more general than that. If one were to compare prices of production with market prices or monopoly prices, then one would quickly discover that the latter would yield profit rates and masses which were different from those of the former, even when the sum of prices is held constant. Neo-Ricardian or neoclassical critics who insist that Marxian value analysis be abandoned because it yields magnitudes which differ from those associated with prices of production generally "forget" to follow through on this aspect of their own argument, for to do so would hoist them on their own petard (Shaikh 1981, n. 38).

Having established that price-value deviations pose no intractable theoretical difficulty for Marxian value theory, it is useful inquire into their empirical significance. In comparing Sraffa-Bortkiewicz prices of production with labor values, it can be shown on theoretical grounds that the deviation between profit and surplus value, and between the uniform rate of profit and the value rate of profit, will be strictly limited in scope. When the system is in balanced reproduction, then the size of the deviation is inversely related to the system's rate of growth. A similar argument can even be made for individual price-value deviations (Shaikh 1984, sec. IV). But the empirical evidence is even more striking. Input-output estimates for the U.S. indicate that labor values account for about 85 percent of the structure of prices of production (as measured by the percentage average absolute deviation), that Marx's own procedure for calculating prices of production (which can be viewed as a linear approximation) captures about 95 percent of the structure of fully transformed prices of production, that the overlap between aggregates such as the Marxian value rate of profit and the uniform rate of profit is greater than 96 percent, and that all empirically estimated aggregate wage-profit curves are virtually linear even when wage shares are relatively low and actual output proportions in the economy are very different from those of Sraffa's standard commodity (Shaikh 1984; Ochoa 1988). Comparisons to *market* prices reveal that labor values account for 88 percent, Marx's prices of production account for 87 percent, and fully transformed (Bortkiewicz-Sraffa) prices account for 86 percent. Recent theoretical and empirical investigations provide even more support for such a Ricardian-Marxian structural approach to the determination of prices (Petrovic 1987; Bienenfeld 1988).

The theoretical and empirical results outlined above cast an entirely different light on the long-standing debate about the determinants of prices of production and of price-value deviations. If our task is to understand how capitalist economies actually function, to show how their characteristic structure regulates their outcomes, and to analyze their real historical, technological, and inter-industrial patterns, then one could ask for no more powerful a foundation than Marx's theory of value.

APPENDIX 1: ACQUIRED VALUES IN SIMPLE AND EXPANDED REPRODUCTION

Simple Reproduction

Table 1A: Production of Value (hours)[a]

Dept.	c_i	v_i	s_i	a_i
I	225	90	60	375
II	100	120	80	300
III	50	90	60	200
	375	300	200	875

Table 1B: Value of Total Use[b]

Total Materials $(c) = \Sigma c_i = 375 = a_1$
Total Worker Consumption $(C_w) = \Sigma v_i = 300 = a_2$
Total Capitalist Consumption $(C_c) = \Sigma s_i = 200 = a_3$

a. Table 1A corresponds to Itoh's Table 1 (Itoh 1980, 75).
b. Table 1B shows the values of the structurally-determined uses of the total product implied by the physical flows in simple reproduction: each department purchases materials to replace those used up in production, with value c; workers expend their wages on consumption goods, with value C_w (assuming workers do not save); and the capitalist class as a whole purchases, for personal consumption, the remaining product, of value C_c (this is the surplus product, whose total value is surplus value s).

Table 2A: Value Commanded by Production Prices (hours)[a]

Dept.	$c_i x$	$v_i y$	p_i	P_i
I	252	84	84	420
II	112	112	56	280
III	56	84	35	175
	420	280	175	875

Table 2B: Value Commanded by Money Expenditures on Total Use[b]

Total Materials $(c^*) = (\Sigma c_i)x = 420 = P_1$
Total Worker Consumption $(C_w^*) = (\Sigma v_i)y = 280 = P_2$
Total Capitalist Consumption $(C_c^*) = \Sigma p_i = 175 = P_3$

a. x and y are respectively the price-value coefficients for materials and worker consumption goods. Table 2A corresponds to Itoh's Table 2, with all money values translated into value commanded-in-exchange by multiplying them by the value of money, defined as the ratio of the sum of values (875 billion hours) in Itoh's Table 1 to the sum of prices ($500 billion) in his Table 2 (Itoh 1980, 75). Itoh's notation has been retained, since rescaling does not alter any basic properties.
b. Table 2B is structurally analogous to Table 1B above; the only difference between them is the valuation attached to the physical flows.

Table 3: Values of Goods Acquired by Expenditure of Departmental Revenues (hours)[a]

Dept.	Value of replacement materials (c_i)	Value of replacement labor-power (v_i)	Value of net investment	Value of capitalist consumption goods $(p_i/p)C_c$	Total value of goods acquired out of department profits $(p_i/p)s$
I	225	90	–	96	96
II	100	120	–	64	64
III	50	90	–	40	40
	375	300	–	200	200

a. Departmental total revenue P_i is spent on materials, labor-power, and capitalist consumption goods. We can always divide the first two into replacement expenditure and net investment (a positive or negative residual which is zero in simple reproduction). For structural reasons discussed in the text, the first two columns of Table 3 are identical to those of Table 1. Moreover, in simple reproduction capitalist consumption absorbs the whole surplus product, so the sum of elements in column 4 above $[\Sigma(C_c)_i]$ will always equal total surplus value (the sum of column 5). The individual elements of column 4 are derived on the assumption that individual capitalist consumption expenditures $(C_c^*)_i$ are equal to individual departmental profits p_i; thus $(C_c^*)_i = (p_i/p)C_c^*$, while $(C_c)_i = (p_i/p)C_c$.

Table 4: Acquired Values (Itoh)[a]

Dept.	c_i	v_i	s_i'	a_i'
I	225	90	96	411
II	100	120	64	284
III	50	90	40	180
	375	300	200	875

$[s_i' = (p_i/p)s]$

a. Table 4 reproduces Itoh's Table 3 (Itoh 1980, 75), which is numerically identical to Table 3 above only in simple reproduction, because only then does aggregate capitalist consumption absorb the whole surplus product, so that $C_c = s$ and thus $s_i' = (p_i/p)s = (p_i/p)C_c$.

Table 5: Simple Reproduction Transfers of Value within the Circuit of Productive Capital[a]

Dept.	Transfer on exports $(p_i - a_i)$	Transfer on imports $[(c_i + v_i) - (c_i x + v_i y)]$	Net transfer (col. 1 + col. 2)	Profit – surplus value $(p_i - s_i)$
I	45	–21	24	24
II	–20	–4	–24	–24
III	–25	0	–25	–25
	0	–25	–25	–25

a. The numbers in this table are derived from Tables 1A and 2A above.

Table 6: Simple Reproduction Transfers of Value within Circuits of Personal Revenue[a]

	Workers			Capitalists	
Dept.	Transfer on exports $(v_i y - v_i)$	Transfer on imports $[(C_w)_i - v_i y)]$	Net worker transfer (col. 1 + col. 2)	Transfer on imports $[(C_c)_i - p_i]$	Net capitalist transfer (–col. 4)
I	–6	6	0	12	12
II	–8	8	0	8	8
III	–6	6	0	5	5
	–20	20	0	25	25

a. Workers' transfers derived from Tables 1A–2B; capitalists' transfers derived from 2A–3.

Expanded Reproduction

Table 7A: Production of Value (hours)[a]

Dept.	c_i	v_i	s_i	a_i
I	275.75	110.30	73.53	459.59
II	110.00	132.00	88.00	330.00
III	32.05	57.70	88.47	128.22
	417.81	300	200	917.81

Table 7B: Value of Total Use[b]
(g = growth rate = 10%)

$$c' = (\Sigma c_i)(1 + g) = 459.59 = a_1$$
$$C_w = (\Sigma v_i)(1 + g) = 330.00 = a_2$$
$$C_c = s - (\Sigma c_i + \Sigma v_i)g = 128.22 = a_3$$

a. Table 7A corresponds to Itoh's (1980, 75) Table 1 for simple reproduction, modified for expanded reproduction at growth rate g = 10%, and scaled so that s is the same (200 hours).
b. Table 7B parallels Table 1B above, for the case of expanded reproduction: in each period, each department purchases 10% more materials and labor-power than the previous period, while capitalist consumption absorbs the remainder of the surplus product.

Table 8A: Value Commanded by Production Prices (hours)[a]

Dept.	$c_i x$	$v_i y$	p_i	P_i
I	303.18	101.07	101.07	505.31
II	120.94	120.94	60.47	302.36
III	35.21	52.86	22.03	110.14
	459.38	274.87	183.57	917.84

Table 8B: Value Commanded by Money Expenditures on Total Use[b]

$$c^{*\prime} = (\Sigma c_i x)(1 + g) = 505.31 = P_1$$
$$C_w^* = (\Sigma v_i y)(1 + g) = 302.36 = P_2$$
$$C_c^* = p - (\Sigma c_i x + \Sigma v_i y)g = 110.14 = P_3$$

a. Table 8A is the price of production equivalent of Table 7A (and the expanded reproduction equivalent of 2A above).
b. Table 8B is the price of production equivalent of Table 7B.

Table 9: Two Measures of Acquired Values (hours)[a]

Dept.	Value of replacement materials (c_i)	Value of replacement labor-power (v_i)	Value of net investment $g(c_i + v_i)$	Value of capitalist consumption $(p_i/p)C_c$	Total value of goods acquired out of department profits (col. 3 + col. 4)	s_i' (Itoh) $(p_i/p)s$
I	275.75	110.30	38.61	70.59	109.20	110.11
II	110.00	132.00	24.20	42.24	66.44	65.89
III	32.05	57.7	8.98	15.39	24.36	24.00
	417.81	300.00	71.78	128.22	200	200

a. The principles behind the calculation of the elements of this table are described in Table 3 above.

Table 10: Expanded Reproduction Transfers of Value within the Circuit of Productive Capital[a]

Dept.	Transfer on exports $(p_i - a_i)$	Transfer on imports $[(c_i + v_i) - (c_ix + v_iy)]$	Net transfer (col. 1 + col. 2)	Profit – surplus value $(p_i - s_i)$
I	45.72	–18.2	27.52	27.54
II	–27.64	0.12	–27.52	–27.53
III	–18.08	1.65	–16.43	–16.44
	0	–16.43	–16.43	–16.43

a. The numbers in this table are deriv4ed from Tables 7A and 8A above.

Table 11: Expanded Reproduction Transfers of Value within the Circuits of Personal Revenue[a]

	Workers			Capitalists-as-Consumers		Investment	
Dept.	Transfer on exports	Transfer on imports	Net worker transfer	Transfer on imports	Net capitalist transfer	Net investment transfer	Net Transfers on Personal and Capital Accounts
I	–10.15	10.15	0	9.955	9.955	–1.820	8.135
II	–12.17	12.17	0	5.958	5.958	0.012	5.97
III	–5.32	5.32	0	2.17	2.17	0.165	2.335
	–27.64	27.64	0	18.083	18.083	–1.643	16.44

a. Workers' consumption occurs at the end of the production period, since we focus on transfers on the circulation of the product (the corresponding transfers on the acquisition of labor-power show up on the input side of the next round of production). There are no exports for capitalists-as-consumers, who consume out of "unearned income." Capitalists are assumed to consume out of individual departmental profits at the same rate as the class as a whole. The elements of each column are calculated as follows: col. 1: $(v_iy - v_i)(1 + g)$; col. 2: $[(C_w)_i - v_iy](1 + g)$; col. 3: col. 1 + col. 2; col. 4: $[(C_c)_i - (C_c^*)_i]$; col. 5: col. 4; col. 6: $[(c_i + v_i) - (c_ix + v_ix)]g$; col. 7: col. 3 + col. 5 + col. 6.

APPENDIX 2: AGGREGATE VALUE FLOWS IN SIMPLE REPRODUCTION

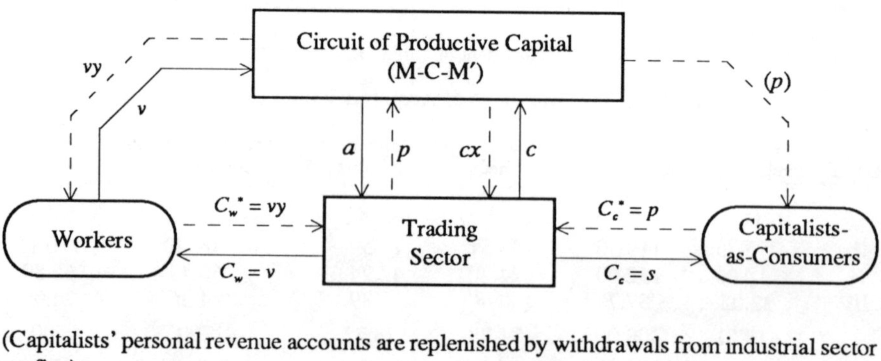

(Capitalists' personal revenue accounts are replenished by withdrawals from industrial sector profits.)

NOTES

1. Itoh lists some works written as late as 1984, but does not comment on them. This pre-1980 focus is most probably due to the fact that his essay here draws heavily on his own earlier work (Itoh 1980), as he acknowledges in n. 4.

2. In my case, his commentary is restricted to my very earliest writing on the subject (Shaikh 1977), and there only to the quantitative aspect of my iteration procedure.

3. I wish to thank Bruce Roberts for his illuminating and extremely helpful comments on an earlier draft of this note.

4. Prices of production regulate market prices by acting as their centers of gravity. But labor values regulate prices of production in a different sense: they form the foundation of production prices (which is the point of the transformation procedure) and also determine their dominant component (see Shaikh 1984, sec. IV).

5. As the universal equivalent, the value of money m is the *general* value commanded by money. Thus m = (sum of values)/(sum of prices) = (875 billion hours)/($500 billion) = 1.75 hours/$ from Itoh's Tables 1–2 (1980, 75). Multiplying all money quantities in Itoh's Table 2 by m gives our Table 2.

6. As we shall see shortly, individual capitalist consumption is not independent of pricing, because it depends on departmental profits which vary with relative prices.

7. We abstract from fixed capital throughout, since the issue here is independent of it.

8. Value is only conserved in exchange if demand and supply match (no realization problems), and if there are no changes in unit values. These are exactly the conditions of the transformation problem, where the issue is the impact of different modes of circulation on the relation between value and its money forms.

9. Ground-rent gives rise to its own form of price-value deviations, because even if we abstract from the difference between value and production price, in ground-rent the price (in value-commanded units) equals the value of output produced on marginal land, whereas value represents the average unit value of all the producers. Thus price differs from (average) value.

10. For example, it exports commodities for $1.6 billion when the value of one dollar is 1/2 hour.

11. The recent debate over the concept of unequal exchange is an area in which the notion of transfers of value has played a crucial role (see Shaikh 1980).

12. Withdrawal of funds by capitalists for personal consumption does not show up in the income statement of the production sector, since that only tallies costs and profits, not the disbursement of profits. It would show up in a sources and uses account. But the discussion of production prices has always utilized input-output and cost-profit types of accounts.

REFERENCES

Bienenfeld, M. 1988. "Regularities in Price Changes as an Effect of Changes in Distribution." *Cambridge Journal of Economics* 12 (2): 247–55.

Itoh, M. 1980. *Value and Crisis*. London: Pluto Press.

——. 1988. *The Basic Theory of Capitalism*. London: Macmillan.

Marx, K. 1971. *Theories of Surplus Value*. Part 3. Moscow: Progress.

——. 1972. "Wage Labour and Capital." In *The Marx-Engels Reader*, ed. R. C. Tucker. New York: Norton.

Ochoa, E. 1988. "Values, Prices, and Wage-Profit Curves in the U.S. Economy." *Cambridge Journal of Economics* 13 (3): 413–30.

Petrovic, P. 1987. "The Deviation of Production Prices from Labour Values: Some Methodology and Empirical Evidence." *Cambridge Journal of Economics* 11 (3): 197–210.

Shaikh, A. 1977. "Marx's Theory of Value and the 'Transformation Problem.'" In *The Subtle Anatomy of Capitalism*, ed. J. Schwartz. Santa Monica, CA: Goodyear.

——. 1980. "On the Laws of International Exchange." In *Growth, Profits and Property*, ed. E. Nell. Cambridge: Cambridge University Press.

——. 1981. "The Poverty of Algebra: Critical Notes on Neo-Ricardian Economics." In I. Steedman et al., *The Value Controversy*. London: New Left Books.

——. 1984. "The Transformation from Marx to Sraffa: Prelude to a Critique of the Neo-Ricardians." In *Marx, Ricardo, Sraffa*, ed. E. Mandel and A. Freeman. London: Verso.

Sweezy, P. 1964. *The Theory of Capitalist Development*. New York: Monthly Review Press.

3 ANALYTICAL MARXISM

E. K. Hunt

Over the past fifteen years, a group of academic theorists has coalesced into a self-described new school of Marxism. Variously labeled "analytical Marxism," "neo-classical Marxism," "game-theoretic Marxism," and "rational choice Marxism," the school's most influential theorists are G. A. Cohen (1989), Jon Elster (1985; 1986) and John Roemer (1981; 1982; 1986a; 1986b; 1988). Others associated with the new school include Pranab Bardhan (1984), Robert Brenner (1989), Alan Carling (1986), Leif Johansen (1972), Adam Przeworski (1986), Ian Steedman (1977), Phillipe van Parijs (1983) and Erik Olin Wright (1982; 1985). I will refer to the ideas of this group as "analytical Marxism" (AM), the label most frequently used.

Although Elster asserts that several of these individuals formed a discussion group in which "some kind of consensus emerged" (Elster 1985, xiv), he fails to enumerate or describe the ideas that were agreed upon. It appears to me that, among the individuals listed above, the ideas of Roemer and Elster have the most direct bearing on Marxian economics, and that their arguments are mutually consistent and, indeed, complementary. However, it seems to me that the ideas of some of these individuals, Brenner in particular, are not only different from but even anti-thetical to those of Roemer and Elster. In this article I will be concerned primarily with the writings of Roemer and Elster. To the degree that Elster is correct and the above individuals have some consensus, then some of my critique will be applicable to the ideas of the other members of the AM school as well. So hereafter, when I refer to the AM school, I take that school to include Roemer, Elster and all others who share their views (probably this would include, for example, Wright, but exclude Brenner). By focusing on the ideas of these two authors, I can avoid the issues of the similarities and differences (which are many) among the above theorists.

The theorists of analytical Marxism argue that it constitutes a significant and unambiguous scientific advance over traditional Marxism. Elster writes that Cohen has "changed the standards of rigor and clarity that were required to write on Marx and Marxism" (1985, xiv). Roemer identifies AM as a "sophisticated" theory that utilizes "contemporary tools of logic, mathematics and model building" in presenting "a non-dogmatic approach to Marxism" (1986, 1–2). Wright sees the essence of AM as the "systematic interrogation and clarification of basic concepts and their reconstruction into a more coherent theoretical structure" (1985, 2).

AM thus appears to its practitioners to be more scientific and rigorous than traditional Marxism—an improved, updated version. But as Marx was fond of stating, essence and appearance can contradict each other. After studying the writings of the AM school, one realizes that, in their efforts to make Marx scientifically rigorous, they have rejected as unscientific nearly every tenet of traditional Marxism. One person's *rigor* appears as another's *mortis*.

One of the first articles to recognize the emergence of the AM school lauded it in glowing terms; John Gray described the creation of a "powerful new school of Analytical Marxism, by such outstanding figures as G.A. Cohen, Jon Elster and John Roemer, with whose works the future of Marxism, if it has any, must henceforth be associated" (1983, 1461). The fact that Gray lauded these theorists while questioning the viability of Marxism reflects Gray's basic ideological identification with the right-wing Austrian school composed of theorists from Von Mises and Hayek to contemporary economists such as Paul Craig Roberts. Gray's sympathy with the AM school is not misplaced. After a long and detailed study of Marx, Elster has, in fact, rejected most of Marx's ideas in favor of those of Marx's Austrian critics, such as Eugen von Böhm-Bawerk.

Elster asserts that any truly scientific analysis of Marx must reject historical materialism, most of the theory of alienation, the theory of the falling rate of profit, the labor theory of value, the theory of the relation between productive forces and the social relations of production, and, indeed, nearly everything that Marx and most traditional Marxists have deemed to be important (1986, 188–94). After more than 500 pages of mocking, condescending derision and imperious pronouncements about the "dead," "intellectually bankrupt," "non-scientific" and "anti-scientific" nature of Marx's writings, Elster finally concludes his *Making Sense of Marx* with this arrogant proclamation: "It is not possible today, morally or intellectually, to be a Marxist in the traditional sense" (1985, 531). It is hardly any wonder that right-wing Austrians wholeheartedly endorse the AM school.

The principal unifying elements of the AM school, in my view, are not a matter of rigor, a non-dogmatic approach, or any imagined scientific merit. The unifying threads of this school are (1) the acceptance of methodological individualism, (2) the belief that all human actions and interactions can be reduced to a single common denominator—rational, calculated, utility-maximizing exchanges, and (3) an uncritical, ahistorical acceptance of certain institutional features of capitalism as the natural, eternal, and ever-present framework within which rational exchanges occur. I shall discuss these three themes, beginning with an examination of the meaning and significance of methodological individualism.

METHODOLOGICAL INDIVIDUALISM AND ITS CONSEQUENCES

Methodological individualism is, as the name implies, a prescriptive method for social analysis. In this view there are no collective entities. Nations do not do anything; classes do nothing; capital does nothing and labor does nothing. The reason is simply that none of these collective entities has any real existence. Only individuals actively make choices and take actions, and thus the concept of a collective entity represents at most a taxonomic convenience rather than an analytical tool. Thus, from this perspective any real and compelling *explanation* of events must begin with the recognition of individuals as agents and proceed to derive behavior from the nature of these individuals—their goals, their capabilities, their circumstances and the nature of the constraints they face.

While it is possible in principle to adopt a methodological individualist approach without imposing any premise concerning human rationality or irrationality, in practice methodological individualist social theory has almost always adopted the assumption of rational maximizing behavior. In this view, if they are to be scientifically understood at all, all human actions in any social context must be reduced to consequences of rational, satisfaction-maximizing choices. Only individuals act, but each individual action is merely a single instance of, a reflection of, the underlying uniformity of all actions as calculatedly rational efforts to optimize subject to constraints. The AM school accepts this melding of rationality and methodological individualism, and then employs it as the standard by which traditional Marxism is judged to be unscientific and obsolete.

For the AM school, the individual's desires and values, her or his endowment of assets, his or her personal knowledge, and all techniques for production (or any other social interaction) are simply taken as exogenously given. *The* essential human problem is that the exogenously given endowments are never optimally distributed so as to maximize the satisfaction of exogenously given human desires. Humans, however, have one main avenue for improvement open to them: exchange. They can exchange some of their initially owned goods or resources for goods or resources owned by other individuals with similarly suboptimal initial endowments. As an alternative to merely exchanging with others, individuals can use owned or acquired resources to produce. In this conceptual context, though, production is nothing more than another sort of exchange—"exchange with nature." Exogenously given preference orderings and production functions are assumed to be quantifiable with appropriate first and second order conditions, and these production functions are expressed in isoquants which are analytically identical to the indifference curves embodying the exogenously given preference orderings of individuals. The problems of cost-benefit calculation for an individual contemplating exchanging assets with another human being are analytically identical to the cost-benefit problems involved in production; exchanges with individuals and exchanges with nature are, analytically speaking, the same. In other words, in this "rational choice" methodological individualism, an individual's most significant relation to another person is indistinguishable from an individual's relation to an inanimate material thing. To say that methodological individualism is asocial would seem to be an understatement.

The AM school, moreover, appears to have only limited knowledge of history, but this lack of historical expertise is, if anything, exceeded by their lack of interest in a truly historical study of society. By assuming that initial endowments, preference orderings, property rights, and "rational" optimizing exchange behavior are "given," methodological individualists such as Elster and Roemer make common cause with neoclassicals in seeking a "social science" with at least a superficial appearance of methodological continuity with physics and chemistry. Given endowments of commodities elicit human desires of specific quantitative magnitudes in a manner analogous to the quantifiably different degrees of magnetic attraction of physical bodies. Utility-maximizing exchange can be described, once and for all, for every person in every society, in every time and place, in the same manner that physicists describe the movements of electrons and other subatomic particles. No particulars need be specified for electrons, and no historical or social and contextual particulars, beyond those subsumed in the given data, need be specified for the individual human being in the theories of Elster, Roemer, and the neoclassical economists. The rejection of history is thus quite conscious and deliberate: it is the *universality* of the choice-theoretic framework, the *independence* of the analytic procedure from any particular form taken by the data, which is seen as its chief virtue in comparison to the historicity of traditional Marxism.

Indeed, as far as I can ascertain, there is only one component of Marx's economic theory that the AM school deems worthy of serious consideration, the theory of exploitation, but the sort of consideration it receives speaks volumes about the approach of the AM theorists. Elster writes of Marx's theory of exploitation that "unlike most of his [Marx's] analytical economics it is worth examining for itself, not just for its place in the history of thought" (1985, 166). But, as is invariably the case for the very few ideas found to be of any value in Marx's writings, the AM theorists argue that the nature of the theoretical explanation of exploitation presented in Marx and traditional Marxism must be fundamentally altered.

Examining that alteration, we find that what they imagine to be Marx's few worthwhile insights can all be explained as merely special cases of the neoclassical theory of constrained optimization. The starting point for analyzing exploitation, for Marx, was the particular social relations of capitalism that gave to capital (and to capitalists, through their hired managers, the agents of capital) control of all labor processes. For the AM theorists the starting point is totally different. Elster's explanation of exploitation begins with:

> a set of individuals all equipped with the same amount of labour-power . . . but differently endowed with other factors of production. In addition to the individuals we must postulate the presence of a state that guarantees property rights and enforces contracts. There are well-defined techniques for producing all goods. (1985, 172)

Similarly, Roemer argues that his theory "explains" phenomena such as exploitation "by deriving them from logically prior data." For Roemer, these data are:

> differential ownership of the means of production, preferences and technology. Everything is driven by these data; class and exploitation are explained to be a consequence of the initial property relations. (1986, 178)

These statements by Elster and Roemer are very significant for an understanding of their critique of Marx. These "logically prior data," these presuppositions, these unquestioned, exogenously determined "facts" are identical with those of neoclassical economics. They follow from the methodological individualism which unites Roemer and Elster with the neoclassical tradition. The data become a "black box" into which one can push all the ideas, desires, motives, values, norms, knowledges, forms of behavior and *forms of control* that characterize a concrete historical set of social relations, in order for the methodological individualist to avoid the observation, description and analysis of the collective entities which are otherwise of such vital importance for understanding human behavior. In other words, the "givenness" of these givens obviates the need for a real social science of the sort that Marxism has always sought to provide.

THE "METHODOLOGICAL COLLECTIVIST" CRITIQUE

In my *History of Economic Thought* (Hunt 1979a), a common theme runs through every chapter. In that book, I attempted at length to show that throughout the history of capitalism there have been two fundamentally different traditions in economic theory: one tradition focuses on exchange as the most fundamental of all human economic activities, while the other looks at social production as most basic. The first approach has invariably led to the conservative conclusion that capitalism is fundamentally harmonious, while the latter has reinforced the more critical conclusion that capitalism is fundamentally conflictual.

Adam Smith is rightly viewed as an important influence on both neoclassical economics and Marxism, in large part because he embraced both of these approaches in a very eclectic and contradictory manner. When he used the exchange approach, his analysis culminated in his famous theory of the "invisible hand" and his well-known conservative *laissez faire* policy conclusions. But Smith also employed the social production approach, and in these writings he arrived at very different conclusions (Hunt 1979a, 34–56).

Unlike the AM school, when Smith used the production approach he did not take property rights and resource endowments as exogenously given:

> The aquisition of valuable and extensive property, therefore, necessarily requires the establishment of civil government. . . . Civil government supposed a certain subordination. But as the necessity of civil government gradually grows up with the acquisition of valuable property, so the principal causes which naturally introduce subordination gradually grow up with the growth of that valuable property. (Smith 1937, 670)

It is important to keep this quotation in mind when I discuss below the Roemer theory of exploitation, the centerpiece of the AM school, since I argue that that school represents an intellectual devolution to a pre-Smithian level of understanding on this point. Smith knew that this subordination necessarily preceded the creation of private property, and that it gave powerful individuals the power to "reap where they never sowed" (Smith 1937, 48). He knew, therefore, that property rights require a very particular form of government:

> Civil government, so far as it is instituted for the security of property, is in reality instituted for the defense of the rich against the poor, or of those who have some property against those who have none at all. (Smith 1937, 674)

Smith goes on at some length to discuss the methods whereby the capitalists control the production process and thereby the process of laboring. Whereas members of the AM school, particularly Roemer and Elster, take the existence and specific nature of government as given, take property rights as given, and assume (tacitly) that the government enforces these rights in a neutral, dispassionate, disinterested manner, Smith's approach was much closer to that of Marx. Smith writes that collusive behaviors by capitalists to enforce stricter controls on labor processes

> are frequently resisted by a contrary defensive combination of the workmen. . . . They are desperate, and act with the folly and extravagance of desparate men, who must either starve, or frighten their masters into immediate compliance with their demands. The masters upon these occasions . . . never cease to call aloud for the assistance of the civil magistrate, and the rigorous execution of those laws which have been enacted with so much severity against the combinations of servants, labourers, and journeymen. The . . . [workers'] combinations . . . generally end in nothing, but the punishment or ruin of the ring-leaders. (Smith 1937, 66–67)

The control of production processes, the origin of and social class domination of government, the control over the specific nature of property rights, and the enormous human costs of workers' coalitions formed to combat these controls were all matters that concerned Smith.

Within the approach of the AM school, though, these Smithian concerns are simply part of the exogenous data for the maximization problems that represent almost the sole concern of this approach. Elster frequently chides Marx for being old-fashioned, which amounts to criticizing him for not being a methodological individualist. But the dispute is not one pitting modern science against out-dated social concerns; Elster's arguments have been made for at least 250 years. Nearly a century ago, Thorstein Veblen clearly and accurately described the neoclassical methodological individualists of his time, and his description is equally applicable to Elster's and Roemer's work. These methodological individualists take their economic categories as given and fixed:

> They are hedonistically "natural" categories of such taxonomic force that their elemental lines of cleavage run through the facts of any given economic situation . . . even where the situation does not permit these lines of cleavage to be seen by men . . . so that, e.g., a gang of Aleutian Islanders slushing about in the wrack and surf with rakes and magical incantations for the capture of shell-fish are held, in point of taxonomic reality, to be engaged in a feat of hedonistic equilibration in rent, wages and interest. And that is all there is to it. Indeed for economic theory of this kind, that is all there is to any economic situation. (Veblen 1961, 193)

Veblen rightly ridiculed this putative science. Human beings are not electrons; they are not born with "given" degrees of attraction to "given" goods with "given property rights" attached to them, goods which can be consumed or transformed in accordance with "given" production functions. In a series of powerful critiques of the AM school, Michael Lebowitz (1984; 1987; 1988) has shown that it is precisely because they take as given nearly everything that Marx attempted to explain that the AM school utterly fails to comprehend Marx.

Human beings, like bees, ants, beavers and many other species, are social animals. We cannot live in isolation. Social interdependence pervades our emotional, aesthetic, intellectual and economic activities, indeed, all human activities. But human social behavior is also quite different from that of other social animals. The specific nature of the social behavior and social relations of ants, bees, and beavers appears to be biologically determined; a given species of bees, for example, exhibits the same behavior and social relations wherever and whenever it is observed. Human beings, however, show considerable plasticity or malleability; our social relations and social behaviors differ significantly from time to time and place to place, and *these behaviors and relations must be learned.*

"Methodological collectivists," as Elster refers to those who do not accept methodological individualism, stress the importance of the fact that every individual human being is born into a particular society at a particular time and place. Any given society has a comprehensible structure of social relations that ensures the perpetuation of the extremely complex set of specific behaviors and human interactions which are necessary to maintain that social system. Most methodological collectivists argue that there are complex and frequently paradoxical relations between the social whole and the individuals who comprise that social whole. Nevertheless, the social whole with its myriad of comprehensible social relations *must* always exist as a necessary precondition for any given individual to learn her or his desires, values, actions and behavioral patterns. This having been said, it must be emphatically stressed that, among methodological collectivists, traditional Marxists insist on a mutual and reciprocal relation between the individual and the social whole. Unlike

Hegelians who tend to reify society and social relations, traditional Marxists focus on the interactive process through which a certain social structure conditions all the learning taking place within it, but that same learning in turn recreates, generation after generation, the relatively stable structure of the society. Moreover, under some circumstances values and skills learned within a social structure can become the basis for consciously changing that structure.

Since social structures are the necessary preconditions for human learning and hence must predate any given individual, and since they most generally outlast any given individual, methodological collectivists argue that a true social science must begin with the specification of a given set of social relations. It must show how that social structure predictably gives rise to certain forms of behavior that are *rational within the prescribed norms, values, rewards and institutions* of that society, even if some of these behaviors appear irrational from within the context of some other set of social relations. It must then show how these socially conditioned behaviors, in turn, recreate the institutional structure of society in each generation. Such an analysis, when successful, shows the dynamic properties or laws of motion of a particular social structure. It also helps to elucidate the real historical possibilities for changing that structure.

We humans are, in addition, animals with a *culture*. Any human being born into a particular, historical social system has a name, a symbolic identity that differentiates her or him sharply not only from the electrons of physical theory but from most other species of animals as well. One has a symbolic self. Most of the objects of human desire are in some manner related to one's sense of self, which is almost entirely based on sociality and symbolism. One's activities, values and desires are based on *learned* and *socially shared* symbols. One's desires are the products of a social process of creation within the context of specific cultural constraints, on the basis of social symbols and values that give one's life a particular and personal meaning. An investigator cannot coherently discuss rationality without understanding real people's real reasons, and reasons are almost always based on values that are symbolically significant for the actor.

The point that is totally missed by Elster and Roemer is that values, motives, actions, practices and, most significantly, social institutions are constituted in part by the social actors' understandings of them, and these understandings are largely symbolic. In the spiraling process of historical interaction, specific social relations, practices and institutions give rise to these values, actions and understandings, but in turn the latter may reproduce, or perhaps fail to sustain, these relations, practices and institutions. Particular desires and actions are possible only within a specific set of beliefs and practices which are always inherently related to the norms, values, assumptions and contradictions of a particular social-economic system in a particular historical era.

The property rights and the behavior of negotiation and exchange that Elster and Roemer simply assume in order to demonstrate their concept of exploitation are connected to a set of material activities peculiar to the capitalist system. Money, bargaining, negotiations, and property rights all require a complex and sophisticated set of understandings, motives and cultural norms, including the institutions of the modern capitalist state, commercial instruments, monetary accounting, economic freedom, individual autonomy, legal contractual obligations, and much more. You cannot grant that these institutions are the product of socially constituted individuals who predate them, and then turn around within theory to claim that these institutions are contemporaneously generated through optimizing behavior on the basis of given endowments, given production functions and an autonomously given will to exchange with other similarly situated, similarly optimizing individuals. Adam Smith understood this. Elster, Roemer, the AM school, and neoclassical economics do not. Thus, I argue that economics, as exemplified by the neoclassical and AM schools, has devolved to a pre-Smithan status.

It is interesting and instructive to note that, in what is arguably one of the most profound books of the twentieth century, Norman O. Brown persuasively marshals his own and others' arguments to demonstrate the ultimately irrational nature of the paradigm of "rational man" (Brown 1959, 234–304). While space constraints prevent me from summarizing what I consider to be Brown's thoroughly brilliant argument, suffice it to say that the AM theorists conception of rationality as simply "given" and known to everyone is as intellectually naive as their notion that all other significant social processes are simply exogenously given.

THE ANALYTICAL MARXIST CONCEPT OF EXPLOITATION

The AM version of exploitation, the single element of Marx's economics that they imagine to be of any value, shows precisely the degree to which their theory is both asocial and ahistorical. Most of the members of this school acknowledge and accept Roemer's revamping of exploitation theory. Roemer enumerates several possible definitions of exploitation, two of which seem to me to be of particular importance in the AM school. I shall label them the "social withdrawal" theory of exploitation and the "factor consumption imbalance" theory of exploitation.

In the former, Roemer considers a "coalition of agents" which he labels *S*. He views the coalition as exploited if the following condition holds:

> If *S* were to withdraw from society, endowed with its per capita share of society's alienable property (that is, produced and nonproduced goods), and with its own labor and skills, then *S* would be better off (in terms of income and leisure) than it is at the present allocation. (1982, 285)

This is the "social withdrawal" approach: we check the income plus leisure of a group in a capitalist society; we then envision them withdrawing from society (with their "share" of commodities and resources) and examine whether their income plus leisure increases. If so, then that group was exploited; if not, then it was not exploited.

Of course, the AM school knows that this hypothetical experiment is impossible.

We would have to imagine a benevolent dictator decreeing a total reallocation, in which the capitalist class moves to Rhode Island with about one percent of total capital; the middle class of small business owners and independent professionals receives the Carolinas, Georgia, Mississippi, and Texas and about 19 percent of all capital; the unemployed and welfare class acquires New York, New England and California and about 25 percent of the capital; and the working class gains the remainder of the country and 55 percent of the capital. Problems remain, however, since we know from the Cambridge controversy that capital in general is not quantifiable except on the basis of prices that result from all of the complex technological, distributional and market interdependencies that prevail under some social regime. Hence we cannot use existing prices because they embody the old, potentially exploitative social and economic relations, and our experiment is supposed to determine this issue independently. Therefore, we could simply use the above-mentioned percentages to divide each category of relatively homogeneous capital goods, so that capitalists get one percent of the shovels, hammers, screwdrivers, etc., and each other class similarly receives its proportional share. For large factories that are very different from each other, we would have to resort to some arbitrary formula or else disassemble the factories and divide the parts.

We would then check the results after a year or two. Each class that experiences an increase in income plus leisure would then be known to have been exploited in the old system. Each class that experiences a decrease would be known to have been an exploiting class. Of course, the absurdity of the idea is so transparent that the cost of the paper and ink needed to print the inanities of this and the previous paragraph would be indefensible, were not these ideas exerting considerable influence today.

The proponents of the AM school would, no doubt, reiterate that the comparison is intended to be strictly mental and hypothetical, an experiment occuring within our thought processes alone. This is, I would argue, even more insane. Productive activity, capital, income and leisure are not simply immutably given data. They are aspects of the capitalist socio-economic system, aspects that require this particular social context to have any meaning whatsoever. Moreover, each of these complex social categories acquires a concrete numerical magnitude only by virtue of its place within the actual functioning of a specific socio-economic system at some point in real historical time.

How much could a worker produce if she or he had never been trained, socialized and educated in a capitalist system? If she or he had none of the values, emotions, and passions that the current system has generated? If she or he had never experienced capitalists or their hired managers waging economic warfare aimed at extracting the maximum labor from a given quantum of labor power purchased at a price that was itself an outcome of this protracted warfare? This AM vision is not science, but science fiction. Yet this is the "scientific rigor" that the AM school proposes to substitute for traditional Marxism.

If the "social withdrawal" theory of exploitation is pure speculative science fiction, the "factor consumption imbalance" theory of exploitation takes us closer to an understanding the real ideological foundations of the AM school. In *A General Theory of Exploitation and Class*, Roemer takes as given the following: consumer preferences and desires, government-enforced property rights, initial endowments of factors of production and a particular distribution of ownership rights over these factors, a set of production functions, and rational, utility-maximizing, exchanging, atomistic individuals. He then shows that, if some individuals have no ownership rights to the means of production, then it is purely rational optimizing behavior for them to sell their labor power to those individuals who do own means of production.

Roemer argues that the labor theory of value with its category of surplus value is unnecessary in deriving this result, and that the labor theory is defective in several ways. My aim here is not to defend the labor theory of value (although I have done so elsewhere; see Hunt 1979a; 1979b; 1982; 1983; 1986; 1989) but to examine what Roemer substitutes for it. His most crucial assertion is that "the fundamental feature of capitalist exploitation is not what happens in the labor process, but the differential ownership of productive assets" (1982, 94–95). In seeking to explain exploitation, Roemer explicitly states his disinterest in the presumably irrelevant issue of the historical specificity of a particular set of social or productive relations: "The historical process which gives rise to the initial endowments where my model begins is not a subject of my analysis" (1986, 138). Instead, he claims that scientific explanation of exploitation requires only (1) different endowments of assets for the atomistic maximizers of his model, and (2) *either* a labor market *or* a credit market.

If a labor market exists, then Roemer demonstrates that optimizing behavior will motivate individuals with small initial endowments to sell their labor power. Those with large endowments buy this labor power and direct the low-endowment individuals in transforming their labor power into labor, i.e., in using the assets of high-endowment individuals to produce commodities which then also belong to the high-endowment individuals. *If* the low-endowment individuals perform all of the productive labor, and *if* we use the quantities of labor embodied in commodities as the measurement standard for commodities, then Roemer's conclusion is simple and obvious: the labor contributed to society's productive processes by low-endowment individuals will *exceed* the labor embodied in the commodities they consume. If high-endowment individuals do not work, then obviously the labor embodied in the commodities they receive will exceed their (zero) labor contribution to the social production process. These differentials, between the labor contributed by an individual and that embodied in the commodities consumed by that individual, are for Roemer the measure of exploitation.

He then proceeds to substitute a credit market for the labor market in the model. Low-endowment individuals now rent capital from high-endowment individuals and use it to produce. Production here is controlled by laborers, who also own the commodities produced, but since they must pay rent to high-endowment individuals, who in turn use this rent to purchase commodities they did not labor to produce, it follows that exploitation, *as Roemer has defined it*, can exist even without a labor market and even where laborers control the production process and own the output produced. He concludes that "exploitation is not what happens in the labor process, but [is explained by] the differential ownership of productive assets" (1982, 94-5).

Once one examines Roemer's model, it comes as no surprise that his notion of exploitation has no connection to capitalist social relations of production. The model resembles Marxist economic theory only in one very superficial and inconsequential way: it uses the words "labor" and "labor-power." If we drop those terms and substitute the letters *a*, *b*, and *c* for the "factors of production," as is often done in conventional models, we can easily see the ambiguous and ultimately trivial nature of Roemer's notion of exploitation.

Assume a Roemer model in which factors of production *a*, *b*, *c* must be combined in certain proportions (defined by the exogenously given production function) to create the commodities that are consumed. Now assume that exogenously given initial endowments are such that one segment of the population (labeled *X*) owns all of *a*, another segment (*Y*) owns all of *b*, and a third segment (*Z*) owns all of *c*. We can further assume that one segment rents assets from the other two segments and proceeds to produce; for example, let *X* rent *b* and *c* from *Y* and *Z*. *Y* and *Z* can now use their rental income to purchase some of the commodities.

If we take factor *a* as the numeriare and measure all commodities in terms of *a*, and if we use Roemer's concept of exploitation, then it is obvious that segment *X* contributes more *a* to production than is embodied in the commodities it receives and that segments *Y* and *Z* contribute less *a* than is embodied in the commodities they receive. Therefore, it follows that *Y* and *Z* exploit *X*. By the same reasoning, however, if we use *b* as the numeraire, then *X* and *Z* exploit *Y*, and if we use *c* as numeraire, then *X* and *Y* exploit *Z*. Moreover, we can arrive at these conclusions with no knowledge whatsoever of the relative quantities of commodities consumed by *X*, *Y*, and *Z*. The poor may exploit the rich, or vice versa—it is of no analytical consequence because who exploits whom changes with every arbitrary change in the factor used as numeraire.

In *The Anti-Capitalist Mentality*, Ludwig von Mises (another methodological individualist) seems to use a model identical to Roemer's. von Mises' four social segments provide labor, abstinence, entrepreneurship and innovation. The providers of labor he considers "non-progressive," while the providers of the other three productive assets are considered by him to constitute the three "progressive" classes. Like Roemer, von Mises has a factor imbalance theory of exploitation:

> The characteristic feature of the market economy is the fact that it allots the greater part of the improvements brought about by the endeavors of the three progressive classes—those saving, those investing in capital goods, and those elaborating new methods for the employment of capital—to the non-progressive majority of people. . . .The market process provides the common man with the opportunity to enjoy the fruits of other people's achievements. It forces the three progressive classes to serve the non-progressive majority. (von Mises 1956, 40)

Roemer is fully aware of this profound ambiguity. In 1981, this seemed to bother him, since, in the conclusion to his *Analytical Foundations of Marxian Economic Theory*, he wrote:

> Another philosophical issue, which has not been dealt with in the book, concerns the choice to privilege labor power as the commodity that is exploited in a capitalist economy. It is well known that one can define corn values or energy values of commodities instead of labor values and show that corn or energy is exploited if there are positive profits. (1981, 204)

All von Mises would have to add to Roemer's statement is that it is not the the factors corn, energy or labor that are exploited but their owners. Roemer (1981, 204) then goes on to ask: "Why, then, do we choose labor power?" His answer is most instructive:

> An analytically convincing answer, as opposed to the plausible, intuitive answers . . . is subtle and not completely worked out at this writing. (1981, 205)

In fact, Roemer has never gotten the answer worked out because to do so would require him to go back to the very Marxian concepts he made his reputation debunking. Property relations, labor markets and credit markets are not given or eternal entities that simply exist. Property relations and markets in antiquity were very different from feudal property relations and markets, and capitalist property relations and markets differ significantly from both. One cannot ascertain what entities would be "assets," what "rights" would be entailed by "ownership" of assets, what types of behavior would be a consequence of these rights, or what behavior would be induced by markets without first specifying the whole system of social relations within which assets, ownership rights, and markets are embedded.

CONCLUSION: MARXISM VERSUS ANALYTICAL MARXISM

In capitalism, as Marx so clearly showed, capitalists *must* ceaselessly accumulate. Yet AM methodological individualists are forced to explain this as an "optimizing choice of portfolio management." For Marx, regardless of capitalists' "preference orderings" or "utility functions," the pressure they face to accumulate always involves class struggle, implying that the economic laws of class struggle can only be understood if one understands the nature and degree of the control that capitalists have over the labor process. But by taking the production function as fixed, Roemer has eliminated from consideration not only most of Marx's concerns in *Capital*, volume 1, but also much of the recent, very important work of Reich, Gordon and Edwards (1973), Piore (1973), Braverman (1974), Marglin (1974-75), Edwards (1976), Gintis (1976), Reich (1981), Bowles, Gordon and Weisskopf (1983), Bowles (1985), and many others.

More significantly, in my view, by rejecting the labor theory of value and surplus value, the AM school has reduced the critque of capitalism to a matter of one's feelings about the fairness or unfairness of the initial endowment of assets. In other essays (Hunt 1982; 1983; 1986), I have attempted to show how the labor theory of value and Marx's analysis of the nature of the labor process under capitalism are the necessary foundations for his profound critique of the damage done to human beings and human development in capitalist society.

Marx's discussion of value as the only expression of the sociality of labor in a capitalist society reflects his views on human nature, the nature of capitalism, and the ways in which human nature is manifested in capitalism. Value is the expression of the sociality of human creativity in an economic system in which that sociality has been alienated to such a degree that it appears to be an abstract quality of an alien, objective entity. And in a capitalist system, money is the general form of all value, considered abstractly. Money is, therefore, the most general, alienated expression of human sociality in a capitalist economy. Marx goes to some lengths to show how and why this state of affairs significantly impairs and distorts human development. His analysis seems to me and, I presume, to most Marxists to be one of his most profound contributions to human knowledge.

Obviously, Roemer and Elster and the AM school are utterly unimpressed with this. Roemer has yet to think of an "analytically convincing answer" to the question of why exploitation is relevant in discussing labor rather than corn or energy. And the only real critique of capitalism that one finds in Roemer is the assertion that the initial endowments of assets may be unfairly distributed.

Neither Roemer nor Elster considers exploitation to be inherently unfair. Each has developed a model which shows how, depending on the nature of individuals' exogenously given preference orderings and initial endowments, rational optimizing behavior results in a situation in which the asset-poor person "exploits the rich person" (Roemer 1986a, 274–77; 1988, 127–31; Elster 1986, 98). Roemer concludes that he has shown "that exploitation is only unethical if that inital distribution of wealth is judged to have come about through means that are not moral" (1988, 127).

Because Elster and Roemer have rejected virtually every tenet of Marxism except for this interpretation of Marxian exploitation theory, this conclusion is particularly significant. Neoclassical textbooks generally contain a standard caveat to the effect that their demonstration of the inherent welfare-optimizing tendency of free market capitalism is premised on the moral acceptance of the initial endowments of assets. The AM school thus appears to be merely the most egalitarian wing of the neoclassical approach to economic theory.

Other neoclassical economists have had egalitarian sentiments, however, sentiments typically held in check by the belief that a significant degree of inequality is necessary for capitalists to make their socially valuable contributions to production. Once again the AM school can be seen as simply a species of neoclassical economics: Elster believes that it is only because the capitalist receives surplus value "that the capitalist has an incentive to create it. Had there been no capitalist, the workers . . . would . . . have nothing that anyone could rob them of" (1985, 225). As with their neoclassical counterparts, the analytical Marxists believe that capitalists are as important as laborers in the creation of value, if not more so. At this point, one can hardly be surprised by Roemer's final conclusion that "there appears to be no reason for an interest in the technical measure of exploitation, calculated in the classical Marxist way" (1988, 131).

If this uninteresting Marxist theory of exploitation is Marxism's most defensible feature, then Marxism would definitely seem to be, as the AM school suggests, intellectually bankrupt. The argument that Marxism is intellectually worthless is certainly nothing new; indeed, this criticism has been made innumerable times over the last 125 years. For these critics to assert, however, that they constitute a "new school" of Marxism is fundamentally dishonest. I can only assume that they believe Marxism to be more vulnerable to a "Trojan Horse" critique from within than to an honest debate between defenders and external detractors. In Roemer's most recent major work, *Free to Lose*, he explicitly rejects the Marxian theory of exploitation (1988, 127–31, 175). This, together with earlier critiques and rejections of virtually every other component of Marxism, makes one wonder how he could subtitle the book "An Introduction to Marxist Economic Philosophy." One gets no help from Elster on this matter. Describing a discussion group that included most of the individuals identified as members of the AM school at the beginning of this essay, Elster wrote:

> An interesting outcome of these discussions is that the sense in which we felt able to call ourselves Marxists has undergone a change over the years. I do not feel that I can speak for others than myself, except to say that there is probably not a single tenet of classical Marxism which has not been the object of insistent criticism at these meetings. Yet some kind of unstated consensus has emerged, even though I feel neither called upon nor competent to explain it here. (1985, xiv)

To my knowledge, no member of the AM school has explained in what sense they are Marxists. Until I am aware of such an explanation and, indeed, find it convincing, I shall consider them to be a part of the long tradition of anti-Marxism—and a particularly virulent part.

REFERENCES

Bardhan, P. 1984. *Land, Labor and Rural Poverty*. New York: Columbia University Press.

Bowles, S.; Gordon, D.; and Weisskopf, T. 1983. *Beyond the Waste Land*. New York: Anchor Press.

Bowles, S. 1985. "The Production Process in a Competitive Economy: Walrasian, Neo-Hobbesian and Marxian Models." *American Economic Review* 75 (1).

Braverman, H. 1974. *Labor and Monopoly Capital*. New York: Monthly Review Press.

Brenner, R. 1989. "Bourgeois Revolution and Transition to Capitalism." In *The First Modern Society*, ed. A. Beur. Cambridge: Cambridge University Press.

Brown, N. O. 1959. *Life Against Death: The Psychoanalytical Meaning of History*. Middletown, CT: Wesleyan University Press.

Carling, Alan. 1986. "Rational Choice Marxism." *New Left Review*, no.160 (November/December).

Cohen, G. A. 1989. "Reconsidering Historical Materialism." In *Marxist Theory*, ed. A. Callinicos. Oxford: Oxford University Press.

Edwards, R. 1976. "Individual Traits and Organizational Incentives: What Makes a 'Good Worker'?" *Journal of Human Resources* 11 (1).

Elster, J. 1985. *Making Sense of Marx*. Cambridge: Cambridge University Press.

——. 1986. *An Introduction to Karl Marx*. Cambridge: Cambridge University Press.

Gintis, H. 1976. "The Nature of the Labor Exchange and the Theory of Capitalist Production." *Review of Radical Political Economics* 8 (2).

Gray, J. 1983. "The System of Ruins." *Times Literary Supplement*, December 30.

Hunt, E. K. 1979a. *History of Economic Thought: A Critical Perspective*. Belmont, CA: Wadsworth Publishing. (Revised edition, forthcoming 1991. New York: Harper and Row).

——. 1979b. "Marx as a Social Economist: The Labor Theory of Value." *Review of Social Economy* 38 (3). Reprinted in *Marxian Economics*, ed. J. E. King. Hants, England: Edward Elgar, 1990.

——. 1982. "Marx's Concept of Human Nature and the Labor Theory of Value." *Review of Radical Political Economics* 14 (3).

——. 1983. "Joan Robinson and the Labour Theory of Value." *Cambridge Journal of Economics* 7 (3/4).

——. 1986. "Philosophy and Economics in the Writings of Karl Marx." In *Marx, Schumpeter and Keynes*, ed. S. W. Helburn and D. F. Bramhall. New York: M. E. Sharpe.

——. 1989. "The Meaning and Significance of the Transformation Problem: Two Contrasting Approaches." *Atlantic Economic Journal* 17 (4).

Johansen, L. 1972. "Labour Theory of Value and Marginal Utilities." In *A Critique of Economic Theory*, ed. E. K. Hunt and J. G. Schwartz. London: Penguin Books.

Lebowitz, M. A. 1987. Review of *A General Theory of Exploitation and Class*, by J. E. Roemer. *Canadian Journal of Economics* 17 (2).

——. 1987. "The Political Economy of Wage-Labor." *Science and Society* 51 (3).

——. 1988. "Is 'Analytical Marxism' Marxism?" *Science and Society* 52 (2).

Marglin, S. 1974-75. "What Do Bosses Do? The Origins and Functions of Hierarchy in Capitalist Production." Parts 1, 2. *Review of Radical Political Economy* 6 (2); 7 (1).

Piore, M. 1973. "Fragments of a Sociological Theory of Wages." *American Economic Review* 63 (2).

Przeworski, A. 1986. *Capitalism and Social Democracy*. Cambridge: Cambridge University Press.

Reich, M.; Gordon, D.; and Edwards, R. 1973. "A Theory of Labor Market Segmentation." *American Economic Review* 63 (2).

Reich, M. 1981. "Economic Theory and Class Conflict." In *Racial Inequality*. Princeton: Princeton University Press.

Roemer, J. E. 1981. *Analytical Foundations of Marxian Economic Theory*. Cambridge: Cambridge University Press.

——. 1982. *A General Theory of Exploitation and Class*. Cambridge: Harvard University Press.

——, ed. 1986a. *Analytical Marxism*. Cambridge: Cambridge University Press.

——. 1986b. "Exploitation and the Labour Theory of Value." *Economic and Political Weekly* 21:3 (January 18).

——. 1988. *Free to Lose*. Cambridge: Harvard University Press.

Smith, A. 1937. *The Wealth of Nations*. New York: Modern Library.

Steedman, I. 1977. *Marx After Sraffa*. London: New Left Books.

Van Parijs, P. 1983. "Why Marxist Economics Needs Microfoundations: Postscript to an Obituary." *Review of Radical Political Economics* 15 (2).

Veblen, T. 1961. "Professor Clark's Economics." *The Place of Science in Modern Civilization and Other Essays*. New York: Russell and Russell.

von Mises, L. 1956. *The Anti-Capitalist Mentality*. New York: D. Van Nostrand.

Wright, E. O. 1982. "The Concept of the Political in the Concept of Class Structure." *Politics and Society* 11 (3).

——. 1985. *Classes*. London: Verso.

THE ANALYTICAL FOUNDATIONS OF CONTEMPORARY POLITICAL ECONOMY: A COMMENT ON HUNT

Herbert Gintis

I do not disagree with E. K. Hunt's admirable description of analytical Marxism, nor do I differ strongly with his characterization of its differences with traditional Marxism. These differences are deep and fundamental, to the point that rational choice Marxism can indeed be considered hostile to many of traditional Marxism's most basic tenets. In this essay I will neither attempt to defend analytical Marxism against Hunt's critique nor will I endorse this critique. I am not analytical Marxist, although I have sympathy with some of its positions. Nor am I a traditional Marxist, having made my peace with Marxism in my joint work with Samuel Bowles, *Democracy and Capitalism: Property, Community, and the Contradictions of Modern Social Thought* (1986). Marxism, I believe, has given us many important insights into the operation of society, but has no monopoly on truth.

Rather than take sides, I propose here to elucidate the differences between the two, and offer an perspective missing in Hunt's critique: the venerable opposition between neoclassical and Marxian economic theory is antiquated and is increasingly of purely historical interest. This is true because both Marxism and neoclassical economics are disintegrating in the face of contemporary political and theoretical concerns. Coming years will involve vast changes in all of economic theory, blurring the old distinctions, validating some concerns traditionally held by Marxists, others conventionally identified with supporters of laissez-faire capitalism, and yet others novel and conflicting with both. The bulk of my remarks deal with two aspects of Hunt's critique of analytical Marxism: its "acceptance of methodological individualism," and its "belief that all human actions and interactions can be reduced to a single common denominator—rational, calculated, utility-maximizing exchanges." Other aspects of his critique, as well as a brief discussion of political implications, will be addressed in the concluding section.

METHODOLOGICAL INDIVIDUALISM

Methodological individualism is a philosophical position holding that all social action should be derived from the atomistic behavior of prima facie isolated social agents. Many neoclassical economists have professed a faith in this philosophical position, and Jon Elster espoused methodological individualism in several of his most influential writings. Yet the position is untenable, I believe, and Marx was quite justified in his derision of the methodological individualists of his day. In particular, no one has ever, to my knowledge, shown that market exchange, private property, or prices, as they are modeled in economic theory, emerge from the atomistic behavior of economic agents. More generally, no one has shown that any particular social institutions are the logical implication of individual action.

Economic theory is not alone in its inability to derive macrostructure from microstructure. Quantum mechanics cannot be used to generate automobiles or computers, microbiology cannot show the necessity of the frog or the tree, and linguistic theory cannot produce syntax and semantics from the linguistic behavior of individuals. The quest for the spontaneous emergence of structure has, by and large, eluded modern science, natural and behavioral alike.

Yet traditional neoclassical economics is not methodologically individualist, despite the frequent lip-service paid to the doctrine by neoclassical economists. The actual methodology of neoclassical theory is to *posit* the existence of certain institutions (prices, markets, etc.) and attempt to show that they are *compatible* with the actions of individual agents. This is the overt position of analytical Marxists in their more recent writings, and Elster's work is an effective defense of this position.

This position, which I accept, may be understood as asserting that *economic theory must have logically consistent microfoundations*. In other words, we cannot have a model of individual action and one of institutional structure that are mutually inconsistent. This appears obvious, but it is often violated in traditional Marxian economic theory. For instance, as Roemer has stressed, the Marxian theory of the falling rate of profit contradicts the assumption that capitalists maximize profits. Similarly, the Marxian premise that labor-power is a commodity subject to the normal laws of market supply and demand is inconsistent with the existence of unemployment as a more than a temporary phenomenon, and the Marxian notion that capital is a commodity is inconsistent with the Marxian assertion that the firm is controlled by owners of capital. Of course, it may be possible to develop more sophisticated Marxian models that avoid these problems. The point that the analytical Marxists are attempting to make in their demand for rigorous thinking is nevertheless incontrovertibly correct: no economic model is acceptable unless its micro and macro reasoning are logically consistent.[1]

Hunt is not sympathetic to this position, arguing that "One person's *rigor* appears as another's *mortis*." But are political models based on microanalytic reasoning really dead? I think not. Roemer's opus, which contains some of the most interesting work in modern economic theory, is a case in point. There are, moreover, many further microanalytic contributions to modern political economy based on assumptions different from those of the analytical Marxists (e.g., Aoki 1984; Bowles and Gintis 1988; 1990; Dow 1986; Epstein and Gintis 1990; Gintis 1989a; 1989b; 1989c). There will doubtless be many more.

SELF INTEREST AND ECONOMIC POWER

It may be thought that affirming the need for microfoundations is a concession to neoclassical economics, and will inexorably lead to the pacification of political economy and its incorporation into neoclassical economics. But neoclassical economics has been just as guilty of microfoundational inconsistency as has Marxian economics. I could give many examples of this, but I will focus on one that I consider of particular importance for political economy: the microeconomic assumption that individuals are self-interested, and the institutional assumption that contracts can be assumed to be enforceable by the state (Bowles and Gintis 1988).

It is clear that many of the most common market exchanges occurring in a capitalist economy cannot be enforced by the state, either because the state does not have the jurisdiction, the proper information, or the incentive to do so. Take, for instance, a typical credit transaction: an agent borrows a sum of money and agrees to repay the loan at a later date. Can the lender depend upon the judicial system to enforce the resulting contractual agreement? If the loan is fully collateralized, the answer is "Yes." But the function of credit in a capitalist economy is to transfer purchasing power from wealth *holders* to wealth *users*, and this is possible only if loans are not collateralized. By the legalities of limited liability, the state cannot attach a debtor's assets beyond the contractually stipulated forms of collateral. Therefore the state cannot enforce capital market transactions (Gintis 1989a).

For another example, take the labor market. A worker agrees, in return for a wage, to submit to the authority of the employer (Gintis 1976). The contract does not specify with any clarity (even if it is negotiated with a labor union) the task to be performed, with what care, and with what intensity. If the employer feels the worker has violated the contract, can she take the worker to court for reparations? The idea is absurd, of course, since such an event almost *never* occurs. First, the cost of pursuing a worker in court would be prohibitive for all but the most highly-paid workers (e.g., the agents of famous actors or musicians). Second, the judicial system lacks the relevant information (the "evidence"). Indeed, if such information were easily available, the employer would have been able to write a more specific contract and to hire an independent agent to carry it out (independent agents are, of course, regularly sued in court for breach of contract). Conclusion: the state cannot enforce labor market transactions.

The above remarks are well-known and not subject to much serious dispute. How then does neoclassical economics manage to render the issue of the violation of the terms of exchange unproblematic? It simply assumes that people are "honest" and spontaneously fulfill their contractual obligations! The homo economicus of neoclassical theory, far from being a self-interested brute, is in fact a perfectly socialized Victorian gentleman, acting from a fundamental sense of honor (Bowles and Gintis 1991).

It follows that neoclassical theory must either drop the assumption of self-interest or that of unproblematic contract enforcement. In realization of this fact, economists in the neoclassical tradition have made important contributions to a theory of endogenous contract enforcement (Stiglitz 1987; Williamson 1985). Similarly, Bowles and I have used models of endogenous contract enforcement to provide the microfoundations for the theory of unemployment, the role of the welfare state in the distribution of income, the existence of economic power in competitive equilibrium, and the basis for the relationship between wealth and power in a capitalist economy (Bowles and Gintis 1990).

BEYOND METHODOLOGICAL INDIVIDUALISM AND COLLECTIVISM

If methodological individualism is incorrect, social structure cannot be inferred from the constitution of economic agents. How then are we to conceive of social institutions? Under the rubric of "methodological collectivism," Hunt argues in favor of the traditional Marxian conception of the primacy of social relations as historically given and internally contradictory. Individual agents in this view are formed by acculturation (social learning through rewards and penalties) to accept, affirm, and defend these social relations under normal conditions, and to reject and overturn them when the structural contradictions become sufficiently grave.

In our book *Democracy and Capitalism*, Bowles and I reject this model of interaction between individual and society in favor of an explicitly game-theoretic formulation: agents pursue personal and group objectives subject to the resources made available by, and the constraints imposed by, the "rules of the game" that comprise the structure of social life (Bowles and Gintis 1986). In the years that have elapsed since this book appeared, it has become even clearer to me that game theory is likely fundamentally to transform all of social theory in coming years.[2] I suspect that most analytical Marxists would have some sympathy with this view.

It should be clear that the traditional Marxian approach to the individual-society interaction is similar to that of traditional liberal sociology à la Durkheim and Parsons: society creates the structures and socializes individuals to accept these structures and work within their parameters. Marxism then adds "contradictions" to the model, either in the form of social relations vs. forces of production (traditional Marxism) or alienated actuality vs. unalienated potentiality (Marxist humanism, critical theory), while liberalism takes a more evolutionary approach.

Once again the future lies in overcoming the joint failures of traditional liberal and Marxian approaches.

There is one central problem in both the traditional Marxian approach and its liberal counterpart: they are incompatible with the notion of autonomous individual strategic action. Agents in these models are socialized into roles, or are members of groups, and blindly act according to their social positions. This may be an acceptable way of treating ants and bees, but human beings *in fact* have extensive information-processing and reasoning abilities, allowing them to act strategically.

One example should suffice to convince the reader of the poverty of the traditional approach. Is it true that individuals accept the norms of society because they are socialized to do so? The answer is a clear "No." American blacks and women have been routinely and universally socialized—in schools, in churches, in popular culture, and in academia— to accept their inferior positions in society. This did not prevent the emergence of the Civil Rights and feminist movements in the 1960s. Similarly, generations of Soviet citizens were propagandized relentlessly as to the virtues of acting as Socialist Man in the Communist system. It is clear now that they did not by and large accept this "socialization."

It is not enough to say that sometimes socialization works and sometimes it does not. The point is *there is no such thing* as socialization in the traditional sense. Individuals accept the cultural tools around them when they conform to the evidence of their senses and contribute to their life projects, as they see them. Otherwise they reject these tools and search for others. A game-theoretic model is perfectly constructed to handle this insight and draw out its macrosocial implications.

Of course for social theory in general we cannot be satisfied with the simple game-theoretic models used in economic theory. In *Democracy and Capitalism*, we proposed that "social games" have four central attributes that are absent from game theory in the von Neumann-Morganstern tradition. First, the rules of the game in social life are normally *asymmetric*: some groups are given positions that ensure their social dominance, while others are relegated to subordinate positions. Second, social games are *recursive*, in that the rules themselves are transformed by the actors, and obedience to the rules occurs only by the strategic choice of agents. Third, social games are *constitutive* in the sense that the objective and the goals of the participants are not pre-given, but are constituted by the process of social participation. Finally, social games are *overlapping* in the sense that there are several distinct sets of rules of the game, for economy, state, family, community, etc., which characteristically conflict in the arenas of social life where they jointly apply (Bowles and Gintis 1986).

RATIONAL BEHAVIOR

Perhaps no aspect of neoclassical theory is more vulnerable to attack than its assumption that human behavior can be understood in terms of the maximization of an objective function subject to constraints. I suspect that ultimately this model will be dropped in favor of some as yet unknown alternative. I have two reasons for this belief. First, it is impossible to treat the agent's objective function (preference structure) as prior to her actions. This is true both because objectives are produced by actions as much as the reverse, and because agents choose their actions with the knowledge that their objectives will be transformed in certain predictable ways thereby.[3] Second, despite its prodigious reasoning capacity, homo sapiens is still a genetically-bound life form. It is not clear that the effect of the genetic constitution of human agents can best be captured, or indeed can be captured at all, in terms of objectives and constraints.

Despite these doubts, and with some reservations that I will address, I think the optimization-subject-to-constraints model is often the best model to apply to economic affairs. My major defense of the proposition is bottom line: I have already referred to the many contributions to political economy using this assumption (some from the analytical Marxism school, others not), and my own assessment of the state of affairs is that they have been quite successful. Opponents of this approach appear to offer little more as an alternative than an exhortation to return to the Great Masters of the Past. Needless to say, neither contributes to the development of a future-oriented, scientifically disciplined political economy.

My first reservation concerning optimization models is that the cost of calculation and the limited information channels available to the agent must, in many cases, be directly incorporated into models of human action. The result of such an integration is that agents will often be best modeled as obeying rule-following as opposed to optimizing behavior (Heiner 1983; 1985). However, rules themselves must be seen as evolving, as transformed according to the "survival value" they lend to their users (Gintis 1991). In this sense it is often the *rule* rather than the individual action based upon it that is explained by an optimizing argument.

My second reservation is that human fallibility, the capacity to act "illogically" for strategically sound reasons, and occasional random behavior must be built into our model of how individuals assess the strategic behavior of other agents. It is well-known in game theory that predicted behavior can change dramatically when the possibility of "illogical" behavior is admitted. Indeed, it can be shown that the very concept of "logical behavior" has a deep internal inconsistency. For instance, in a finite, repeated Prisoner's Dilemma game, it is illogical to cooperate on the first round. Thus by cooperating on the first round, an agent may be able to induce her opponent to abandon logical reasoning, since such reasoning has been incontrovertibly incorrect on the first round. The result may benefit the first agent.[4]

A third problem with the game theory paradigm is in its treatment of individual behavior towards risk. On the one hand, the modern choice-theoretic analysis of risk is surely one the great successes of economic theory in the twentieth century, and the absence of a cogent theory of risk and uncertainty is a major absence in Keynesian, Marxian, and institutional economic theories. While post-Keynesian economists have roundly criticized this analytical tradition (e.g., Shackle 1968), I find their criticisms unpersuasive. The future lies, I believe, in refining rather than supplanting the choice-theoretic treatment of risk. However, there are well documented and systematic tendencies for agents to deviate from the predictions of the expected utility hypothesis, and some of these are of the greatest importance for social theory and social policy (Machina 1987; Tversky and Kahneman 1974; 1981; Tversky and Thaler 1990).

Finally, while optimization models do not necessarily presume self-interested agents, there are as yet no fully acceptable models of human "altruistic" behavior. There are, however, several interesting approaches to this question (Axelrod and Hamilton 1981; Boyd and Richerson 1985; Caporael 1987). Political economists should begin to contribute to this branch of knowledge in coming years.

CONCLUDING REMARKS

The most serious mistake radical economics can make in the closing years of the twentieth century is to prolong the futile attempt to breathe fresh life into defunct doctrines. In this respect I agree with the iconoclastic research paradigm of the analytical Marxists. But I believe Hunt is correct in his claim that the analytical Marxists have too uncritically borrowed from neoclassical doctrine. As I have suggested, this doctrine is no more likely to survive the contemporary "microfoundations revolution" than is traditional Marxism.

There was a time, not too many decades ago, when it was still reasonable to hold that working class revolutions are the likely medium of progressive social change in the advanced capitalist world, and that Marxism (properly interpreted, revised, and updated) is the theory of such change. That time lies squarely in the past. The labor theory of value, the Marxian theory of exploitation and alienation, and the Marxian theory of the state are part of that defunct tradition. The issues facing the oppressed in the present and future include nuclear holocaust, environmental destruction, racism and sexism, the exploitation of the Third World, the violation of human rights, and the suppression of national self-determination, among others. These issues come together in the vision of a global world community based on equality, dignity, reciprocity, ecological balance and democratic accountability. We need new theories for new times.

Twentieth century political philosophy was steeped in the opposition between capitalism and socialism, and progressives posed total alternatives to the existing order as the only visions worthy of the name "radical." But we have no more total alternatives (we never did, but no one could possibly have known that). Radical economists in the twenty-first century must *develop, and demonstrate to the world the viability of, new egalitarian and democratic instruments for the control of economic life*. I have a deep faith in the possibility of a socialist economy promoting dignity, equality, freedom, and democratic accountability. We do not yet know what social institutions would look like in such a society, and we should admit this. We should also admit that traditional economic theories do not answer these questions, and thus we must develop new ones. The concepts I have discussed in this essay may, in the end, be inadequate to the task. But if they are rejected, it will be in favor of even more untraditional and forward-looking forms of scientific reasoning. The past cannot be recovered.

NOTES

1. Of course if Marxian theory were an excellent predictor of economic phenomena, it might be acceptable even if it had serious methodological imperfections. But it is not.

2. For recent game-theoretic contributions to political philosophy, see Hardin (1982), Sugden (1986), Taylor (1987), and Elster (1989). For similar contributions to sociology, see Hechter, Opp and Wippler (1990) and Friedland and Robertson (1990).

3. For a more complete discussion, see Bowles and Gintis (1986), chaps. 5 and 6.

4. Careful analyses of some of these problems are presented in Campbell and Sowden (1985).

REFERENCES

Aoki, M. 1984. *The Co-operative Game Theory of the Firm*. London: Clarendon.

Axelrod, R., and Hamilton, W. D. 1981. "The Evolution of Cooperation." *Science* 211 (March): 1390–96.

Bowles, S., and Gintis, H. 1986. *Democracy and Capitalism: Property, Community and the Contradictions of Modern Social Thought*. New York: Basic Books.

———. 1988. "Contested Exchange: Political Economy and Modern Economic Theory." *American Economic Review* 78 (2): 145-50.

———. 1990. "Contested Exchange: New Microfoundations of the Political Economy of Capitalism." *Politics and Society* 18 (2): 165–222.

———. Forthcoming, 1991. "The Revenge of *Homo Economicus*: Post-Walrasian Economics and the Revival of Political Economy." *Journal of Economic Perspectives*.

Boyd, R., and Richerson, P. J. 1985. *Culture and the Evolutionary Process*. Chicago: University of Chicago Press.

Campbell, R., and Sowden, L., eds. 1985. *Paradoxes of Rationality and Cooperation*. Vancouver: University of British Columbia Press.

Caporael, L. R. 1987. "*Homo Sapiens, Homo Faber, Homo Socians*: Technology and the Social Animal." In *Evolutionary Epistemology: A Multiparadigm Program*, ed. W. Callebaut and R. Pinxten. Boston: Reidel.

Dow, G. 1986. "Control Rights, Competitive Markets, and the Labor Management Debate." *Journal of Comparitive Economics* 10 (1): 48–61.

Elster, J. 1989. *The Cement of Society: A Study of Social Order*. Cambridge: Cambridge University Press.

Epstein, G., and Gintis, H. 1990. "International Capital Markets and the Limits of National Economic Policy." In *Financial Openness and National Autonomy*, ed. T. Banuri and J. Schor. Oxford: Clarendon.

Friedland, R., and Robertson, A. F. 1990. *Beyond the Marketplace: Rethinking Economy and Society*. Hawthorne, NY: Aldine de Gruyter.

Gintis, H. 1976. "The Nature of the Labor Exchange and the Theory of Capitalist Production." *Review of Radical Political Economics* 8 (2): 36–54.

———. 1989a. "Financial Markets and the Political Structure of the Enterprise." *Journal of Economic Behavior and Organization* 1 (2): 311–22.

———. 1989b. "The Principle of External Accountability in Financial Markets." In *The Firm as a Nexus of Treaties*, ed. M. Aoki, B. Gustafsson, and O. Williamson. New York: Russell Sage.

———. 1989c. "The Power to Switch: On the Political Economy of Consumer Sovereignty." In *Unconventional Wisdom: Essays in Honor of John Kenneth Galbraith*, ed. S. Bowles, R. Edwards, and W. Shepherd. New York: Houghton-Mifflin.

———. 1991. "The Emergence of Money in General Equilibrium: An Artificial Life Simulation." Working paper, University of Massachusetts, January.

Hardin, R. 1982. *Collective Action*. Baltimore: Johns Hopkins.

Hechter, M.; Opp, K.; and Wippler, R. 1990. *Social Institutions: Their Emergence, Maintenance, and Effects*. Hawthorne, NY: Aldine de Gruyter.

Heiner, R. A. 1983. "The Origin of Predictable Behavior." *American Economic Review* 73 (4): 560–95.

———. 1985. "The Origin of Predictable Behavior: Further Modeling and Applications." *American Economic Review* 75 (2): 391–96.

Machina, M. J. 1987. "Choice Under Uncertainty: Problems Solved and Unsolved." *Journal of Economic Perspectives* 1 (1): 121–54.

Shackle, G. L. S. 1968. *Expectations, Investment and Income*. Oxford: Oxford University Press.

Stiglitz, J. E. 1987. "The Causes and Consequences of the Dependence of Quality on Price." *Journal of Economic Literature* 25 (March): 1–48.

Sugden, R. 1986. *The Economics of Rights, Cooperation, and Welfare*. Oxford: Basil Blackwell.

Taylor, M. 1987. *The Possiblity of Cooperation*. Cambridge: Cambridge University Press.

Tversky, A., and Kahneman, D. 1974. "Judgment under Uncertainty: Heuristics and Biases." *Science* 185 (September): 1124–31.

———. 1981. "The Framing of Decisions and the Psychology of Choices." *Science* 211 (January): 453–58.

Tversky, A., and Thaler, R. H. 1990. "Preference Reversals." *Journal of Economic Perspectives* 4 (2): 201–11.

Williamson, O. 1985. *The Economic Institutions of Capitalism*. New York: Free Press.

4 MARXIST–FEMINIST CONTRIBUTIONS TO RADICAL ECONOMICS

Julie Matthaei

In the last twenty years, a new and rich school of economic analysis has developed—Marxist-Feminist thought—as part of what many historians now call the "second wave" of feminism (the first was in the mid- and late-nineteenth century). This resurgence of feminism was both the result and cause of a growing breakdown in the traditional sexual division of labor as more and more married women entered into the paid labor force, and as women began to demand entrance into men's jobs (Matthaei 1982). In the early 1970s, grass-roots feminist groups sprung up all over the U.S. to study, criticize, and fight to break down gender straightjackets, including the exclusion of women from positions of power.

Marxist-feminism developed in the early seventies, with roots in radical feminism and the New Left. Some women came to Marxism and radical economics as a result of their participation in radical feminist study and organizing groups. Others had been

---

I developed many of these ideas, especially the unitary systems approach, while working with Teresa Amott on *Race, Gender, and Work: A Multicultural Economic History of Women in the United States* (1991). Marcellus Andrews and the editors of this volume provided very helpful comments, criticisms and editorial suggestions. I presented earlier versions of this paper at the Union for Radical Political Economics Summer meetings (1988), the Harvard University Seminar in Non-neoclassical Economics (1988), the "Marxism Now: Traditions and Difference" Conference (1989), and various meetings of Marxist-Feminist 1, and benefited from the comments and questions of these audiences. Chris McGee, Gwynne Wiatrowski and Jennifer Schoenstadt provided invaluable research assistance.

active participants in the New Left and its economics in the sixties; growing feminist consciousness led them to split off, due both to the sexist practices of the New Left and to the inadequacy of its Marxist theory for explaining women's oppression (Sargent 1981). Marxist-feminism arose, then, both to study and explain women's subordination to men and the recent changes in gender relations and to inform an active and multi-faceted women's movement.

Marxist-feminism is part of the larger Women's Studies movement, which began during this period and has continued to grow and develop. The contributions of Marxist-feminism to radical economics and political organizing also parallel those of Women's Studies in general to academia and politics in general. In this essay I will discuss two broad themes: (1) the introduction of new concepts and areas of study into radical economic theorizing, and (2) the transformation (now only in its early stages) of the entire body of radical/Marxist economics, stemming from the recognition that the actors within capitalist society are gendered and raced. My aim is not to provide an encyclopedic survey of the burgeoning literature but rather to elucidate the main contributions of Marxist-feminist thought and point out useful directions for its future development.

MARXIST-FEMINISM ENLARGES THE SCOPE OF MARXIST ECONOMICS

Marxist-feminism has enlarged the scope of radical economics in three ways: adding new topics or areas of study, developing the concept of patriarchy as a lens through which to analyze the economy, and adding feminist organizing to the discourse on radical social movements.

New Areas of Study

An early and major contribution of Marxist-feminism was simply to undertake and encourage the study of women and women's work. Early Marxist-feminist writings correctly faulted Marxist theory for being "sex-blind." Marx and his more recent followers divided people into two economic categories or classes: workers and capitalists. Men, women, whites, and blacks were nowhere to be found; implicitly, the assumption was that all economic actors were white men. The first contribution of Marxist-feminism was to bring into radical economics questions concerning women's roles in the economy and economic history, both in the labor force and union organizing, and in the family, particularly in housework and childcare. Books such as *Womanhood in America* (Ryan 1975), *America's Working Women* (Baxandall et al. 1976), *We Were There* (Wertheimer 1977), *A Heritage of Her Own* (Cott and Pleck 1979), and *The Economics of Women and Work* (Amsden 1980) began to redress the exclusion of women and women's work from economic scholarship.

One necessary adjunct of this addition of women was more intensive study of the economic aspects of the family, given that the bulk of women's work has been done within the household. This study has led Marxist-feminists to uncover the changing relationship between family and economy in U.S. history, the early conflation and growing separation of these spheres with capitalist development, and the continued centrality for the reproduction of capitalism of women's work in the home and women's roles as consumers and reproducers of the labor force (Scott and Tilly 1978; Matthaei 1982).

A second and related aspect of this study of women was the study of women's oppression, of inequality between the sexes. For Marxist-feminists, the first step in this process was to document the existence of sexual inequality, particularly economic inequality between the sexes. In capitalism, Marxist-feminists noted, women's relegation to unpaid work in the home and to the lower-paid jobs in the labor force has reduced our access to income relative to men and created economic dependency within marriage. This economic and marital inequality has been further compounded by men's monopolization of political power, of management positions, and of academia and the media. When male radicals argued in response that sexual inequality was a creation of the ruling class to divide workers and hence should be ignored as secondary, both theoretically and in radical political movements, Marxist-feminists pointed to (and worked on) studies which showed that sexual inequality preceded capitalism and persists in all existing socialist countries (Scott 1974).

The study and critique of sexual inequality necessarily led Marxist-feminists to the study of sexual differentiation, both to document and to explain it. A series of studies by Marxist and non-Marxist feminists has shown the universality of the sex-typing of jobs, indeed of all work. The question then became one of explaining this. The then-current explanation for women's lesser pay or assignment to housework was that women are biologically better suited for these tasks, and that men are, similarly, biologically better suited for higher paid managing and directing work. To attack this biological-determinist rationalization of sexual inequality, Marxist-feminists (like other feminists) drove a wedge between biological sex and the social identities of the sexes. In doing so, Marxist-feminists made use of a central principle of Marxist social science—that social relations determine and differentiate individuals, i.e., that society shapes the individual in the first instance, not vice versa. Rubin (1975) was among the first to apply this insight to the sexes with her concept of a "sex/gender system." Later studies have focused in particular on the sexual division of labor as the social mechanism which, by assigning the (biological) sexes to different and complementary work, transforms them into different and complementary social beings, or "genders" (e.g., Matthaei 1982; Young 1981).

As feminist scholars began to conceptualize gender as a social product, the feminist critique of sexual inequality was extended, for many, to criticism of gender roles in general—as straightjackets which force each sex into distorted, less-than-fully-human identities. In our society, feminine self-seeking means subordinating oneself to the needs of one's family, serving, whereas masculinity means competing with other men, striving to subordinate or better them. Neither, some Marxist-feminists argue, are adequate ways of being. Women's liberation, then, does not simply involve equality with men or the empowerment of women but, I would argue, the end of gender differentiation—and the emergence of a new ungendered individual involved in relations of mutuality (Gould 1983). The critique of gender roles becomes a lens through which social institutions can be analyzed and criticized, since they all involve and construct gendered individuals; one political goal then becomes envisioning and developing new, ungendered social institutions and practices.

Attempts to locate the roots of sexual inequality led Marxist-feminist anthropologists to cross-cultural studies, which found gender and a sexual division of labor everywhere. Early studies (Rosaldo 1974) concluded that sexual inequality was a universal consequence of the assignment of women to private (intrafamilial) activities dominated by the public (interfamilial) activities of men. More recent studies have disputed this claim; women are not universally excluded from interfamilial activities (e.g., women traders in West Africa) and women's assignment to the home doesn't always bring social inferiority (Leacock 1981; Coontz and Henderson 1986). In other words, as Rosaldo (1980) argues, "woman's place in human social life is not in any direct sense a product of the things she does (or even less a function of what biologically she is) but of the meaning her activities acquire through concrete social interactions." So apparently sexual inequality is tied to, but not necessarily the product of, the sexual division of labor and gender itself.[1] Marxist-feminists need to avoid projecting characteristics of the present onto the past. Nevertheless, there is agreement that, in capitalism, gender differentiation (masculine/feminine and public/private) and gender inequality (the domination of public over private) are clearly linked. In other words, women's primary assignment to the private, home sphere and concomitant exclusion from paid and high-paid labor is at the root of sexual inequality in capitalism. There is no agreement on whether or not the social differentiation of the sexes must be abolished if women's oppression is to cease.

Patriarchy: A New Way to Analyze the Economy

Marxist-feminists have used the term "patriarchy" or "patriarchal" to characterize social systems which both differentiate the sexes and place men above women. Patriarchy thus involves relations and institutions of gender differentiation, in which feminine activities are devalued relative to masculine ones and men are given power over women. However, the relationship between inequality/power and differentiation is different for different theorists. Some see men's successful struggles to subordinate and terrorize women as the origin of patriarchy; here, men organize to force women into devalued and low-paid activities and the unpaid service of men. Others (myself among them) begin instead with gender and the sexual division of labor, as unconscious or semi-conscious social systems which place men (as economic and political beings) above the family-centered women in most societies. Either way, patriarchy reproduces itself by creating sexual difference and inequality through different levels of consciousness, from the subconscious to the self-conscious.

The Subconscious Reproduction of Patriarchy by Mother-Dominated Parenting. Dinerstein (1976), Chodorow (1978), and Harding (1981) have given psychoanalytic accounts of the ways in which mother-dominated parenting accounts for both gender differentiation and for men's need to dominate women. Daughters mold their identities after their mothers; sons out of differentiation from their mothers. Children by an early age acquire "gender identities" which they pursue as a given by striving to engage in the activities proper to their sex and by shunning the activities thought proper for the "opposite" sex (Eichenbaum and Orbach 1983). Not only does the feminine role exclude women from economic and political power, mother-dominated parenting creates in men a subconscious need to dominate women. These theorists argue that, unless both sexes participate equally and similarly in parenting, gender differerentiation and inequality will continue. Sexist language is another subconscious force in reproducing gender difference and inequality: third person pronouns must specify gender, the masculine "he" or "men" represents "the generic," and sexist occupational titles have overtly dictated the sex of the worker, from "chairman" to "stewardess" to "men working" (Lakoff 1975).

Patriarchal Institutions and Social Practices. A second interrelated way in which patriarchy reproduces itself is through institutions and practices. Central among these for Marxist-feminists is the job structure, which includes jobs that require and reproduce masculine or feminine workers. Marxist-feminists have intensively studied the historical development and contemporary landscape of the labor market. White masculine jobs pay a family wage, involve progression upward through seniority, often in competition against other white masculine workers, and include the direction of other men and of women. Feminine jobs pay secondary wages, neither demand much continuity nor reward it, and often involve performing wifely or motherly functions, such as waitressing, nursing, or personal secretary. The job structure institutionalizes gender by objectifying it in jobs to which individuals then have to accommodate themselves through training. Other institutions noted by Marxist-feminists as central to the reproduction of patriarchy include: property laws (which formerly denied married women the right to their property or wages); marriage laws and laws against homosexuality (which dictate heterosexuality); divorce law and practice (which assign children and property); laws and practices concerning sex-uality, birth control, and sterilization (which reduce women's control over their own bodies); the educational system (with its "masculinist" textbooks and scholarly work); and the welfare and child support systems (which prop up "broken," i.e., husbandless, families without empowering women).

Self-Conscious Choice and Struggle. Certain aspects of patriarchy are the result of self-conscious individual and collective actions. Many Marxist-feminists have simplistically assumed individualistic, materially-oriented "utility-maximization" from the sexes, viewing everything from marriage to union organizing as the result of such self-conscious, self-interested struggle. I would argue instead that most people, now and in the past, have accepted their gender identities and roles without thought, rather than having come to them as the result of struggle and choice. However, given the constraints of their subconscious minds and existing social institutions, individuals are still left with a good deal of choice as to how to live out their gender roles, or whether to do so at all. Many have been individually and collectively involved in the continual effort to redefine, refine, and sometimes attenuate patriarchal practices. These openings for action within a seemingly given sex/gender system occur when: (1) the system is internally contradictory, (2) new social practices are coming into being, particularly within the context of the rapid change brought by capitalist development, and (3) the gender interests of two or more groups are in conflict. Often two or all of these openings for change occur simultaneously.

An example of the first case is women's higher education. Nineteenth century white women (and some white men) viewed higher education for middle-class women as necessary training for their vocation of mothering. Yet once these women went to college, a substantial portion of them wanted to work in paid professions to use their developed knowledge and abilities. This conflict caused growing numbers of these women to choose to be "career girls" and later to try to enter white masculine jobs. Another example of an internal contradiction in gender is the nineteenth century white feminist argument that women should be able to vote in order to express their special feminine sensibility; in other words, women's special abilities in the domestic or private sphere were said to qualify them for participation in the public political sphere (Matthaei 1982, pt. II).

An example of the second case is the sex-typing of new jobs according to employers' needs and technological options, their views of "proper" gender roles, their perceptions of the different abilities of the sexes, workers' views and perceptions, and the relative supply and cost of the genders. At the turn of the century, firms chose to replace male clerks with female typists equipped with typewriters (Davies 1979; Rotella 1981), a decision which, with this century's explosion of clerical employment, has helped draw white women into the labor force in increasing numbers. The managers of multinational corporations have chosen to employ mostly women and girls in their labor-intensive shops in the Third World, leaving men in those communities with high unemployment. Such decisions, which extend, reproduce, and perhaps problematize the sexual division of labor by breaking down separate sexual spheres, involve numerous historical factors and are thus historically contingent. Gender is not given in biology or in men's diabolical minds, but produced, transformed, and now attenuated by the confluence of a variety of social forces.[2]

An example of the third case is the development of the family wage system, the much debated practice of excluding women from high-paid jobs which evolved in the nineteenth century with the expansion of wage labor (Hartmann 1979; 1981; Humphries 1977;1981; Brenner and Ramas 1985; Benenson 1984).[3] Hartmann presents the process as a power struggle between women seeking entrance into such jobs (albeit for slightly lower wages) and men defending themselves against women's low wage competition. However, others have pointed out that these men may have been fighting for family wages to help their families as well as to retain their positions as heads of households. Furthermore, we must recognize that the individuals involved were also members of families, with whom they pooled income. We can suppose that the families of these women, including husbands, fathers and sons, may have supported them in their attempts to gain employment and enhance family income, whereas the families of the employed men, including wives, daughters and mothers, most likely would oppose women's employment in this case. But these were not the only parties in conflict—potential employers also lined up in support of women's employment, while opposing it also were upper-middle-class women reformers who wanted to "protect" poor women from exploitation by the capitalists and to impose their own definition of womanhood upon them. If we realize that the workers in question also had gender identities to shore up, we can conclude that on the whole men and women may have supported the family wage system because it maintained, even strengthened, the social differentiation of the sexes. Since homebound women were the opposite of job-centered men, a family wage allowed for a clear sexual division of labor in marriage. Further, as Humphries (1977) has pointed out, households may have decided it was in their best interest to keep one sphere of production, housework, outside of the control of capital, which would also force capitalists to pay higher, family wages to men in order to reproduce the labor force.

A final important instance of the third case of self-conscious organizing occurs when feminists attempt to challenge established patriarchal practices. Most (but not all) of the defenders of these patriarchal practices will be men, upon whom such practices confer special privileges and powers. Yet from this we cannot infer that men's self-interested organizing necessarily created these institutions—only that patriarchal institutions, by giving men power over women, give men a vested interest in their defense. In this way, the three levels at which patriarchy is reproduced—subconscious, institutional, and self conscious—reinforce one another. Thus, any struggle against patriarchy must involve all three levels if it is to be successful.

Marxist-feminist Contributions to the Feminist Movement

While feminist political practice is not the subject of this paper, I want to note the important role played by Marxist-feminists not only in developing an analysis of patriarchal oppression that could support feminist movements for change but also in shaping the directions that movement has taken. In the U.S., Marxist-feminists were active in "Socialist-feminist groups" formed in Berkeley, Chicago, and New Haven, among others; they have been central participants in the struggle for comparable worth, and also reproductive rights (in particular, with the Reproductive Rights National Network and the Coalition for Abortion Rights and Against Sterilization Abuse). In this, they have had to fight the opposition of their male left colleagues, many of whom have dismissed feminist action as "reformist." Further, because feminist organizing often brings together women across class, racial-ethnic, and sexual preference lines, organizing activity has forced Marxist-feminists to deal with the difficult question of the relationship between women's gender oppression and these other sources of oppression (Molyneux 1985). This has led many Marxist-feminists to argue that class, race, and gender oppressions are intrinsically linked and must be simultaneously addressed by any progressive movement (Hooks 1984). Thus the Marxist-feminist interest in the political links among these different oppressions has reinforced the need for theoretical and historical study of these same links, and has raised the question of the relationship between Marxist-feminist theory and Marxist theory, which we will now explore.

BEYOND THE UNHAPPY MARRIAGE OF MARXISM AND FEMINISM: MARXIST-FEMINISM AND THE TRANSFORMATION OF MARXIST ECONOMICS

How have Marxist-feminists related their new areas of study to the traditional corpus of Marxist theory? Marxist-feminists' starting point was the analysis of capitalism based on Marx's method of historical materialism. But Marxist theory and method were not only gender-blind, they also enabled traditional Marxists to argue that the topics of interest to Marxist-feminists represented a diversion into non-economic, "superstructural" and therefore secondary theoretical territory.

Marxist-feminist theory has built upon Marxist theory in three distinct ways: (1) fitting the topics of Marxist-feminist concern into traditional Marxist analysis and categories, (2) developing a set of separate and parallel theoretical constructs to analyze patriarchal relations, and (3) transforming fundamental Marxist concepts to produce a more adequate analysis of economic and social reality. To some extent, these different strategies can be seen as chronological stages. The first stage took the form of an analysis of patriarchy as part of the capitalist mode of production, with a particular focus on women's work in the home. The second meant analysis of patriarchy as a system or mode of production distinct from and parallel to capitalism, without challenging Marxist theories of the latter. The third and current stage involves analysis of class, gender, and white supremacy as interconnected, inseparable systems of differentiation and oppression within our historically specific social structure. I argue that the latter is the only correct way to grasp gender and class issues.

Fitting Women's Work in the Home into the Capitalist Mode of Production: Housework as Domestic Labor or Ideology-Generator

When women Marxists first became feminists, we faced the task of justifying and pursuing our interest in women's lives and feminist struggles within our accepted theoretical and political framework, Marxist economics. This was no easy task.

Marxist theory took class as its central category, and in the theoretical world populated by ungendered capitalists and workers, women, and men's domination over them, didn't fit. Neither did feminist struggles for women's liberation; Marxist men saw them as reforms, which at best did nothing to further the struggle for socialism and at worst divided the working class and put off the coming of socialism, as capitalists wanted.[4] Instead, we were told, women should organize with men workers to overthrow capitalism; our liberation could and would only come after the revolution, in socialism. To make things worse, women's unique and central activity, homemaking, takes place in the family, a site which Marxist historical materialism relegated to theoretical and political insignificance as part of the superstructure.

The task early Marxist-feminists set for themselves thus was to fit women and our work into this framework. This meant either placing women's work in the home in the material base, by conceptualizing it as labor, or placing it in the superstructure, by conceptualizing it as the production of ideology. Both routes were tried.

The "domestic labor debate," which raged in the 1970s, concerned the relationship of housework to the capital accumulation process. Marxist-feminists argued for the centrality of housework, as domestic labor, to capitalist production.[5] Theorists pointed out that housework maintains capitalism by reproducing the labor force, both daily and generationally. When a capitalist hires a male worker, he is also buying with the wage the unpaid services of a housewife/mother which both maintain that worker and produce new workers. The debate focused on whether or not domestic labor produced surplus value, since if this could be shown, it then followed that housewives were also exploited by capital and their struggle would be the same as that of wage workers. Housewives would be part of the revolutionary working class. Dalla Costa (1973), in particular, argued that housewives were workers like men, could equally disrupt capitalism by striking, and should be paid wages in recognition of the value they produce. The upshot of the domestic labor debate was a strong "wages for housework" movement, despite the theoretical conclusion that housework could not be said to produce surplus value.

One contribution of the domestic labor debate was its discovery that the household work of women—both as producers of labor power and as consumers of capitalist products—is central to capitalist production (Weinbaum and Bridges 1979). As Miller (1976) pointed out, male supremacy rests in part on the denial of men's dependence on women's work; standing, as it were, on the shoulders of the women who fulfill their everyday needs, both physiological and emotional, men act as if they are only abstract thinkers, commodity producers, capital accumulators—not flesh and blood individuals. Capitalism in particular relies on the existence of unpaid labor, whether generated through women's housework or subsistence modes of production (Mies 1986, ch. 2). After the domestic labor debate, one hopes that Marxists will never again be able to pretend that capitalist production exists independent of women's household work.

However, this first Marxist-feminist attempt to bring women into Marxist analysis was a very partial advance. It viewed women only as housewives, ignoring their position as wage workers. It viewed housework and family life inadequately, since analysis based on economic categories like labor, exploitation and surplus value stresses their material, physical aspects, not the social relations surrounding them. It provided no real explanation of the forms of domestic labor other than as means to fulfill capitalism's needs, and hence tended to functionalism. Finally, although some mention was made of men's privileged role in the home, the focus on the relationship between housework and capitalism obfuscated the issue of gender domination.

A second, early route to integrating women into traditional Marxist economics involved using its historical materialist method to analyze the family as the generator and reproducer of capitalist ideology, preparing children for lives as workers or capitalists. Marxist-feminist theorists, most notably Mitchell (1974) and Chodorow (1979), used psychoanalysis and object-relations theory to analyze the role of the family and of women's work within it in producing and reproducing ideas and personalities compatible with capitalist production. This analysis began to explore the psychological aspects of women's work, and indeed of gender roles and inequality, in counterposition to the domestic labor focus on the physical production aspect. Nevertheless, as ideology-production, women's housework was construed as superstructural and secondary, essentially shaped to satisfy capital's needs.

Conceptualizing women's work in the home as part of the capitalist mode of production, either as base or as superstructure, meant assessing its role in filling capitalism's needs. The subject of male domination and its connection to women's work in the home remained slighted. In their desire to give more weight to the patriarchal aspects of women's work, Marxist-feminists began to examine patriarchal institutions with a set of new concepts which they put on par with Marxist concepts of class and exploitation; Marxist-feminists added onto the capitalist mode of production a second system or mode, one which organized and reproduced sexual inequality.

Adding Another Sphere or System to the Capitalist Mode of Production: Patriarchy, Reproduction, and the Patriarchal Mode of Production

Patriarchy. In their attempt to "wed" an analysis of sexual inequality and oppression to the Marxist class-based analysis, one group of Marxist-feminists has suggested that our economy is best conceived as two systems, capitalism (characterized by class exploitation and struggle) and patriarchy (characterized by sex exploitation and struggle). Here, Marxist-feminists have built on analyses of "radical feminists" such as Firestone (1970) and Millet (1969), who had developed a conception of patriarchy as a system of domination. Indeed, Firestone had used modified Marxist categories to understand sexual inequality: history, she argued, was the history of struggle between the sexes (not the classes); male domination (not class domination) was based on male control over the means of reproduction (not the means of production).

Since Marxist-feminists were already convinced of the importance of Marxist class analysis, the logical development was a "dual systems" approach, adding a conception of patriarchy to the traditional Marxist notion of capitalism.[6] Extending and transforming Marx's historical materialist method, Marxist-feminists have constructed conceptions of patriarchy which, like Firestone's, paralleled the Marxist notion of capitalism. Each system produces its own form of social differentiation and domination: in capitalism, class and capitalist exploitation; in patriarchy, gender and male domination. Each has a "material base" comprised of an exploiting/oppressing group (capitalists or men) which extracted unpaid labor (surplus value or unpaid housework) from the exploites/oppressed group (workers, women). Each is maintained and reproduced by struggle between the groups (class struggle, sex struggle). Capitalism and patriarchy, Marxist-feminists argued, sometimes reinforce, sometimes conflict, depending on historical circumstances. Hartmann (1981), a major advocate of this approach, argued that the "family wage" system was a compromise between capitalism and patriarchy (embodied by male workers, wishing to exclude women from their high-paid jobs). Ferguson and Folbre (1981) argued that capitalism has been breaking down patriarchy by reducing the economic benefits of child-rearing, hence freeing women to work in the labor force, beyond their husbands' patriarchal power.

Production and Reproduction. Another form of dual systems theory instead focused on reproduction as counterposed to and interconnected with production. Taking off from Engels' (1972) statement that a society is a "mode of production and reproduction," these Marxist-feminists argue that Marxist analyses of capitalism should be expanded to include the family and women's work within it, the sphere of "reproduction." Building on the earlier analyses of housework as domestic labor or ideology-producer, these Marxist-feminists posit the mode of reproduction as different from but interconnected with and necessary to capitalist production. With a material base of its own (domestic labor physically reproducing labor power) and an ideal (psychological) aspect, the arena of reproduction is conceptualized as a different "mode" or "sphere" which is at least semi-autonomous from capitalist production. Marxist-feminists (e.g., Humphries 1981) conceptualize family relations as involving shared income and concerns as well as sexual inequality and antagonism. Humphries and Rubery (1984) have begun to explore the effects of the organization of reproduction on the capitalist labor market. Others such as Beneria (1979) have emphasized the patriarchal nature of the relationships of reproduction.

The Patriarchal Mode of Production. Another group of Marxist-feminists has wedded these two approaches, adding both patriarchy and reproduction to their analysis through the conception of a patriarchal mode of production or reproduction. In these theories, the capitalist and patriarchal modes of production can be distinguished by their objects (one produces commodities, the other human beings), their sites (workplace, family), and their relations of domination (class, gender). Folbre (1982) actually formalized an analysis of patriarchal exploitation parallel to that of worker exploitation, based on the number of labor hours each family member works and consumes. The conception of a patriarchal mode of production builds on the insight that the central locus of women's oppression is in the family: in the sexual division of labor in marriage, in women's assignment to reproductive labor, and in men's control over the latter. For such theorists, the material base of women's oppression lies in women's physical production of children, with men in control of the means of reproduction. While some, such as O'Brien (1981) and Brenner and Ramas (1985), root the patriarchal mode in women's unique abilities to reproduce, thus tending towards biological determinism, others, such as Ferguson (1984) and Delphy (1984), acknowledge the social and particularly the emotional, aspects of what Ferguson calls "sex-affective production" and account for women's assignment to it as the result of struggle, not biology.

The strength of dual systems theory is its full-blown analysis of (1) the relationships and divisions of labor which differentiate the sexes and give men power over women, and (2) the family, especially in economic terms, as a source of determinate effects, rather than a superstructural expression of the needs of capital. Marxist-feminists made this progress by placing gender on an equal footing with class, setting it up as a parallel phenomenon. Thus, the dual systems approach allowed us for the first time to inquire into the nature of this system which most of us have chosen to call patriarchy. As seen in the variety of insights surveyed above, this has resulted in a rich literature.

Production/reproduction analyses which differentiate the product of each system (commodities vs. labor power) can accommodate a unified theory of the economy encompassing both production and reproduction; however, these formulations tend to collapse into the domestic labor position—an enlarged view of capitalism in which gender domination is underemphasized (e.g., Humphries and Rubery 1984). Theories which, on the other hand, emphasize reproduction as the sphere where gender domination originates tend to limit patriarchy to the sphere of reproduction and class to that of production. One interesting insight of the production/reproduction analyses concerns how, with men's domination in both the economy and the family, the requirements of the production sphere (capital accumulation) have come to prevail over the needs of the feminine sphere of reproduction (Himmelweit 1984).

Problems with Dual Systems Theory and the Tri-Systems "Solution"

The most evident problem with dual systems theory was pointed out by Marxist-feminists of color—what about race? As Joseph (1981) noted, the concept of patriarchy as a system through which men dominate women makes sense only if race is ignored. Black men do not have power over white women; indeed, the reverse is usually the case. Similarly, black women rarely feel a unity of interest with white women, who have often been their race and class enemies. Similar critisms of "race-blindness" and "white bias" were aimed at the feminist movement by women of color, many of whom decided to form autonomous groups (Hooks 1984). History was replaying itself in short succession: white Marxist-feminists, who had accused white Marxists of being gender-blind and sexist, were now being accused by Marxist-feminists of color of being race-blind and racist. And both accusations were correct.

One response to these criticisms has been to add race as a third system of oppression. In tri-systems theory, as advocated by Ferguson (1984), race, sex and class are conceptualized as distinct social systems of differentiation and oppression. But once one has opened the door to other oppressions suffered in our capitalist system, where does one stop? Other groups within the feminist movement have argued that their oppressions are similarly ignored: lesbians and gay men are oppressed by heterosexism or homophobia, older women by agism, disabled women by "able-ism," Jews by anti-semitism, Third World by First World. Where do we stop? If we truly wish to encompass each type of oppression created within our economic system, do we need an eight-systems theory?

I believe not. "Multiple-systems" theory is certainly superior to a Marxist theory which recognizes only one kind of oppression within capitalism: class. However, besides being extremely unwieldy, multiple-system theory is conceptually faulty. It is, I argue, impossible to conceptualize adequately *any* of these types of social differentiation/oppression—class, gender, race, sexual preference, age—while "abstracting from" or "controlling for" the others (see Amott and Matthaei 1991, ch. 2).

Let us take the example of class. Marx defines it as determined by one's relationship to the means of production, a clear concept for distinguishing the white male craft worker from his boss. But what about the white woman who is married to this industrial worker? She doesn't own the means of production, but neither is she necessarily a wage worker selling her labor power to capital.[7] And what about the black woman who does laundry for the white woman married to the craft worker? Or the prostitute who services his sexual needs?

The concepts of patriarchal theory are similarly problematic. This theory focuses on the unpaid labor which housewives do for their husbands as the essence of their gender oppression. But what if this housewife uses her husband's income to pay another woman to do her domestic labor? And what if this other woman not only performs all of her employer's domestic labor (except actually bearing children for her) but also serves as her personal maid? Where is the housewife's unpaid labor? Where is the material oppression of the housewife, when her husband may actually be laboring many more hours than she is? In the "mode of reproduction," are men oppressing women, or women oppressing women, or women oppressing men by oppressing women?

Finally, let us attempt to discuss race as a distinct conceptual category. First, can we compare the racial oppression of blacks with that of Native Americans, Chicanas, Puerto Ricans, Japanese, and Filipinas, other than by noting in a qualitative sense that these groups were all in some way oppressed/exploited/disinherited by whites? How can we analyze the roots of black oppression in their enslavement without discussing slavery as a class system? Can we understand contemporary race without class — or, as Wilson (1987) has argued, must we recognize that the basis of the current economic oppression of most blacks lies in their separation from wealth, income, and human capital, from the means of production?

When we as Marxist-feminists confine our study of patriarchy to a separate conceptual sphere, we leave intact the central conceptions of Marxist economic theory. When we focus on patriarchal oppression, we are then forced to downplay class and race differences among women What is needed for the further development of Marxist-feminist theory and Marxist theory in general is analysis of race, class, and gender differentiation and inequality as integral parts of our complex economic system—one which, for lack of a better word, we can still call capitalism. Thus, rather than adding race and gender systems of oppression to Marxist theory's race- and gender-blind categories of class, Marxist-feminists must work to transform the conception of capitalism to encompass its historically patriarchal and white supremacist nature. And this, I believe, means revising Marxist methodology as well.

Transforming Marxist Methodology

There are two basic ways in which Marxist methodology must be transformed: first, its theorizing must become explicitly historical; second, it must abandon its insistence on differentiating material from ideal, privileging the former. It is my view that we can understand the present workings of race, class and gender oppression only by studying them as they have historically developed, viewing the U.S. or any other country as part of an increasingly world-wide system. In other words, we have to locate our theory in time and space.[8]

Despite the clear precedent in the wedding of history and theory in Marx's historical materialism, Marxists constantly deny the historical nature of the economy in their theoretical practice. First, Marxists (including Marx) incorrectly project into the past our present institutions and practices—such as the primacy of the economic ("material") and the universality of overt and self-conscious, self-interested struggle over the surplus—and then view these as central, transhistorical forces. Second, there is still a tendency for Marxist theorists to "abstract" from history, presenting capitalism as a timeless universal force unaffected by its historical grounding in patriarchal and racist social relations;[9] the fact that all relations within capitalism are both gendered and raced becomes, for them, simply a matter of historical contingency, one which need not be incorporated into the theory in any explicit way. When theory proceeds without specifying a particular era in capitalist history, it is easier to ignore race and gender in the economy. Marxist-feminist theorists have similarly been guilty of ignoring historical change, particularly in our early positing of universal sexual inequality, as discussed above.

In order to locate our theorizing in space, we must acknowledge that capitalism does have a different nature in different parts of the world (with pressures both for homogenization and differentiation of regions) and that capital has always been involved in relations with non-capitalist systems which play a non-trivial role in the explanation of its development (see Mies 1986). We cannot simply study the U.S. economy and assume that what we find characterizes the rest of the world, or even the rest of the capitalist world. Here we can learn from Marxist-feminists, who have discovered the extreme variability of the sexual division of labor across cultures, even among capitalist countries, and who, as well, have been soundly criticized by Third World feminists for projecting issues and political programs on them.[10]

If, rather than projecting the present onto the past, we see how the present has grown out of past and qualitatively different social relations, we arrive at a very different result. This historical approach allows us to see how pre-capitalist patriarchal relations (relations of male and parental dominance) were built into capitalism from its inception, preventing any of capitalism's social relations of production from being "gender-blind" (Matthaei 1982, ch. 5, 9). If we also locate early capitalism in space, noting that capitalism developed among white Western Europeans, in Europe and in their settler colonies, we can see that early wealth accumulation was based on the displacement, destruction, and/or subordination of societies and peoples of color; indeed, the rapid growth of capitalism involved the underdevelopment of much of the rest of the world. Thus western capitalism is not only white supremacist, in that it spread white social relations and culture while destroying or subordinating non-white peoples and their ways of life; it is also inherently white supremacist in that its practices reproduce racial difference and white superiority (Amott and Matthaei 1991).

A second needed transformation of Marxism is the abandonment of materialism, which has been a central barrier to the incorporation of Marxist-feminist insights into Marxism. Since women's work is centered in the family and materialism views the family as "superstructural," Marxist-feminists have attempted to extend the "economic base" to include the family as the site of domestic labor or reproduction. Doing so has meant violating the distinctiveness and sociality of familial and economic relations, reducing them to a nondescript "labor" which physically produces either commodities or people (e.g., O'Brien 1981). We must not give up the distinctiveness of familial relations as the price for making them important. Family relations involve a level of love and sharing and indeed of fusion of personality absent from production relations. Yet the family should be of central importance to Marxist economists. Historically, the family played a pivotal role in structuring early capitalist relations; currently it is crucial both to the distribution of income and wealth and the construction of gendered, raced and classed personalities who can then fit within an authoritarian classed, raced and gendered work structure. Further, we must be open to the real historical relationships between economy and family, rather than impose an assumption that the economy dominates at all times and in all ways. It is not at all clear that all of the forces for change in present day capitalism come from the economy, and it certainly is clear that, in earlier systems, familial and kinship relations often played a determining role.

A second problematic aspect of materialism is the very attempt to characterize activities as material or ideal. Women's work of mothering is the perfect example of an activity which is neither material nor ideal but both—as are, I would argue, all social practices. Marxist-feminists have shown how women's actual physical production of children, from pregnancy and childbirth to breast-feeding, is at the same time a social and ideal process in which children develop their consciousnesses and identities.[11] Similarly, men's participation in wage labor is not simply a physical or material expenditure of energy which can be exploited but also a social and ideal relationship, one critically structured by their gender and race identities, as has been shown in the family wage controversy discussed above. We must, as Marxists, find a way to acknowledge in our theories the centrality of social relations in constituting subjectivity. Otherwise, we are reduced to viewing individual motivation in the most simplistic sense, as the "material" struggle for a larger piece of the pie, ignoring individuals' struggles, for example, to prove or defend their gender or racial or sexual identities, or to fulfill themselves, or to aid their families, or to establish their solidarity with others who are oppressed in different ways.[12]

This rejection of materialism allows Marxists to have a more complicated understanding of consciousness and social action, both individual and collective. Instead of simplistically assuming that individuals always engage in self-interested struggle against the "opposed" racial, gender or class group, we can look at individual subjectivity as structured by the complex web of social relations we call capitalism. The Marxist-feminist analysis of the psychological production of gendered beings needs to be extended to encompass the class and race and sexual dimensions of identity. Such an analysis would necessarily include another important aspect of personality formation: the process of repression of a child's true self and feelings created by Western parenting, repression which then prepares him or her for life in a world of authoritarian work, family and political relations.[13] Issues like these deserve attention, since the transformation of parenting and family life is crucial to the success of a radical movement for democracy.

Further, Marxists should learn from Marxist-feminism's exploration of women's identities and political consciousnesses. Marxist-feminists have identified the ways in which individuality is blurred in familial relations, especially for a woman who sees her goal as caring for her husband and children, and who (correctly) identifies her economic position with that of her husband rather than defining herself solely by her own relation to the labor market. We have learned that women's opposition to the feminist movement can result from: (1) the "internalization" of patriarchal oppression—something which can be "exorcised" through consciousness-raising; (2) the fact that some women actually see themselves as privileged by patriarchy because it has given them access through their husbands to high income and to the domestic labor of other women; or (3) the fact that feminism, focused typically on gender oppression alone, cannot adequately deal with patriarchy as experienced by working-class women or women of color, or with the racism and classism often present in the feminist movement. Class and worker struggles can be similarly understood as impeded by: (1) internalized oppression on the part of the worker, in particular a childlike relationship to the employer as the authoritarian parent against whom one rebels or demands or even struggles, but in whose hands one leaves authority; (2) the worker's potential identification with capitalism as a system which has benefitted him (particularly if the worker is male and white) by placing him very near the top of the world wealth distribution (see Baron 1985); and (3) the fact that working class struggles, traditionally focused on class oppression alone, do not deal with the class experiences of white women or workers of color, or with the racism and sexism of the union movement. In other words, individuals do not struggle just as workers, or women, or people of color—they take with them all parts of their identities, and these include their multifaceted relationships with both oppressor and subordinate groups (Spelman 1988).

This more complicated look at socially-constructed identity allows for a more sophisticated and promising sort of progressive political practice. Once we recognize the complexity of each group's position within a system incorporating multiple dimensions of oppression, then even a successful struggle by one oppressed group to increase its share of income may not lead to the breakdown of any of the dimensions of oppression. Consider, for example, white male workers' successful struggles to monopolize the best jobs, at the expense of the majority of workers and without challenging the capitalist-worker relationship. Or what about upper-class white women's "feminist" struggle to gain access to the top men's jobs by acting masculine and capitalist (à la Maggie Thatcher or Jeane Kirkpatrick)? True progressive change is not brought about if one subgroup increases its income share at the expense of others who are more oppressed, or if some females or people of color fit themselves into the white, masculine, upper-class mode by acting white, masculine and upper-class.

The only clearly progressive action is action which takes all dimensions of oppression into account simultaneously, as a truly feminist or radical political movement must. This means that a major goal for any progressive movement must involve building "solidarity interests," i.e., the willingness of individuals to fight against oppressions from which they do not directly suffer, even at the expense of their narrow self-interest, in the larger self-interest of building a whole, healthy and ethical community. This also means that the multiply oppressed, those most marginalized (Hooks 1984), are best able to take the lead in envisioning a radical movement which is truly progressive.[14] The issue from a radical perspective is to abolish the class, gender and race divisions themselves, by transforming our institutions and consciousness. Progressive political work means (1) making people aware of their internalized oppression, usually through meeting with others of their group, (2) recognizing the systemic enemy, rather than viewing the privileged as individuals who "have what I want," and (3) developing solidarity interests, including an awareness of the interconnectedness of us all and a vision of the fulfillment that could come from a more just social and economic order (Hooks 1984).

Reconceptualizing U.S. Capitalism as Inherently Patriarchal and Racist

Here I will suggest and briefly explore the directions for Marxist research which would correct the white and masculine bias of its economic theory. As I have suggested above, what is needed is a unitary theory of capitalism.[15] I will discuss three major areas: (1) competition between capitals, (2) the job structure, and (3) the present family/economy connections.[16]

Capital as White and Masculine. Capitalism began as competition between propertied, white, patriarchal familial lineages in Western Europe and in its colonies;[17] families of color in the colonies were excluded from property ownership, indeed robbed of their lands and/or forced to be property themselves. Whereas the feudal family inherited from its ancestors a fixed social position, the early capitalist family inherited property, a social position which could be enlarged or diminished by the family's efforts. Hence families could, through hard work and luck, elevate their social position and pass their accumulated wealth and influence on to their children; we can think of the early motivation for capital accumulation as tied to lineages' efforts to better their social positions. In fact, we can think of the energy unleashed by the developing market economy as that of lineages freed to elevate their social position (or threatened with deterioration of the same) and that of sons freed from determination by their fathers (Barker-Benfield 1976).

Given that white families at that time were patriarchal, headed by the fathers, it was the adult white man's assignment to direct this competition, with children and wife as his aides. In this way, white masculinity was increasingly defined in the competitive struggle to best other men, as household heads and individuals. With the concentration and centralization of capital and the declining availability of "free" land, more and more white men were proletarianized; their white masculine competition became "bread-winning" (as they called it) in the labor market.

As capitalism developed, it broke down the conception of blood which had sustained a permanent and recognized hierarchy among white families. However, ideas of aristocratic and plebian blood were replaced by new types of "blood" as marks of status: nationality, the shared characteristic distinguishing all classes of a society from members of other nations (Ward 1966, 48: Ehrenreich 1983), and race, the innate superiority of whites over all non-whites (Cox 1948, pt. II). These new conceptions spread from Europe to North America with the formation of colonies of wealth-seeking, entrepreneurial white families who recognized as property-owning competitors only other white families. They robbed, displaced or killed the non-white natives they encountered and used African slave labor in their striving for wealth. On the other hand, whites without sufficient property in the means of production (land, tools, or capital) to take part in this entrepreneurial competition were only temporarily subordinated to propertied whites as servants or hired hands; they could eventually gain land and property of their own and enter the competition.

As the family firm was replaced by the corporation, this white masculine competition became institutionalized in the form of competition of corporate capitals.

The corporate form allowed family firms increased access to capital from shareholders, and protected the family's economic position with limited liability. At the same time, the family lost its ownership of the firm to a more diffuse body of stockholders and gave up control of the production process to hired managers. From our standpoint, the resulting system of competing corporations represents the abstract institutionalization of lineage: now, instead of white patriarchal families competing with other families to improve their relative position across the generations, we have corporate individuals, reproduced across generations of employees, competing to be the biggest and best. In both cases, the energies of family or corporation members are aimed, through authoritarian control, at perpetuation and growth of the enterprise within the system of competing enterprises. The process of familial competition is transformed into competition between corporations, and hired managers are now the corporate entrepreneurs. The past practice of using marriage to create business alliances is reproduced in the common practice of corporate mergers.

This brief sketch suggests a few important insights for further investigation. First, structured as it is by competition for relative position and led as it is by white men, capital is disjointed and distanced from the process of actually filling needs, which is allocated to women as homemakers. Although the selling of commodities is inherent in the process through which capitals expand, this is simply a means to an end, and expansion in the marketplace commonly involves producing products which are useless or even harmful to consumers, with technologies which are often harmful to life. Because managers are white and masculine and thus preoccupied with self-advancement as opposed to "feminine" care-taking, they provide little or no check on this dangerous process.

Second, we can study the issue of corporate motivation from a new perspective. Marxists have traditionally seen firms as bent on profit and growth, but it appears that other patriarchally and racially motivated processes are involved, at least in a subconscious manner. Firms reproduce gender, race and authority hierarchies not because these practices have been scientifically examined and found optimal, but because these hierarchies, present in the white patriarchal family system, are understood to be natural and given. Managers, as white men,[18] seek their own advancement in the white masculine competition and thus that of the corporation for which they work, not some abstract notion of profitability, growth, efficiency or productivity. Indeed, since the managers are no longer the owners, it is reasonable to expect that they would experience the profit motive and the ensuing pressure to minimize costs as less compelling (Lauterback 1954). The recent flurry of corporate take-over bids may be at least partially motivated by a masculine competition to dominate others. Kanter's (1983) study of technological innovation showed that corporations are excessively hierarchical and authoritarian, alienating workers and stifling innovation; this suggests that corporations are at least partially structured to provide the hierarchies in which white men can compete. There is also evidence that the masculinity of management blinds it to the centrality of feminine work within the corporation, for example, the importance of the caring work of nurses in the production of health.[19] Such findings are consistent with my contention here that, besides consciously defending and perpetuating their sex, race and class privilege, corporate managers are indeed fulfilling another and related unconscious assignment—that of perpetuating the patriarchal legacy inherited from the family.[20] These pressures, reinforced by self-conscious protection of white and male privilege, make capital a powerful generator of race and gender inequality.

Patriarchy and Race in the Job Structure. Another area of Marxist economics in need of revision is its analysis of the job structure. First, we need to broaden our conception of wage labor beyond the capitalist-worker relationship. White women and people of color have been and still are importantly employed in other types of wage work—domestic work, work for the state and non-profits, and tenant-farming[21]—and such work relationships are central in reproducing gender, race, and sexual and racial inequality. Limiting our theoretical and historical analyses of labor markets to consideration of capitalist firms means ignoring key aspects of the job structure.

Second, as I have hinted above, we need to think of the internal labor markets within firms as inherently patriarchal, racist, agist and authoritarian. These characteristics are historical legacies from the patriarchal white family. Some early firms, especially craft producers or merchants, were actually families; the early textile mills employed entire families (like Slater's mills) or established paternalistic and patriarchal job structures for their white workers (the Waltham/Lowell system).[22] This pattern of using family-like structures in the workplace has continued through the present; indeed, it is problematic for firms to place their workers in relationships antithetical to those common in their families and communities.[23] Job structures need to be "familiar" to workers—the Oxford English Dictionary's first definition of "familiar" is "of or pertaining to one's family or household"!

Many key aspects of contemporary job structures can be traced to patriarchal family[24] and racist community systems, for these have provided the context for the origin and persistence of capitalist firms: (1) the authoritarian power wielded by the white male boss (as father) over workers (as wives, sons, daughters) in commanding and overseeing their behavior; (2) the paternalistic responsibility of the boss for the worker, first construed somewhat broadly (including housing and education), later reduced essentially to providing workers with the wages with which to fill their consumption needs; (3) the development of a chain of command which delegates to older and male white workers (sons) their boss's (father's) authority over younger, female, and/or non-white workers;[25] (4) the sex-race typing of jobs, at least by firm or region, which maintains gender and racial difference and inequality (Amott and Matthaei 1991, ch. 10); (5) the struggle of adult white men to monopolize and preserve "family wage jobs" which reproduce their patriarchal positions of power in their families; (6) the establishment of "job ladders," allowing white men to move up in the hierarchy with age ("seniority"), benefiting in terms of pay and/or position and level of authority and status, often through competition against other white male "siblings" (white male employees at the same level); (7) the practice by white male workers of uniting in fraternal organizations (unions);[26] (8) the employment of women workers in dead-end auxiliary positions without authority over men, based on the expectation that they will leave the firm's "family" with marriage; (9) the efforts of white managers and workers to exclude non-whites from membership in the work family or, failing this exclusion, their segregation in clearly subordinate secondary jobs (Williams 1987). More research is needed to explore these links.

The key point is that patriarchy and white supremacy have been built into job structures and the firm. Race and gender are not merely mechanisms for allocating a predetermined set of jobs, or for dividing the labor force. This perspective on the significance of race and gender in labor markets makes it easier to understand why white working class men have not been a revolutionary force in the U.S., and why a movement to give "workers" control of the means of production, without changing inter-worker relationships, has limited appeal for white women and people of color.

Family and Economy. We can see, from the above discussion, that radicals cannot afford to ignore the role of the family in the reproduction of difference and inequality. First, Marxist-feminist analysis has made great strides in showing how the present family system reproduces patriarchal domination which is then both reflected onto and reinforced by gendered economic relations and institutions. Indeed, although gender divisions in family life may be breaking down, this breakdown cannot itself produce an alternative, non-patriarchal family system without the elimination of patriarchy from the economy, that is, without the elimination of capitalism. Second, we must note that the pooling of incomes and the passing of wealth across generations which occurs in the family is a central, if not *the* central, mechanism by which systematic race and class differences and inequality are reproduced. If the inheritance of income-producing property were banned and instead such property were appropriated by the state for collective use or distributed equally across the population, class, in the formal Marxist sense, would be abolished in one generation; racial differences and inequality would also be greatly reduced. Finally, we must keep in mind the fact that authoritarian parenting practices create individuals incapable of participating in truly democratic institutions, economic or political, while reinforcing the masculine mandate to seek inequality (i.e., to outdo or subordinate others); any socialist movement which does not take this into account is bound to fall far short of its goals. Marxist-feminists have drawn attention to the family and argued for its importance in capitalism; now that we have begun to study it seriously, it is clear that changes in family organization are crucial not only to the feminist movement but also to all progressive change (Matthaei 1988).

CONCLUSION

The contributions which Marxist-feminists have made to Marxist theory and practice are impressive. But the work of Marxist-feminists is far from over. As I have tried to show, the struggle to develop a truly Marxist-feminist anti-racist theory will help us both to understand the nature and contradictions of capitalism and to construct a truly radical and liberatory political movement. I hope all Marxists become Marxist-feminists.

NOTES

1. Although, as Young (1981) points out, many feminists continue to confuse gender differentiation with gender inequality.

2. In Matthaei (1982, pt. III), I explore the complicated process through which twentieth century capitalist development contributes to the breakdown of the sexual division of labor.

3. This debate has essentially been race-blind, whereas, in fact, white men monopolized family wage jobs, excluding both white women and people of color; see Joseph (1981).

4. The Left and Marxist press was full of articles to this effect in the mid-seventies. For example, it was argued that, according to Mao's theory of primary and secondary contradictions, sexual inequality is a secondary contradiction in the contemporary U.S. and must be put aside until "after the Revolution." One Marxist-feminist response was, as noted above, to stress the persistence of sexual inequality in all socialist countries.

5. Most of this debate took place in *New Left Review* in the 1970s. Good reviews are Himmelweit and Mohun (1977), Gardiner (1981), and Seccombe (1986).

6. Hartmann's work, particularly her (1981) essay "The Unhappy Marriage of Marxism and Feminism," best typifies this dual systems approach. The essays in Sargent (1981) explore the implications of her ovular essay and of the dual systems approach in general.

7. Nicholson (1986, 195) argues that gender relations are class relations since they involve differential access to and control over the means of production (i.e., the making of food and objects).

8. In this, I agree with Nicholson (1986, 6) who argues that "feminist theory, to fulfill its potential for radical challenge, must adopt an explicitly historical approach," rather than looking for cross-cultural laws or for *the* cause of women's oppression.

9. The "Social Structures of Accumulation" school is somewhat of an exception; however, it assumes that the central dynamic of capitalism is accumulation (hence class and exploitation), ignoring capitalism's other intrinsic processes, such as the reproduction or transformation of race and gender.

10. See Cagatay (1986) for a discussion of the evolving dialogue between First and Third World feminists, and for constructive suggestions for future interactions.

11. Convinced of the significance of these consciousness-producing activities for gender oppression, yet wedded to a materialist analysis, Mitchell (1974) and Delphy (1984, 159, 171) have come up with the unlikely conception of these processes as material ideology, referring to Althusser's discussion of ideology as a distinct and semi-autonomous level of practice. For a good explication, see Beechey (1979, 72-4).

12. Balbus (1982) and Nicholson (1986), also interested in integrating class and gender, present excellent arguments against materialism.

13. Miller (1981) gives an excellent discussion of authoritarian parenting; see also Chodorow (1979) and Hodges (1975).

14. Hartsock's (1983) discussion of the particular theoretical strength of work done from

the "standpoint" of the oppressed is also relevant here, although she considers only the promise of the "feminist" standpoint.

15. Other Marxist-feminists have worked on unitary theories; however, they have tended to posit patriarchy as a transhistorical force which takes different forms: Mies (1986) sees different societies as different "predatory modes of production"; Al Hibri (1981, 174) posits a universal need of men to make up for their "feeling of inadequacy and mortality vis-à-vis the female." Young (1981) argues the need for a unitary theory, but doesn't develop one.

16. I explore the first two points in much more detail in Matthaei (1987), which examines patriarchal capital. See also Rose (1986), for an excellent discussion of other ways in which gender was an intrinsic part of early capitalist work relations.

17. By lineage, I mean the transgenerational transmission of a family's social status, the cross-generational existence of a family, as expressed by a family surname.

18. We might expect that white women or people of color would behave differently in management; however, for them to make it into top positions in the existing structure, they must, for the most part, act white and masculine.

19. For example, hospital administrators try to increase "efficiency" in health care delivery by time-saving, cost-cutting methods, which in fact make nurses less productive by cutting down their "caring" time with patients. Kanter (1976, 45) claims that the importance of women's work in the corporation is ignored or devalued by its nature as maintenance and support rather than production.

20. Lauterback (1954, 2) writes: "actual or expected profit is seldom the ultimate determinant of business activity in the psychological sense, even though profit is ordinarily the most direct and conscious incentive for such activity." As Marcellus Andrews has pointed out to me, individual advancement is more and more achieved at the expense of the corporation being managed.

21. Through 1900, the majority of employed women did private domestic work; in 1940, 60% of black women were still employed in this work. Blacks and Native Americans are greatly overrepresented in state employment, as are women.

22. See Lown (1983) for an excellent analysis of the patriarchal characteristics of the early British mills.

23. Joyce (1980) argues that such use of familial work structures was central in the maintenance of class harmony in late nineteenth century Britain: "Because of its family aspect, the new distribution of authority and status in work served to accomodate the whole of the workforce, skilled and unskilled, male and female, in the prevailing order of industrial society. And it did so . . . by making people's own sense of communal identification a source of the employer's domination over their lives" (quoted in Rose 1986, 127).

24. See Weinbaum (1983) for a somewhat similar analysis of work relations in terms of family life.

25. Chandler (1977) treats the managerial hierarchy as copied from the military, ignoring the family.

26. Clawson (1980) discusses early fraternal organizations among workers as based on partiarchal kinship relations (I see unions as a later form of this fraternalism. She writes: "The use of kin relations of fatherhood and brotherhood as the model for other social relations results, in turn, in a model of authority in which age and sex appear to be the basic sources of domination and subordination—even in those situations in which property and control over labor power or the use of force are the actual basis of inequality" (380).

REFERENCES

Al-Hibri, A. 1981. "Capitalism Is an Advanced Stage of Patriarchy: But Marxism Is Not Feminism." In *Women and Revolution*, ed. L. Sargent, 165–94. Boston: South End Press.

Amott,T., and Matthaei, J. 1991. *Race, Gender, and Work: A Multicultural Economic History of Women in the United States*. Boston: South End Press.

Amsden, A. H., ed. 1980. *The Economics of Women and Work*. New York: St. Martin's Press.

Balbus, I. 1982. *Beyond Domination*. Princeton: Princeton University Press.

Barker-Benfield, G. J. 1976. *The Horrors of the Half-Known Life: Male Attitudes to Women and Sexuality in Nineteenth Century America*. New York: Harper and Row.

Baron, H. 1975. "Racial Domination in Advanced Capitalism: A Theory of Nationalism and Divisions in the Labor Market." In *Labor Market Segmentation*, ed. R. Edwards et al., 173–216. Lexington, MA: D. C. Heath.

Barrett, M. 1980. *Women's Oppression Today: Problems in Marxist Feminist Analysis*. London: Verso Editions and NLB.

Baxandall, R., et al., eds. 1976. *America's Working Women*. New York: Random House.

Beechey, V. 1979. "On Patriarchy." *Feminist Review* 3: 66–82.

Benenson, H. 1984. "Victorian Sexual Ideology and Marx's Theory of the Working Class." *International Labor and Working Class History* 25 (Spring): 1–23.

Beneria, L. 1979. "Reproduction, Production, and the Sexual Division of Labour." *Cambridge Journal of Economics* 3 (3): 203–25.

Brenner, J., and Ramas, M. 1985. "Rethinking Women's Oppression." *New Left Review*, no. 149: 33–71.

Cagatay, N., et al. 1986. "The Nairobi Women's Conference: Toward a Global Feminism?" *Feminist Studies* 12 (2): 401–12.

Chandler, A. D., Jr. 1977. *The Visible Hand: The Managerial Revolution in American Business*. Cambridge: Harvard University Press, Belknap Press.

Chodorow, N. 1978. *The Reproduction of Mothering: Psychoanalysis and the Sociology of Gender*. Berkeley: University of California Press.

———. 1979. "Mothering, Male Dominance, and Capitalism." In *Capitalist Patriarchy and the Case for Socialist Feminism*, ed. Z. Eisenstein, 83–106. New York: Monthly Review Press.

Clawson, M. A. 1980. "Early Modern Fraternalism and the Patriarchal Family." *Feminist Studies* 6 (2): 368–91.

Coontz, S., and Henderson, P., eds. 1986. *Women's Work, Men's Property: The Origins of Gender and Class*. London: Verso.

Cott, N. F., and Pleck, E. H., eds. 1979. *A Heritage of Her Own: Toward a New Social History of American Women*. New York: Simon and Schuster.

Cox, O.C. 1959. *Caste, Class, and Race: A Study in Social Dynamics*. New York: Monthly Review Press.

Dalla Costa, M. 1973. "Women and the Subversion of the Community." In *The Power of Women and the Subversion of the Community*, ed. M. Dalla Costa and S. James, 21–56. Bristol, England: Falling Wall Press.

Davies, M. 1979. "Woman's Place is at the Typewriter: The Feminization of the Clerical Labor Force." In *Capitalist Patriarchy and the Case for Socialist Feminism*, ed. Z. Eisenstein, 248–66. New York: Monthly Review Press.

Delphy, C. 1984. *Close to Home: A Materialist Analysis of Women's Oppression*. Amherst, MA: University of Massachusetts Press.

Dinerstein, D. 1976. *The Mermaid and the Minotaur*. New York: Harper and Row.

Ehrenreich, J. H. 1983. "Socialism, Nationalism, and Capitalist Development." *Review of Radical Political Economics* 15 (1): 1–42.

Eichenbaum, L., and Orbach, S. 1983. *Understanding Women: A Feminist Psychoanalytic Approach*. New York: Basic.

Engels, F. 1972. The Orig*in of the Family, Private Property and the State*. New York: International.

Ferguson, A. 1984. "On Conceiving Motherhood and Sexuality: A Feminist Materialist Approach." In *Mothering*, ed. J. Trebilcot, 153–82. Totowa, NJ: Rowman and Allanheld.

Ferguson, A., and Folbre, N. 1981. "The Unhappy Marriage of Patriarchy and Capitalism." In *Women and Revolution*, ed. L. Sargent, 313–38. Boston: South End Press.

Firestone, S. 1970. *The Dialectic of Sex: The Case for Feminist Revolution*. New York: Bantam Books.

Folbre, N. 1982. "Exploitation Comes Home: A Critique of the Marxian Theory of Family Labour." *Cambridge Journal of Economics* 6 (4): 317–29.

Fox, B. 1986. "Never Done: The Struggle to Understand Domestic Labour and Women's Oppression." In *The Politics of Diversity*, ed. R. Hamilton and M. Barrett, 180–89. London: Verso.

Gardiner, J. 1979. "Women's Domestic Labor." In *Women and Revolution*, ed. L. Sargent. Boston: South End Press.

Glazer, N. Y. 1984. "Servants to Capital: Unpaid Domestic Labor and Paid Work." *Review of Radical Political Economics* 16 (1): 61–88.

Gould, C. 1983. "Private Rights and Public Virtues: Women, the Family, and Democracy." In *Beyond Domination: New Perspectives on Women and Philosophy*, ed. C. Gould, 3–20. Totowa, NJ: Rowman and Allanheld.

Harding, S. 1981. "What is the Real Material Base of Patriarchy and Capital?" In *Women and Revolution*, ed. L. Sargent, 135–64. Boston: South End Press.

Hartmann, H. 1979. "Capitalism, Patriarchy, and Job Segregation by Sex." In *Capitalist Patriarchy and the Case for Socialist Feminism*, ed. Z. Eistenstein, 206–47. New York: Monthly Review Press.

Hartmann, H. 1981. "The Unhappy Marriage of Marxism and Feminism: Towards a More Progressive Union." In *Women and Revolution*, ed. L. Sargent, 1–42. Boston: South End Press.

Hartsock, N. C. M. 1983. "The Feminist Standpoint: Developing the Ground for a Specifically Feminist Historical Materialism." In *Discovering Reality*, ed. S. Harding and M. B. Hintikka, 283–310. Boston: D. Reidel Publishing.

Himmelweit, S. 1984. "The Real Dualism of Sex and Class." *Review of Radical Political Economics* 16 (1): 16–84.

Himmelweit, S., and Mohun, S. 1977. "Domestic Labour and Capital." *Cambridge Journal of Economics* 1 (1): 15–31.

Hodges, J., et al. 1975. *Cultural Bases of Racism and Group Oppression*. Berkeley: Two Riders Press.

Hooks, B. 1984. *Feminist Theory: From Margin to Center*. Boston: South End Press.

Humphries, J. 1977. "Class Struggles and the Persistence of the Working-Class Family." *Cambridge Journal of Economics* 1 (3).

——. 1981. "Protective Legislation, the Capitalist State, and Working Class Men: The Case of the 1842 Mines Regulation Act." *Feminist Review* 7: 1–33.

Humphries, J., and Rubery, J. 1984. "The Reconstitution of the Supply Side of the Labour Market: The Relative Autonomy of Social Reproduction." *Cambridge Journal of Economics* 8 (4): 331–46.

Joseph, G. 1981. "The Incompatible Ménage à Trois: Marxism, Feminism, and Racism." In *Women and Revolution*, ed. L. Sargent, 91–108. Boston: South End Press.

Joyce, P. 1980. *Work, Society, and Politics*. New Brunswick, NJ: Rutgers University Press.

Kanter, R. M. 1976. "Women and the Structure of Organizations: Explorations in Theory and Behavior." In *Another Voice: Feminist Perspectives on Social Life and Social Science*, ed. M. Millman and R. M. Kanter. New York: Octagon Books.

——. 1983. *The Change Masters*. New York: Simon and Schuster.

Lakoff, R. 1975. *Language and Women's Place*. New York: Harper and Row.

Lauterback, A. 1954. *Man, Motives, and Money: Psychological Frontiers of Economics*. Ithaca, NY: Cornell University Press.

Leacock, E. 1981. *Myths of Male Dominance*. New York: Monthly Review Press.

Lown, J. 1983. "Not So Much a Factory, More a Form of Patriarchy: Gender and Class During Industrialization." In *Gender, Class, and Work*, ed. E. Gamarnikow et. al., 28–45. London: Heinemann Educational Books.

Matthaei, J. 1982. *An Economic History of Women in America: Women's Work, the Sexual Division of Labor, and the Development of Capitalism*. New York: Schocken Books.

——. 1987. "The Patriarchal Structure of Capital: A Feminist Analysis of the Development of the Firm in the U.S." Paper presented at the Berkshire Conference of Women Historians, Wellesley, MA, June.

——. 1988. "Political Economy and Family Policy." In *The Imperiled Economy, Book II: Through the Safety Net*, ed. R. Cherry et al., 141–50. New York: URPE.
Mies, M. 1986. *Patriarchy and Accumulation on a World Scale: Women in the International Division of Labour*. London: Zed Books.
Miles, A. 1986. "Economism and Feminism: A Comment on the Domestic Labour Debate." In *The Politics of Diversity*, ed. R. Hamilton and M. Barrett, 168–79. London: Verso.
Miller, A. 1981. *The Drama of the Gifted Child*. Trans. Ruth Ward. New York: Basic Books.
Miller, J. B. 1976. *Towards a New Psychology of Women*. Boston: Beacon Press.
Millet, K. 1969. *Sexual Politics*. New York: Avon Books.
Mitchell, J. 1974. *Psychoanalysis and Feminism*. New York: Pantheon.
Molyneux, M. 1985. "Mobilization without Emancipation? Women's Interests, the State, and Revolution in Nicaragua. *Feminist Studies* 11 (2): 227–54.
Nicholson, L. 1986. *Gender and History: The Limits of Social Theory in the Age of the Family*. New York: Columbia University Press.
O'Brien, M. 1981. *The Politics of Reproduction*. Boston: Routledge and Kegan Paul.
Rosaldo, M. Z. 1980. "The Use and Abuse of Anthropology: Reflections on Feminism and Cross-Cultural Understanding." *Signs* 5 (3): 389–417.
Rosaldo, M. Z., and Lamphere, L., eds. 1974. *Woman, Culture, and Society*. Stanford: Stanford University Press.
Rose, S. O. 1986. "'Gender at Work': Sex, Class and Industrial Capitalism." *History Workshop Journal: A Journal of Socialist and Feminist Historians*, no. 21: 113–31.
Rotella, E. 1981. *From Home to Office: U.S. Women at Work, 1870-1930*. Ann Arbor: University of Michigan Research Press.
Rubin, G. 1975. "The Traffic in Women: Notes on the 'Political Economy' of Sex." In *Toward an Anthropology of Women*, ed. R. R. Reiter, 157–210. New York: Monthly Review Press.
Ryan, M. 1975. *Womanhood in America: From Colonial Times to the Present*. New York: New Viewpoints.
Sargent, L. 1981. "New Left Women and Men: The Honeymoon is Over." In *Women and Revolution: A Discussion of the Unhappy Marriage of Marxism and Feminism*, ed. L. Sargent, xi–xxxii. Boston: South End Press.
Scott, H. 1974. *Does Socialism Liberate Women?* Boston: Beacon Press.
Seccombe, W. 1986. "Reflections on the Domestic Labour Debate and Prospects for Marxist-Feminist Synthesis." In *The Politics of Diversity*, ed. R. Hamilton and M. Barrett, 190–207. London: Verso.
Sen, G. 1984. "Subordination and Sexual Control: A Comparative View of the Control of Women." *Review of Radical Political Economics* 16 (1): 133–42.
Spelman, E. V. 1988. *Inessential Woman: Problems of Exclusion in Feminist Thought*. Boston: Beacon Press.

Tilly, L. A., and Scott, J. W. 1978. *Women, Work and Family*. New York: Holt, Rinehart and Winston.

Ward, B. 1966. *Nationalism in Ideology*. New York: Norton.

Weinbaum, B. 1983. *Pictures of Patriarchy*. Boston: South End Press.

Weinbaum, B., and Bridges, A. 1979. "The Other Side of the Paycheck: Monopoly Capital and the Structure of Consumption." In *Capitalist Patriarchy and the Case for Socialist Feminism*, ed. Z. Eisenstein, 190–205. New York: Monthly Review Press.

Wertheimer, B. 1977. *We Were There*. New York: Pantheon Books.

Williams, R. 1987. "Capital, Competition, and Discrimination: A Reconsideration of Racial Earnings Inequality." *Review of Radical Political Economics* 19 (2): 1–15.

Wilson, W. J. 1987. *The Truly Disadvantaged*. Chicago: University of Chicago Press.

Young, I. 1981. "Beyond the Unhappy Marriage: A Critique of the Dual Systems Theory." In *Women and Revolution*, ed. L. Sargent, 43–70. Boston: South End Press.

METHOD, MATERIALISM, AND MARXIST-FEMINISM: A COMMENT ON MATTHAEI

Jane Humphries

Julie Matthaei's review of Marxist-feminist contributions to radical economics is thorough and thoughtful. As a survey it cannot be faulted. But—and of course partly because it seeks to provide a comprehensive guide—it passes rather too hastily over some still contentious issues and provides perhaps too glib a solution to the outstanding problem for Marxist-feminists: to move from influencing the content of radical economics to influencing its methodology. The unitary theory of capitalism to which Matthaei gives allegiance falls short of a useful framework for pursuing our future research agenda. I hope to show that an alternative theoretical framework, a variant of the dual systems theory which Matthaei herself finds wanting, is more promising for the task.

FROM CONTENT TO METHOD: THE IMPACT OF MARXIST-FEMINISM

Matthaei begins with the separation of the contributions of Marxist-feminism into: (1) the addition of new topics/areas essential for understanding women's economic experience but hitherto neglected by radical economists; and (2) the transformation of radical economic theory in the light of Marxist-feminist critiques. Initially, Marxist-feminist interest in certain new questions seemed to require a reformulation of Marxist theory and method, which had not been intended for such analysis and did not exactly fit it. For example, the need to locate women's domestic labour in capitalist relations of production initially promised a reformulation of Marxist theory: the domestic labour debate pushed authors to revise Marxian value categories designed to analyze exploitation in capitalist relations of production so as to accommodate unpaid labour time in the home.

But the expansion of the content of radical political economy has failed to impact on the mainstream: the transformation of Marxist theory has been limited at best. Take the hard core of Marxist economics, the general labour theory of value, which shows that value in commodity exchange is grounded on exploitation in production, and which leads on to the special labour theory of value, which postulates a link between the prices of commodities and the hours of direct and indirect labour that went to produce them. Despite the challenge of the domestic labour debate, this core, as described in two recent encyclopedic accounts, has been untouched by Marxist-feminism (Nell 1985; Roemer 1988). What about other important aspects of Marxist economics, particularly issues which have attracted attention in recent years, such as the labour process and the study of modes of accumulation? It appears that developments in these areas can be written up without reference to even the *experience* of women, let alone *how that experience must force a reorientation or reconceptualization* (Glyn 1988).

It is not so much that the transformation of Marxist method is "only in its early stages," as Matthaei contends, as that orthodox Marxism has established a kind of coexistence with its feminist critique: it lives and lets live. Perhaps the imperviousness of radical economics to its feminist critique is itself a sign of male dominance and control, here of the ideas which constitute the theoretical core. Alternatively, I shall argue that the resistance of radical economics relates to the particular form taken by the Marxist-feminist theoretical challenge, a form which, although initially useful, proved ultimately to be problematic.

THE PATRIARCHY MODEL

Within the mainstream Marxist paradigm, one problem had emerged as a key stumbling block. Although it was easy to show that in advanced economies, women workers, either as cheap wage labourers or as housewives, benefited capital, there was a glaring gap in the analysis: why was it that women did these jobs (Young, Wolkowitz and McCullagh 1981)? We needed to move beyond explanation solely in terms of the benefits of women's work for capital; thus, by the mid-1970s, the feminist critique changed tack. At this point the most influential challenge involved not the reformulation and extension of standard theory but the establishment of a separate and parallel theoretical construct which could be used to analyze topics and questions crucial to feminists. Thus patriarchy was conceptualized as a separate system of dominance and subordination (see Matthaei above, 126).

My concern here is not with the strengths and weaknesses of the patriarchy model per se (on this, see Beechey 1979; Edholm et al. 1977; Walby 1986; Humphries forthcoming), it is rather with how the patriarchy model has contributed to the "ghettoisation" of women's experience, blocked the integration of our understanding of that experience back into the mainstream, and, in particular, reduced the pressure to revise radical theory.

The conceptualization of patriarchy as a separate system relieved pressure on orthodox theorists and feminist critics alike. For orthodox theorists, patriarchy was a *parallel* system, important enough perhaps for lip service to be paid to the idea, but it did not require them to rethink their own perspectives. For feminist critics, patriarchy provided an independent and ahistorical explanation of sexual inequality. In patriarchy, men as men oppress women as women, often an obvious truth at the visible level of social reality. But often, too, it was a gross oversimplification which stymied the need to investigate whether men behaved as the model predicted, let alone whether their actions were instrumental or whether the consequences were intended. As Martha Gimenez has argued, to locate sexual inequality at the level of appearances is not to minimize its importance but to establish a distinction between levels of analysis (Gimenez 1987). Excess female mortality, wife-battering, rape, and sexual discrimination in employment are tragically real even if produced through a social dynamic which is not immediately observable (Wright 1978). To understand why women are oppressed in these ways requires an investigation of the underlying social and economic structures. My argument is that the concept of patriarchy *as a separate structure* stood in the way of such an investigation.

FROM PATRIARCHY TO DUAL SYSTEMS THEORY

This is not to deny that most authors, beginning with the seminal contributors to the debate (Hartmann 1979; Barrett 1980), believed that the sex/gender system related to the organization of production, but their focus was on the surface links between capitalism and women's oppression rather than their underlying mutual causes. As a result, instead of a careful and subtle study of the historically evolving relationship between women's oppression and other social forces, because capitalists were (are) male it was all too easy to see male workers and employers in unholy alliance against women, the former motivated to protect their patriarchal privileges and terms and conditions of employment, and the latter by the need (at least for capital as a whole) to fragment the labour force so as ultimately to beat down wages and increase exploitation. Intentional and functional models of explanation neatly coincided. Capitalism and patriarchy fitted only too well (see Matthaei above, 124–26).[1]

Criticisms of this version of *dual systems theory* on the grounds of its reductionism and functionalism are well known (Humphries 1977). But let us look once again at the model of explanation implied. The patriarchy model assumes that men have the vision and the power to shape history in their favor, transcending the opacity of social reality and mastering both the intended and unintended consequences of their actions (Gimenez 1987). Implicit too are other questionable assumptions about human behavior. Patriarchy theory shares with neoclassical economics and some vulgar interpretations of materialism a foundation in utilitarianism and methodological individualism. Men are assumed to act rationally and instrumentally in pursuit of their own material well-being. Asymetrically, feminist scholarship has demolished this as a serious model of women's behavior, and not just because of false consciousness or social conditioning. It is not only that, for example, family relationships involve "a level of love and sharing and indeed fusion of personality absent from production relations" but that to envisage men as struggling to "subordinate and terrorize" women, either as an end to itself or so as to extract unpaid domestic service, is to outdo the neoclassical economist in his/her vision of motivation by rational selfish self-interest. Matthaei seems to agree: "We must, as Marxists, find a way to acknowledge in our theories the centrality of social relations in constituting subjectivity" (above, 132). However, this is not an argument against materialism as a method of understanding a particular social form, as Matthaei contends, but only a criticism of the crude reduction of materialism to a social anthropology in which individual motivation is dominated by "the 'material' struggle for a larger piece of the pie, ignoring individuals' struggles, for example, to prove or defend their gender or racial or sexual identities, or to fulfill themselves, or to aid their families, or to establish their solidarity with others who are oppressed in different ways" (132). Unfortunately, by collaborating with this distorted presentation of materialism, patriarchy analysis has not only inhibited the challenge to Marxist economics but also contributed to its vulgarization.

Response to these and other problems with early formulations of the articulation of capitalism and patriarchy has taken several forms, as Matthaei's survey notes. Some authors have rejected dual systems theories altogether in favor of an insistence on the crucial determining role of production in the analysis of women's oppression (Gimenez 1987); others have also rejected dual systems theory, but in favor of a *unitary approach* which shifts our focus to the question of how gender is implicated in all social processes. Matthaei is in this camp (see also Acker 1989). Yet other authors are still unwilling to abandon dual systems theory, and seek instead to sharpen our understanding of the articulation between capitalism and patriarchy, often by reformulating and complicating our understanding of patriarchy so as to accommodate the empirical reality of historical and cross-cultural variation in women's subordination (Waters 1989; Walby 1989).

My approach falls into the final category above and derives from my particular criticisms of discussions of the articulation of capitalism and patriarchy which lodge the theorization of patriarchy at the empirical level of the relations between the sexes. What is required is a variant of dual systems theory which goes beyond tracing the empirical links between a separate system of sex oppression and a particular form of economic organization, a theory which uncovers the dual dynamic of both sex and class exploitation in the historically specific interaction between the relations of production and human reproduction.[2]

PRODUCTION AND HUMAN REPRODUCTION: THE DUAL DYNAMIC

Elsewhere I have argued that within classical Marxism there is a distinguished tradition of dualistic thinking about the oppression of women, but that the key dualism is not capitalism/patriarchy but production/reproduction (Humphries 1987a). Both Marx and Engels located human reproduction and the social relations of human reproduction in the material base of society, and one variant of dual systems theory has just such an expanded concept of the material as its starting point. Historical analysis must emphasize the interaction between these *two* aspects of material life, that is, between the changing organization of production and the changing form of the family. Unfortunately, in the course of his influential analysis of the family and the the position of women, Engels abandoned reproduction as a second autonomous, if interrelated, moment of the material; consequently, his analysis collapsed into an economism of which feminists have been rightly suspicious, since it conveniently identified women's struggle with struggle against private property, and so against capitalism (Humphries 1987a; Stolcke 1981).

But there are insights in Engels' method, if not in his analysis. An approach which sees human reproduction and production as relatively autonomous and equivalent in analytical status can handle the important but historically specific roles of women as mothers and potential mothers without falling into biological essentialism (Young, Wolkowitz and McCullagh 1981; Kuhn and Wolpe 1978; Fahy Bryceson and Vuorela 1984; Humphries forthcoming). Women's oppression has emerged from the confrontation between the demands of economic production and the structures of human reproduction (Brenner and Ramas 1984; Mackintosh 1981).[3] This approach has proved useful in explaining, for example: the sexual division of labour in agrarian West African societies still dominated by non-wage labour (Mackintosh 1979); otherwise problematic characteristics of capitalist labour markets (Humphries and Rubery 1984); the genesis of the sexual division of labour in capitalism (Humphries 1987b); cyclical and secular trends in women's employment in advanced industrial economies (Rubery 1988); and the sexual division of labour in feudal England (Middleton 1979; 1981).

DUAL SYSTEMS THEORY AND RACE

But what of the problems that Matthaei sees with dual systems theory in general and the production/reproduction dualism in particular? Let us look at these within the context of what Matthaei agrees is a major weakness in radical economics: the inadequate analysis of racial oppression. Inability to handle the question of race is acute in the patriarchy model because, as explained above, it *begins* with the oppression of women by men and not with the underlying organization of production and reproduction as fundamental determinants of relations between people. Consequently, the extension of the patriarchy model to accommodate racial as well as sexual oppression implies a proliferation of "systems" which Matthaei rightly regards as not only unwieldy but conceptually faulty. But the alternative is *not* simply to recognize only one sort of oppression, that of class. Marx and Engels *used* materialism to understand inequality between classes, but this does not mean that it cannot be used to understand other systematic oppressions; indeed, I argued above that if we begin with the material processes of reproduction as well as production, historical materialism has proved a powerful model for understanding the oppression of women. Much less work has been done on a materialist approach to racial oppression, but I believe that a materialist analysis could be insightful.

Beginning with the conditions of scarcity characteristic of societies with both underdeveloped economies and meager contraceptive technology, the associated inequality, in terms of access to both productive resources and their fruits, can be traced through to characteristic patterns of sexual and racial oppression. Thus Verena Stolcke (1981) has shown that when social hierarchies are rationalized implicitly or explicitly in terms of natural attributes (such as race or biologically transmitted capacities, for example), rather than exposed as the material product of environmental factors (such as unequal access to the means of production, for example), heredity becomes a fundamental concern. The importance of heredity has immediate consequences for women as well for the relations between races. She points out that in Germany, in the second half of the nineteenth century, elites responded to the polarization of society with various types of racist rationalizations, all of which attributed social inequalities not to a functioning division of labour but to inherent (racial) differences between human beings.

Stolcke also uses a materialist analysis to unravel the role of marriage and the family in two explicitly racist societies: nineteenth century Cuba and Nazi Germany. In Cuba, a slave society, an individual's social condition was not exclusively determined by ascription, and although the norm was racial endogamy, the very existence of legislation outlawing interracial marriage indicates its existence, which heightened the concern of the dominant class with racial "purity." As well as wealth, the marks of superior status were whiteness and racial purity. The perpetuation of class supremacy depended not only on the transmission of property according to the prevalent rules of inheritance but equally on the preservation of racial purity through control of heredity. This, in turn, was achieved through the rigid control by upper-class men of the sexuality of women of their class, and through women's domestic seclusion.

Germany differed from Cuba because of the rapid increase in the 1920s in the employment of women, especially white collar workers recruited predominantly from among the lower middle and middle class. But economic crisis at the end of the decade abruptly interrupted this trend. Simultaneously there had been changes in fertility, and by the early thirties birth rates were steadily declining. These two factors found expression in the fascists' violent reassertion of the traditional role of woman as mother and its translation into policy when they seized power. By 1937, however, with rearmament, this policy was reversed and women were encouraged to participate in the war effort. But the growing involvement of women in production did not seem to have a marked effect in altering society's image of women as subordinate. Women remained excluded from positions of power, a result both consistent with the Nazi emphasis on motherhood and the home and expressive of Nazism's aggressive and racist ideological underpinnings (see also Koonz 1988).

But if all racist rationalizations of inequality are bound to attach particular importance to women's procreative role, with negative implications for women's position, paradoxically domestic hierarchies which have no material base in the organization of production and reproduction tend to whither away, which leads to another interesting observation on racial oppression. Ellen Meiksins Wood (1988) has linked political rights in precapitalism to the extra-economic coercion characteristic of economic privilege in such societies. She argues that households must reproduce and reflect the hierarchical relations between exploiter and exploited, and that, as the organizer of production, the head of household acts as the agent of his own exploitation. The organization of human reproduction, she acknowledges, helps us to understand why such hierarchical structures should take the form of male dominance. But a predisposition in this direction is also inherent in the relation between precapitalist peasant households and the state. In particular, the fact that the exploitative powers confronting the peasant household are typically extra-economic (juridical, political, and military) links them inescapably to the one social function which has been most universally a male monopoly: armed violence. "In other words the organization of society in general and specifically the nature of the ruling class places a special premium on male domination" (Meiksins Wood 1988, 16). Meiksins Wood proposes a test of her hypothesis which is particularly interesting from our point of view. Imagine a dependent family of producers within which the male has no such political role outside the family and for which the surrounding social relations are not of the same kind. Then we might not expect the family to be characterized by male domination. Her empirical example of just such a family is the slave family in the American South, whose distinctive characteristic was, of course, the unusual authority of its women.

Clearly these fragments do not constitute a theory, but they indicate the way in which a material analysis can begin to unravel the meaning of racial oppression. If we begin instead not with the organization and interaction of production and human reproduction, but with the empirical object of our study, the miseries of racism, we might end up none the wiser about its causes and persistence.

This brings me to my final point, a point implicit in the arguments above.

Matthaei has presented a variety of approaches to the study of exploitative and oppressive social relations, all of which share something with Marx's own interest and (perhaps less clearly) his method. In the end the approach which helps us most to understand the patterns of dominance and subordination that we seek to root out must be the one we prefer. One disappointing aspect of Matthaei's survey is her failure to show that her chosen framework, the unitary theory, could provide new insight and understanding. Hence my emphasis here has been to try to suggest the ways in which a materialist approach can be used to try to understand particular aspects of the oppression of women, and indeed to contribute to a theory of racial oppression.

NOTES

1. It is now generally accepted that these early models overestimated the harmony between capitalism and patriarchy (see Walby 1986, 42–47).

2. Reproduction has been a very vexing concept in feminist theory. It has been used with a variety of different definitions, and its meaning and content is still much debated (see Edholm et al. 1977; Harris and Young 1981). My emphasis is on human reproduction and the relations which circumscribe and determine fertility, sexuality and the rearing of children (see Mackintosh 1981).

3. In practice, the approach I favor is similar to that of Brenner and Ramas (1984) who also want, for example, to introduce a "biological countertow" to the Marxist emphasis on the inevitable proletarianization of women in capitalism. However, they reject the dual systems approach which I think provides the best framework for accommodating the exigencies of biological reproduction, on the grounds that it descends into a bourgeois theory of multidetermination (for a similar criticism, see Gimenez 1987).

REFERENCES

Acker, J. 1989. "The Problem with Patriarchy." *Sociology* 23 (2): 235–40.

Barrett, M. 1980. *Women's Oppression Today*. London: New Left Books.

Beechey, V. 1977. "Some Notes on Female Wage Labour in Capitalist Production." *Capital & Class*, no. 11: 45–66.

Brenner, J., and Ramas, M. 1984. "Rethinking Women's Oppression." *New Left Review*, no. 144: 33–71.

Edholm, F.; Harris, O.; and Young, K. 1977. "Conceptualising Women." *Critique of Anthropology* 3 (9/10): 101–30.

Fahy Bryceson, D., and Vuorela, U. 1984. "Outside the Domestic Labor Debate: Towards a Theory of Modes of Human Reproduction." *Review of Radical Political Economics* 16 (2/3): 137–66.

Gimenez, M. 1987. "Marxist and Non-Marxist Elements in Engels' Views on the Oppression of Women." In *Engels Revisited: New Feminist Essays*, ed. J. Sayers, M. Evans, and N. Redclift. London: Tavistock.

Glyn, A. 1987. "Marxist Economics." In *The New Palgrave*, ed. J. Eatwell, M. Milgate, and P. Newman. London: Macmillan.

Harris, O., and Young, K. 1981. "Engendered Structures. Some Problems in the Analysis of Reproduction." In *Anthropological Analysis and Pre-Capitalist Societies*, ed. J. Llobera and J. Kahn. London: Macmillan.

Hartmann, H. 1979. "The Unhappy Marriage of Marxism and Feminism: Towards a More Progressive Union." *Capital and Class*, no. 8: 1–33.

Humphries, J. 1977. "The Working Class Family, Women's Liberation and Class Struggle." *Review of Radical Political Economics* 9 (3): 25–41.

———. 1987a. "The Origin of the Family: Born Out of Scarcity Not Wealth." In *Engels Revisted: New Feminist Essays*, ed. J. Sayers, M. Evans, and N. Redclift. London: Tavistock.

———. 1987b. "The Most Free From Objection . . .The Sexual Division of Labour and Women's Work in Nineteenth Century England." *Journal of Economic History* 47 (4): 929–50.

———. Forthcoming. "The Sexual Division of Labour and Social Control: An Interpretation." *Review of Radical Political Economics.*

Humphries, J., and Rubery, J. 1984. "The Reconstitution of the Supply Side of the Labour Market: The Relative Autonomy of Social Reproduction." *Cambridge Journal of Economics* 8 (4): 331–46.

Koonz, C. 1988. *Mothers in the Fatherland: Women, the Family and Nazi Politics*. London: Methuen.

Kuhn, A., and Wolpe, A. M., eds. 1979. *Feminism and Materialism.* London: Routledge and Kegan Paul.

Mackintosh, M. 1981. "Gender and Economics: The Sexual Division of Labour and the Subordination of Women." In *Of Marriage and the Market*, ed. K. Young, C. Wolkowitz, and R. McCullagh. London: CSE Books.

Mason, T. 1976. "Women in Nazi Germany, 1925-1940." Parts 1, 2. *History Workshop Journal*, no. 1, 2: 74–113, 5–32.

Meiksins Wood, E. 1988. "Capitalism and Human Emancipation." *New Left Review*, no. 167: 1–21.

Middleton, C. 1979. "Sexual Division of Labour in Feudal England." *New Left Review*, no. 113–114: 147–68.

———. 1981. "Peasants, Patriarchy and the Feudal Mode of Production in England: A Marxist Appraisal." *Sociological Review* 29 (1): 105–54.

Nell, E. 1985. "Marxian Economics." In *The Social Science Encyclopedia*, ed. A Kuper and J. Kuper. London: Routledge and Kegan Paul.

Roemer, J. 1987. "Marxian Value Analysis." In *The New Palgrave*, ed. J. Eatwell, M. Milgate, and P. Newman. London: Macmillan.

Rubery, J., ed. 1988. *Women and Recession.* London: Routledge and Kegan Paul.

Stolcke, V. 1981. "Women's Labours: The Naturalisation of Social Inequality and

Women's Subordination." In *Of Marriage and the Market*, ed. K. Young, C. Wolkowitz, and R. McCullagh. London: CSE Books.

Walby, S. 1986. *Patriarchy at Work.* London: Polity.

———. 1989. "Theorising Patriarchy." *Sociology* 23 (2): 213–34.

Waters, M. 1989. "Patriarchy and Viriarchy: An Exploration and Reconstruction of Concepts of Masculine Domination." *Sociology* 23 (2): 193–211.

Young, K.; Wolkowitz, C.; and McCullagh, R., eds. 1981. *Of Marriage and the Market.* London: CSE Books.

Wright, E. O. 1978. *Class, Crisis and the State.* London: New Left Books.

5 RADICAL THEORIES OF ACCUMULATION AND CRISIS: DEVELOPMENTS AND DIRECTIONS

Bruce Norton

The capital accumulation process holds a privileged place in most radical frameworks, providing for many a uniquely important key to the dynamics of capitalist economies. Various frameworks, however, theorize the process in quite different terms. The result is a somewhat fractured body of thought whose major fault lines are a focus of this essay.

From another angle my topic is theories of economic crisis, for understandings of the latter both shape and are shaped by general theories of accumulation. Whether the term is used to indicate abrupt and violent cessations in the process of accumulation or, as is now more common, prolonged periods of impaired capitalist growth, we shall see that a central characteristic of various radical traditions is their attempt to demonstrate that economic crises are products of accumulation's fundamental workings. Indeed, in a mode of reasoning I seek to question below, crises are generally conceived as uniquely visible expressions of the basic nature of the contemporary accumulation process as a whole.

The analysis which follows is at a general level: it concerns general theories of changes in profit and investment rates thought to underlie crisis periods, rather than any detailed analysis of the mechanisms by which crises are spread, inflation produced, or state activities constrained. Advocates of virtually every framework considered below develop richer and more concrete analyses than I shall be able to recount.

It is useful as well as customary to begin crisis theory discussions by emphasizing an initial distinction Marx himself stressed (see, for example, Alcaly 1978, 17).

The general characteristics of capitalist economies which produce the possibility of crisis differ from the forces which, as he argued, produce their actuality. As recent authors have particularly underlined (Kenway 1980; Crotty 1985), the possibility of crisis is suggested at an abstract level in Marx's framework: indeed the general possibility is already "contained in the metamorphosis of commodities," the necessity for commodities to be sold (Marx 1968, 502). Capitalist commodities must be transformed into money, but the very existence of money implies that the sale may not take place as expected, for money may be held rather than spent. These considerations suggest that for Marx crises always involve monetary and financial dynamics, though this by no means leads directly to analysis of the general forces which might provoke a widespread inability of commodities to realize their values. Instead radical theorists most often turn to the capital accumulation process.

Here again Marx delineated a basic approach whose outlines are still shared by most schools of radical thought. In *Capital* 1, Marx depicts the accumulation of capital (initially defined as the "employment of surplus-value as capital, or its reconversion into capital") in the context of the several circuits through which productive capital must pass. First, money must be spent on means of production and labor-power. Second, the process of production must take place. The produced commodities must then be sold, at which point a portion of the realized profit may be returned to production in the form of new means of production and labor-power (Marx 1976, 709). The circuit of productive capital then looks as follows:

$$M - C\,(MP, LP) \ldots (P) \ldots C' - M'$$

Money (M) is invested in commodities (C), means of production and labor power (MP and LP), which are used in the production process (P) to create new commodities (C′). These are sold for (M′), a sum of money greater than (M).

The introduction of accumulation into this circuit involves tracing the disposition of M′. We can write out an extended circuit, numbering the consecutive processes undergone in production and accumulation of capital in order to facilitate analyses below.

$$\underset{(1)}{M - C\,(MP,\ LP)} \ldots \underset{(2)}{(P)} \ldots \underset{(3)}{C' - M'} \begin{cases} \text{–non-accumulation distributions} \\ \text{–accumulation distributions} \\ \quad \text{(renewed M—C (MP, LP))} \quad (1') \end{cases}$$

As indicated, part of M′ is allocated to various non-accumulation purposes. Part is reinvested, or accumulated as productive capital.

An initial general consideration sets the stage for radical accumulation and crisis theory. Abstractly considered, profit reinvestment, or accumulation, may have implications which will shape any or all of the processes constituting the circuit of capitalist production: purchase of inputs (1), the production process (2), or the ability of capitalists to sell their produced commodities at full value (3). Any such effects, of course, may in turn redound back upon the rate of capital accumulation, first of all by changing the rate of profit reaped by capitalist enterprises. Thus the characteristic general vision of radical macrotheory: accumulation changes the conditions of surplus value production and realization, and thereby modulates its own continued course. Theories of the "actuality" of crisis generally elaborate conceptions and positions not yet indicated. These form distinct general frameworks amounting to contending visions of capitalist economies. We shall try to see why each wins passionately committed partisans, looking not only at differences among them but, imbricated in the differences, repeated general themes.

THE DOMINANCE OF PRODUCTION: FALLING RATE OF PROFIT THEORY

Conceptions of accumulation and crisis are defined in part by the way they construe relations among (and therefore the makeup of) the spheres of production, circulation or "exchange," and distribution. An important interpretation of Marxian economic theory, old in comparison with other current frameworks, begins by asserting that basic characteristics of capitalist production shape and determine the course of capital accumulation as a whole. The school came to prominence in English-speaking radical thought in the early 1970s with works by Mattick (1969), Yaffe (1973a), and Cogoy (1973). The general tradition was then strongly buttressed by the English publication of Rosdolsky's interpretation of the logic of Marx's writings (1977). More recent variants of the framework, elaborated by Shaikh, Fine and Harris, Weeks, and others, are now prominently represented as the Marxian interpretation of capitalist crisis in encyclopedias of economic thought, dictionaries of Marxism, special publications of the Union for Radical Political Economics, and so on (see, e.g., Shaikh 1983; 1987a; Fine 1983).

In certain respects the position was originally advanced in the 1920s and 1930s by Henryk Grossman, who considered his interpretation of Marx's method as perhaps his most important contribution to Marxism (Jacoby 1975, 32; Mattick 1981, 103).[1] The method he identified consists of a gradual movement from abstract to concrete through a series of "successive approximations," in which additional aspects are taken into account in order to approach further "concreteness" (Sweezy 1968, 11-20; Jacoby 1975, 33).

For Grossman, the method of successive approximations is, however, highly structured. Marx began with production for good reason: production is capitalism's ultimately determinant sphere. Accordingly, while the analysis developed in *Capital* changes as it develops, it does so in a particular way: Marx identifies the general character of capitalism's essential nature in Volume 1, elaborates aspects of capitalist circulation in Volume 2, and shows in Volume 3 how the essential productionist logic earlier developed asserts itself in capitalist development as a whole, through the laws of accumulation and crises. As Howard and King render

Grossman's argument, "economic crisis must be explained in terms of 'the inner nature of capital' itself" (1988, 292; quote is from Grossman).

This thesis aptly summarizes a common position linking otherwise diverse theorists in this tradition. A truly Marxian economic theory must understand capitalist crisis as the inevitable expression of the basic makeup—or "laws of motion" — of capitalist production relations. To do otherwise is to fail to grasp the nature of Marx's method and, disarmed, to fall into both bourgeois forms of theory and reformist and evolutionary politics.[2]

Rosdolsky's scholarly reconstruction of the development of Marx's thinking added new dimensions to the productionist interpretation of Marx in the late 1960s. *The Making of Marx's Capital* (1977; German edition, 1968) uses the long unavailable *Grundrisse* to reinterpret Marx's own conception of the logic of his theory, again taking up first of all "Marx's method." His thesis is that Marx's "general concept of capital"—in Rosdolsky's view the focus of the *Grundrisse* as well as *Capital* 1 and 2—corresponds to and bears determinate implications for the course of capitalist development (1977, 49). Rosdolsky thus adds a self-consciously rationalist epistemological perspective to the more implicit rationalism already at work in Grossman's formulation. Publication of the *Grundrisse* irrevocably clarifies the method at work in *Capital*: in however "materialist" and "inverted" a form, it is Hegelian (Rosdolsky 1977, xii–xiii). Thus Marx starts with a general analysis of the production of surplus value not simply because that is his special concern; he seeks to establish capitalism's structuring dynamic, the general concept of capital.

What is this concept? Production theorists share a first approach to this question. Yaffe draws strongly on Rosdolsky in arguing that capitalist production "has as its aim and driving force the production of surplus-value as additional exchange-value" (1973b, 193). Capital seeks more—both more surplus value in production and more expansion in the form of accumulated surplus value. But the source of capital's growth is living labor, and living labor—more precisely that portion of living labor performed in excess of what is needed for the living standards of productive workers ("necessary" labor)—is limited. To show this, Yaffe summarizes the development of Marx's treatment of the labor process in *Capital* 1 along lines Rosdolsky had earlier traced. The working day cannot be extended beyond certain limits. Other means for raising surplus value must be found: those involved in Marx's "relative surplus value" production, by which labor productivity in wage goods production is increased and the necessary portion of the work day correspondingly shortened (if real wages don't rise as rapidly as productivity). While raising the intensity of labor can produce such results, after a certain point there are limits to its further application. Mechanization then looms by default as the sole long-run means to satisfy the unceasing search for additional surplus value implied by capital's general nature (Yaffe 1973a, 193–94; Rosdolsky 1977, 220–49).

Yaffe, like others, utilizes the aggregate rate of profit expressions Marx deploys in *Capital* 3. If r, C, V, and S are respectively the value rate of profit and annual flows of constant capital, variable capital, and surplus value, then the rate of profit is given by $r = S/(C + V)$.[3] Dividing by V, $r = (S/V)/((C/V) + 1)$.

Yaffe's contention is that the innate drive to mechanize the labor process will be expressed in a rising "organic composition" of capital, which he equates with the value composition (C/V). This cannot, on algebraic grounds, be permanently offset by the rise in the rate of surplus value (S/V) produced as technical change raises labor productivity and thereby lowers the value of the wage bundle. Therefore in the long run the aggregate rate of profit must fall, and when this fall proceeds so far as to undermine growth of the mass of surplus value, more concrete phenomena in the sphere of circulation produce the crisis itself.

Thus, for Yaffe as well as Rosdolsky, the notion that accumulation must eventually undermine its own further progress by driving down the rate of profit is no mere conjecture. It is a necessity, once one grasps "Marx's method" and more specifically the role played by mechanization in capital's struggle to expand regardless of limits posed by the supply of living labor.

Since 1978, Shaikh has further developed productionist theory. When he set out to "trace Maurice Dobb's theory of crises, and to demonstrate its substantial difference from that of Marx" (1978b, 246), it was in outline Rosdolsky's reading which he construed as the theory "of Marx." Dobb, in Shaikh's view, was wrong to construct accumulation as a process bearing no determinate implications for the organic composition of capital unless and until it proceeds so far as to seriously diminish the reserve army of unemployed, thereby pushing up real wages and provoking systematic substitution of machines for workers. For it is not real wage pressures which are responsible for mechanization, it is the "immanent" nature of social relations within the capitalist labor process itself.

But if mechanization is nourished by the basic nature of capitalist production, how is it actually implemented in the world of capitalist competition? Shaikh balances a basic tension on this point. On one hand, he maintains the tradition's distinctive claim that accumulation is subject to general laws established outside itself, in production's capital-labor dynamics. Competition itself "does not explain these laws, nor produce them, but rather lets them become visible (albeit in inverted form, for circulation is the mirror of production)" (Shaikh 1978b, 240). At the same time Shaikh is not ready to assert that mechanization and a rising value composition of capital come about simply because competition must "execute" a law to that effect. Distinct imperatives operating at the level of capitalist competition undoubtedly act as a "filter" screening certain types of technical change and admitting others. Hence the question Shaikh confronts: "What is the scope and effect of this filtering process?" (1978b, 240–41).

By posing the question in this way, Shaikh produced a moment of some drama in radical economics as a whole. The question forms a point of contact between two contending schools, the productionist tradition on one hand, and Sraffian economics (with its well developed theory of the "choice of technique") on the other. Hegel and Sraffa meet head on, one might say, and somewhat on the latter's home ground.

As Shaikh well knew, a line of thought stemming from Okishio (1961) was confidently ready to answer his question, having indeed already posed it and reached a conclusion directly contrary to the one he sought. Okishio used a Sraffian model to investigate whether a firm's choice to adopt a new technique which lowers its costs per unit of output (raising the profit it makes at the initial prices and real wage) might thereby lower the rate of profit in the system as a whole, once prices have changed to their new equilibrium levels. The "Okishian" answer is that it can't. With an unchanged real wage, any innovation which lowers the cost of a commodity can ultimately only raise (or leave unchanged) the general money rate of profit. Competition seems to "filter out" the force productionist theorists believe propels capitalism's basic trajectory.[4]

Shaikh, of course, continues to disagree. After extensive debate, during which his position changed, he now challenges the theorem's relevance on the basis of the neoclassical concept of competition on which it relies. The choice of technique literature construes current prices as the basis on which capitalists evaluate investment projects. Techniques will be adopted in that framework if the "transitional" profit they yield—that is, the profit at the price structure associated with the techniques initially prevailing—is maximized. In contrast, Shaikh maintains that capitalists both anticipate and actively effect falling prices: they strive to maximize survival probabilities by minimizing unit production costs, defined as depreciation, materials and labor costs per unit output (1987b, 116; cf. Shaikh 1978b, 234–35; 1980, 83). For Marxian theory, "competition is war," a continual battle to be the first to lower production costs, not an adjustment to reigning relative prices.

Given this different conception of competition, a rising value composition can still be seen to follow from capitalist production if, as Shaikh then asserts, ever-larger investment in fixed capital is the means to cheapen unit production costs. If so, then "the same factor which fuels the competitive struggle among individual capitalists also produces a *slow but steady downward drift in the economy wide average rate of profit*" (Shaikh 1987b, 116; emphasis in original). More precisely, the floor to the value composition of capital, defined as C/L where $L = V + S$, rises over time, bringing with it at some point the value composition itself.[5] Paralleling Yaffe, Shaikh further contends that "any sustained rise in C'/L (where C' is the stock of fixed capital) can be shown to give rise to an actual falling rate of profit, *no mat-ter how fast the rate of surplus value is rising*" (1987a). Once the non-Marxian conception of competition associated with Sraffa-style analysis is jettisoned, the laws of accumulation envisioned in the productionist tradition may still be seen to hold.[6]

Without attempting to evaluate the argument as a whole, we might note that it places a heavy burden on a particular thesis about technological change. In effect, the cost-cutting criterion enforced by capitalist competition favors "capitalization" only because more capital-intensive techniques are assumed to dominate the available supply of technical possibilities. This hypothesis uneasily and uncertainly fills the gap left when, parting from Rosdolsky and Yaffe, Shaikh set out to analyze the sphere of competition in terms not a priori reducible to capitalist production's asserted essential logic.

The productionist interpretation of Marxian theory has a noteworthy immediate implication for the theory of *accumulation*. In the narrow sense of the word, accumulation takes place in the sphere of circulation, as surplus value is used to purchase constant and variable capital. However, this tradition folds the circulation process securely and explicitly into the productionist logic it believes dominates capitalist economies.[7] From this perspective both the expansion of value in capitalist production and the use of surplus value for reinvestment are conjoint aspects of the general concept of capital. The drive to expand exchange-value, the inner nature of capital, encompasses both more or less at once. In effect, the circuit of production and accumulation is thus "closed" at point (1′) in our diagram above.

This closure is also effected on a less abstract level. Mechanization, the phenomenon thought directly implied by capital's basic urge to extract surplus value in production, also operates to enforce maximum possible capital expansion in the realm of circulation/distribution. Hence, even when considered at the level of incentive structures, the capitalists' behavior at step (1′) in the circuit is univocal: profitability permitting, the maximum portion of available funds must be used for new investment in physical capital.[8] Fixed capital becomes both the key condition for reaping surplus value and its key destination once reaped.

The move by which production and accumulation are merged into a seamless whole (whether referred to as "the concept of capital," the "accumulation of capital," or other titles) bears consideration from a more general angle. It is linked with—related to and supportive of—a larger philosophical and political vision which these theorists embrace. The history of the capitalist mode of production, in this view, is informed by an essential contradiction between the forces of production and the social relations of production. For productionist theorists the unified drive to accumulate represents precisely the latter term in this contradiction, the *relations* of production. The drive to expand, embedded in production relations, ceaselessly develops the productive forces (the social productivity of labor), constantly requiring and nourishing new and more productive techniques. These very changes, however, also necessarily lower the rate of profit, the very heart of the production relations themselves. The contradiction erupts; crises of ever-growing severity ensue (Shaikh 1983, 142); the *necessity* to overthrow capitalism is manifest.

From the perspective of its advocates, it is productionist theory's larger backing which ensures political implications quite different from those of other accumulation frameworks. As Mattick and Yaffe proclaimed near the end of the post-war boom, Keynesian notions of stabilization are illusory. In the long term, the growth of the state sector simply *adds* to capitalism's problems, taking surplus value out of capitalists' hands as taxes when the basic problem is a shortage of surplus value to begin with. Both taxation and deficit spending ultimately represent "a decline in accumulation and a decline in the rate of growth of the productivity of labor" (Yaffe 1973b, 218). The economic theory itself implies determinate limits on the power of economic policy.

Generally speaking, falling rate of profit theorists seem to care less about precise analysis of the state than about the overall conclusion just traced. This they contrast—in virtually every work on crisis theory—to both Keynesian theory and the perspectives on state intervention provided by underconsumption and profit-squeeze theories (e.g., Yaffe 1973a; Shaikh 1978a). Indeed, Shaikh structures a recent reference volume entry on economic crises around this point, classifying Marxist crisis theories as either "possibility theories" (underconsumption and wage-squeeze theories) or "necessity theories" ("Marx's falling rate of profit theory"). The latter, he contends, follow Marx in construing "laws of motion" as tendencies which "arise out of the very nature of the system itself" (1983, 139). In contrast, he concludes, it is "characteristic of possibility theories in general that because they end by endowing the state with the power to determine the basic laws of motion of capitalism, both the expectations and the promises of their proponents come to depend heavily on the notion that even under capitalism politics can command the system" (1983, 141).

The strict bifurcation of historical dynamics instituted by Grossman remains. Capitalist history is composed of two forces: "laws of motion," utterly unchangeable within the confines of capitalism and at a certain point of development utterly destructive, and the "subjective" element, class struggle, the further ingredient necessary if the dying mode of production is to be surpassed. Perhaps an odd couple on the face of it, the two forces are quite complementary within the political perspective of this tradition.[9] The proposition that capitalism's fundamental nature expresses itself in unavoidable and growing crises (whether secularly, as for Yaffe, or in periodic long-wave downturns, as for Shaikh) is thought to be important not simply because it is scientifically correct; it is an insight which is politically essential, opening, as Grossman at least hoped, a third path between the embrace of capitalism, on one side, and adherence to the twentieth century's bureaucratically administered workers' movements, on the other.

ANOTHER VERSION OF PRODUCTIONIST THEORY: CONTRADICTIONS BETWEEN PRODUCTION AND EXCHANGE

In the late 1970s a provocative *cyclical* variant of the productionist interpretation of Marxian accumulation theory emerged. Fine and Harris (1976; 1977;

1979) took as raw materials many of the basic propositions just encountered, though the theory they constructed differs substantially in two general respects. First, Fine and Harris emphasize that exchange and distribution processes are distinct spheres of capitalist economies, not simply mirrors of production. If they are ultimately determined by production (which Fine and Harris also firmly assert), that does not eliminate their "relative autonomy." They also mold the complex "structured whole," influencing its laws of motion by responding to and influencing production's own effects (Fine and Harris 1979, 3–6). Fine and Harris cite Marx's well-known "Introduction" (1973, 81–111) in support of these theses.

Second, *Rereading Capital* (Fine and Harris 1979) pays renewed attention to the levels of abstraction through which, in their view, scientific theorizing proceeds. But Fine and Harris interpret the significance of this progression quite differently than prior productionists. One result: a "law" of motion such as the law of the tendency for the rate of profit to fall need not be a direct empirical prediction. It may instead indicate relationships sketched by the theory at a certain still abstract level of analysis, whose empirical significance depends on the further elaboration of the theory.

Readers familiar with recent controversies in Marxian theory might detect the influence of Althusser and Balibar. Indeed, Fine and Harris cite Althusser directly and engage his work through their use of terms such as "overdetermination" and "structured wholes" composed of "relatively autonomous" spheres, and so on (e.g., 1979, 6, 88). In this context, however, what may be most striking about their theoretical framework is the basic *continuities* it nevertheless shares with other productionist theories. Althusser's critique of traditional epistemologies, for example, is in no way endorsed: Fine and Harris stick to a strict rationalism much like prior authors. If, as they argue, human thought is produced by the elaboration of concepts rather than as a simple reflection of "reality," the concepts used in that process of scientific thought are nevertheless specially grounded: they correspond to a logic thought to structure the world.

In capitalist societies that logic reflects the confrontation of two great classes, workers and capitalists, in production. Once again, however, one may substitute the term "accumulation" for capitalist production.[10] Perhaps this conflation is assisted by the fact that, for Fine and Harris as for Yaffe, "capital" by definition encompasses both the production and *accumulation* of surplus value. In any case the general point is clear: if production is the determining realm, accumulation (strictly speaking an exchange process) is both part of that realm and a summary title for the whole (1979, 3–20, 76, 77, 133). It is then accumulation which, "for Marx," "is the essence of capitalism" (1979, 58).

So far we seem to be on familiar territory, yet the crisis theory produced in this theoretical setting differs substantively from Yaffe's or Shaikh's. The "fundamentalists," as Fine and Harris refer to Yaffe and associates, err by confining to the level of production the analysis of the contradictions produced by accumulation's progress. Once that is corrected, their basic argument no longer holds. Certainly capitalist technical change necessarily raises the "technical composition of capital," the mass of machinery and materials set in motion by a single laborer (1979, 62). But since the rise in labor productivity associated with this technical change reduces the value of both constant and variable capital within circulation, there is no necessary trajectory for the value composition of capital, and hence no long term tendency for the rate of profit to decline (1979, 73; cf. Fine 1982, 111).

Nevertheless, as Fine and Harris argue, Marx's theory, once properly formulated, does indeed imply that the organic composition of capital necessarily rises with the progress of accumulation. But here, contrary to Yaffe, the organic composition of capital is quite distinct from its value composition. Marx defines the "organic composition" in order to trace the direct implications of technical change *at the still abstract (conceptual) level of production.* It measures the ratio of constant to variable capital, *C/V*, where the commodities entering into both numerator and denominator are valued at their "old values"—the values obtaining before the technical change in question raised labor productivity. Hence Marx's definition makes sense: the organic composition measures the value composition "insofar as it is determined by its technical composition and mirrors the changes in the latter" (Marx 1976, 762). In contrast, the value composition takes account of the change in values which accompanies technical change; it "is only formed on the basis of the complex articulation of production, exchange and distribution." The failure of "fundamentalists" to adequately distinguish between organic and value compositions is thus part of their larger failure to adequately theorize both spheres of exchange and distribution and the *complex* relationships through which production's ultimate determination is expressed in those spheres (1979, 60–61).

Nevertheless the law of the tendency of the rate of profit to fall (LTRPF) is still the centerpiece of Marxian accumulation theory and the key to understanding capitalist crises. Once the confusion between organic and value compositions is rectified, Fine and Harris argue that Marx's LTRPF is both redefined and reaffirmed, as is the productionist claim that this law is the source of all capitalist economic crises. In a passage from *Capital* 3 stressed in their interpretation, Marx suggests that the normal course of accumulation produces contradictions sufficient to interrupt the circuit of capital. Discussing the development of productivity, the depreciation of existing capitals, the growth of relative overpopulation, and so on, Marx concludes:

> These different influences may at one time operate predominantly side by side in space, and at another time succeed each other in time. From time to time the conflict of antagonistic agencies finds vent in crises. The crises are always but momentary and forcible solutions of the existing contradictions. (1967, 249)

The passage fittingly describes Fine and Harris' interpretation of crisis theory. The LTRPF now concerns short-run rather than secular phenomena, and involves issues not raised at all in "fundamentalist" theory: the contradictory tensions which "result from the fact that accumulation inevitably causes both the TRPF and the counteracting influences to develop in such a contradictory way that smooth accumulation is impossible" (1979, 84).

Production is first of all constantly changing as new techniques are instituted which raise the organic composition of capital. This may, if not offset, lower the profit rate sufficiently to halt accumulation. But in any case, as labor productivity rises with technical change, exchange relations must adjust as well. Values are reduced, indeed both commodity values and the value of fixed capital are constantly subject to revision and attack by accumulation itself. Crises thus involve, in general terms, "the reorganization of production in its interaction with exchange" (1979, 84; cf. Weeks 1981, 204–12). As Fine suggests, more concrete development of this analysis would require both elaboration of the role of money in accumulation and introduction of "more historical elements" specifying the forms of capital reorganization and competition molding these dynamics at a particular time (Fine 1982, 121).

In 1982, Harvey's influential *The Limits to Capital* added a further voice to this tradition. More wide-ranging than Fine and Harris' work, particularly on questions of space, Harvey's scholarly Marxian exegesis builds on substantially the same foundations. Like Fine and Harris and Weeks, Harvey staunchly defends the position earlier adopted by Mattick, Yaffe, et al., that *every* crisis *expresses* the contradiction between production relations (accumulation) and the contradictory development of the productive forces (labor productivity) under accumulation's lead.[11] The claim, of course, cannot be directly shown: it follows rather from the position as a whole, its belief that "Marx's method" captures an essential logic and thereby uncovers those "hidden, inner characteristics" of capitalist production which structure economic events (Fine and Harris 1979, 58).

ACCUMULATION AND EPOCHAL STAGNATION

A competing radical framework differs from the productionist tradition in part because it systematically elaborates certain similar basic assumptions—but in another direction. In the theory of capitalist maturity or monopoly capitalism, accumulation is again thought to bear abstractly determinate implications for the course of capitalist development as a whole: accumulation eventually produces conditions which undermine its continued progress, thereby initiating an epoch marked by slowed and halting capitalist growth. In this case though, it is not production but circulation which is the immediate site of capitalism's inner expansion dynamic and the realm in which contradictions also emerge.

As I shall argue, one condition for the certain broad similarities between productionist theory and the theory of monopoly capitalism is that the two share certain general conceptions of the nature of science. For productionists, the world is made up of appearances and essences. For monopoly capital theorists like

Steindl and Baran and Sweezy, it divides into "endogenous" or essential forces and "exogenous" or conjunctural processes. Thus, for both traditions, science has one task: to identify the essential or endogenous determinants and show how they express themselves (and are modified) in the world of appearance or historical phenomena.

While for both traditions these essential determinants stem from the inner nature of accumulation, there agreement ends. Indeed, monopoly capital theorists begin by reversing productionist principle: they take capitalist production as a generally solved issue. In contemporary conditions, leading capitalist firms are thought readily able to reap high profit margins per unit of sales.

This has immediate implications for analysis of the circuit of accumulation. If production processes (at step 2 in our diagram) are readily controlled by capitalist firms, the dynamic forces which propel and disturb accumulation's pace must lie elsewhere, namely, in the sphere of circulation (step 1′). In this respect, monopoly capital theory neatly inverts the "fundamentalist" production theory of Mattick, Yaffe, and Shaikh. We saw that for the latter theorists the capitalists' need to reinvest profit, which can be taken for granted except in crisis conditions, in effect solves the problem of aggregate demand; hence everything depends upon profitability conditions in production itself. Monopoly capital theory reverses this logic. It is now accrual of profit in production which is smoothly predictable, leaving demand (more precisely, certain demand-side implications of the capitalist firm's expansion process) in the position of regulating the system's ups and downs.

Its focus on exchange phenomena leaves the theory of monopoly capitalism with certain of its basic assumuptions exposed in a readily accessible form. For what is now the source of the primal force constituted by "'accumulation for accumulation's sake'"? We have seen how the productionist notion that accumulation is a *primus agens* (Harvey 1982, 176) is surrounded by several levels of argument: general assertions about "Marx's method," the causal priority of production, the unique role of fixed capital in the struggle for surplus value appropriation, and so on. Avoiding this entire apparatus, Steindl maintains the centrality of the notion in a simpler way: he takes it as a starting point, ensured and effected not by production-level determinants but directly at the level of circulation, as an unmediated expression of the basic nature of capitalist firms. Capitalist firms inherently seek to expand, Steindl argues, an urge expressed in the way they save and reinvest out of gross profit income.

The framework's conception of science enters at this point to give this abstract principle particular shape. If both productionist and monopoly capital theorists set out to uncover capitalism's essential determinants, the two schools' conceptions of the method of inquiry appropriate to this task are quite different. We have seen that for productionists scientific method involves elaborating concepts through successive "levels" of analysis to show how the basic nature of capitalist production ultimately shapes economic crises and other phenomena. For monopoly capital theorists the process of conceptual elaboration is somewhat simpler. Science proceeds in two basic steps: construction of a *model* of society's essential logic, and deployment of that model (in conjunction with concepts of historically specific "exogenous" forces) to explain actual events (Steindl 1976, 132, 210; Baran and Sweezy 1966, 14). Baran and Sweezy express the point clearly and simply: "a good model . . . provides the key to understanding reality" (1966, 14).

Monopoly capital theorists present their case accordingly. We will consider Steindl's model of "long-run endogenous development" first, both because of its precedence and because it most visibly presents certain of the framework's most basic principles.

Steindl's is a non-monetary model which centers on firms' reinvestment of accrued profit income. Proceeding in two steps, he first represents firm savings as a determinate fraction of profit, then depicts investment spending as a stable fraction of resulting (past-period) firm savings, subject to the further influences of firm indebtedness rates and capacity utilization rates. Taken together these contentions constitute a thesis about capitalism's "internal" nature. Steindl's explanation

> starts from the conviction that in order to explain the historical phenomenon of growth of capital it is not necessary to have recourse to external influences, such as innovations, population growth, wars, etc. The growth of capital is, on the contrary, viewed as something inherent in the nature of capitalism, and to be explained by much simpler assumptions. The concrete hypothesis which explains growth is this: the mere fact that business concerns accumulate savings is sufficient to induce them (after a certain time) to invest. The internal accumulation, by itself, generates investment. (1976, 193)

Profit thus pushes later-period investment. But for Steindl profit in turn is the product of demand, and particularly spending by capitalists. Indeed, it is above all investment (along with the more passively determined capitalist consumption) which creates profit. On this principle, the basic linkages structuring accumulation are all enclosed inside a self-determining and self-reproducing "endogenous" space. "If there has been growth in the past sufficient to enable entrepreneurs to accumulate funds internally," Steindl concludes, "then this will in itself produce a further growth. The growth of capital is in this sense self-perpetuating" (1976, 193).

This "endogenous" self-determination clearly appealed to Steindl for more than purely theoretical reasons. From one angle, *Maturity and Stagnation* can be viewed as a focused and systematic effort to link the devastation of the 1930s Depression to capitalism— not to this or that conjunctural development enabled by capitalism (such as a possible decline in the pace of technological innovation), but to *inner necessities* of capitalist growth.

Shaping the effort is an observation: Kuznets' initial national income estimates had recently revealed that the growth rate of the U.S. capital stock peaked toward the end of the 19th century and fell progressively thereafter (Steindl 1976, 156, 160; cf. Abramowitz and David 1973). For Steindl, this decline in "the most important variable in long run economic development"(156–57) had enormous significance. He set out to build a model which could, first, explain it as "a necessary consequence of the development of certain essential features of capitalism" (1976, 191) and, second, link both the decline and its causes to the Depression itself.

Whatever the mix of political and theoretical forces at work, once taken seriously, the idea that capitalist growth is structured by inner forces of a sort representable by an abstract model has consequences. Clearly all the sites immediately "determining" the rate of accumulation—profit rates in relation to capital stock operation rates, firm savings rates, profit reinvestment rates, and so on—must be thought to take their quantitative determination primarily from one another. Otherwise the parametric and functional stability implied by a model thought to represent long-run forces makes no sense.

All social processes not directly represented in the model are then necessarily exogenous or secondary factors. While these may modify the historical expression of the logic represented by the endogenous model, thereby in certain cases playing important historical roles, as Baran and Sweezy stress regarding issues such as waves of technical change or war (1966, ch. 8), they are irrelevant to that logic itself. The basic outlines of capitalist growth are established and fixed well prior to any consideration of social processes as a whole: they are an expression of the essential nature of units of capital.[12] This quality extends even to the quantitative course of actual economic events: in Steindl's variant of this perspective, accumulation is a sort of "'independent variable.'"[13] Once set at a given long-term pace, it tends to maintain that pace of its own accord. This at least is the argument he sees and approves of in *Capital* 1, as he elaborates in *Maturity and Stagnation*'s final chapter.

What then accounts for the slowdown identifiable in Kuznets' estimates of capital stock growth? Far from contradicting Steindl's "theory of endogenous long-run economic development" (1976, 226), this secular decline is said to be a fundamental part of it. For as Steindl argues it was endogenously produced by developments in a central dimension of the accumulation process not yet considered—market structure. The growth process eventually produced oligopoly (during the 1890s in major U.S. manufacturing industries), and that change accounts for the simultaneous downturn in capital stock rates Kuznets finds.

This argument is part of a more general conception in which, by transforming the size structure of firms, capitalist growth produces epochal changes in its own dynamic. The causal determinacy allotted to market structure in monopoly capital theory is nourished by this larger framework. Like the urge to reinvest profit, changes in market structure are "endogenous" aspects of capitalist development. Produced by growth, they then redefine the structure of its inner determination.

Steindl concentrates on two epochs, a period of competitive capitalism he terms "absolute concentration," and the succeeding period of capitalist maturity.[14] In the first era, large and small firms coexist within each industry. Benefiting from economies of scale, the larger firms earn higher profits and consequently reinvest more rapidly. To enlarge their market they cut prices, driving higher-cost competitors out of existence. Hence this period's hallmarks: fierce price competition and rapid capital stock growth. This dynamic, however, eventually produces its logical result, the elimination of smaller, high-cost firms within major industries. Thus the period of absolute concentration gives way to its successor, capitalist maturity. At this point a new problem arises. Large firms are no longer so readily able to create expanded markets for the capital stock expansion they seek. According to Steindl, price competition no longer suffices to solve this problem, since their competitors are now themselves large in size and therefore not easily driven under. Hence, Steindl argues, price competition no longer occurs.[15]

The excess capacity argument in Steindl's endogenous investment function then assumes new prominence. Indeed, it now regulates the pace of the accumulation process as a whole. The issue is not simply that undesired capacity within an industry is no longer directly remediable by firm strategy. As Steindl suggests, the relationship is now perverse: facing undesired capacity, firms reduce investment spending (though not, in a key characteristic of Steindl's endogenous model, their rate of saving out of profits). By cutting spending, they raise the level of excess capacity in the economy as a whole. The endogenous growth process thus places its own product, oligopoly, in a critical role. The accumulation epoch dominated by oligopoly is marked by slowed capital stock growth and a structurally enforced tendency toward stagnation.

For purposes of historical interpretation the endogenous model must be supplemented by concepts of more conjunctural forces at work in any given period (Steindl 1976, 210). We might briefly review the way in which Baran and Sweezy flesh out the "crisis theory" analysis implicit in this framework in their enormously influential book, *Monopoly Capital* (1966).

Baran and Sweezy's macroeconomic analysis begins by describing a pattern of pricing and savings behavior said to result from the basic nature of contemporary giant firms. Put simply, prices no longer fall, but production costs do. The book's "law of rising surplus" stems from these forces, more precisely the widening profit rates they imply at given operating rates. A simple analysis of demand then completes their model of "the 'elementary logic' of the system" (1966, 108). There are only two "normal" forms of spending out of gross profit income, capitalist consumption—spending funded by dividends—and investment.[16] Normally these are insufficient to sustain cyclical booms. In a boom, profits accrue rapidly, fueled both by secularly rising profit margins and cyclically high operating rates. But capitalist consumption, they argue, does not keep pace, since "a deeply rooted aspect of corporate behavior" is the tendency to adjust dividend payments to changes in profits only with a lag (1966, 80–81). With capitalist consumption capped by the limited disbursal of dividends, investment spending is left to fill an ever larger demand gap. Eventually it is unable to soak up retained earnings, excess capacity levels rise, and stagnation begins.

The similarities to Steindl's framework should be apparent. In oligopolistic capitalism, production problems are solved; accumulation dynamics stem from enterprise behavior regarding savings and reinvestment of profit. Namely, at high levels of capacity utilization, monopolistic corporations tend to save more than they can find spending outlets for. Hence either further types of spending out of profit income must be found or firms are condemned to operate at capacity utilization rates low enough to prevent high levels of actual profit accrual, that is, a state of stagnation. Of course, as Baran and Sweezy continue, wasteful forms of profit spending, from advertising to financial speculation, do exist; the United States is pervaded by them. Further, "external" factors, from wars to "epochal" innovations such as the automobile, periodically stimulate demand sufficiently to offset the system's inner tendency.

Nevertheless accumulation's wasteful inner logic shapes the whole. *Monopoly Capital*'s powerful final chapters thus elaborate a general critique of every aspect of American life, from politics and marriage to sexual dysfunction and moral decay. If, as the quote from Hegel which prefaces the book indicates, "The truth is the whole," the whole which Baran and Sweezy theorize is a totality whose every aspect expresses its irrational essential core. There can therefore be, they argue, but one political goal, since "behind the emptiness, the degradation, and the suffering which poison human existence in this society lies the profound irrationality and moral bankruptcy of monopoly capitalism itself." Hence "the only true rationality lies in action to overthrow what has become a hopelessly irrational system" (1966, 363).[17]

"Production" theorists criticize monopoly capital theory in part on political grounds: it fails to show that capitalism necessarily encounters increasingly devastating crises as it develops, thereby failing to recognize that capitalism is now being ushered out by the limits which its social relations of production place on continued growth in the productive forces. What merits emphasis in the present context is, however, not this difference but a general similarity between the two approaches. Both tie general critiques of capitalism to developmental trajectories thought necessarily implied by Marxian theory's basic concepts of capitalism's "inner" nature. The theory of monopoly capitalism locates forces which destroy meaning, morality, and efficiency, rather than produce a necessary progression of deepening economic crises, so that its associated political perspective is somewhat different.[18] But it poses the same general requirements for its accumulation theory: accumulation must be shown to follow an abstractly determinate inner logic which then shapes other aspects of social life without being shaped by them in return. Thus the political critique which each framework offers presupposes what might be termed an essentialist theory of the workings of the capital accumulation process. Although the essential forces depicted by the two traditions differ, as do the conceptions of scientific method through which each links essence to concrete appearance, this should not obscure the more general theoretical strategy they share.

Until well into the 1970s these two schools dominated radical theories of accumulation and crisis; in the United States certainly they did so almost exclusively, with monopoly capital theory perhaps the more influential among academic social scientists. The field has become more variegated from the mid-1970s on, however. In what follows I am particularly concerned to explore the ways in which, and degrees to which, in breaking from these older traditions the newer theories which have emerged have also stepped somewhat outside of the theoretical strategy traced above, in which political critiques of capitalism are constructed by linking essential dynamics of the accumulation process to their eventual expression in irremediably destructive results.

VARIANTS OF THE MONOPOLY CAPITAL TRADITION AND EMERGING FRAMEWORKS

In the framework elaborated by Steindl and Baran and Sweezy, the "inner logic" of capitalism is sited not in production or an eternally fixed logic of capitalist class relations, but in what many have interpreted as a roomier and more historically variegated space, the accumulation process "considered as a whole." This may be the broadly defining characteristic of the position which Sweezy has advanced in debates with radical economists from Cogoy to Steedman: economic events, including crises, must be "envisaged as integral to an overall conception of the nature and function of the capitalist accumulation process" (Sweezy 1979; cf. Sweezy 1974). If I have concentrated on the "abstractly fixed inner logic" dimension of his views, the other side—the concern to theorize interrelated aspects of accumulation as a whole, from financial dynamics to international competition—should not be forgotten. Several important schools of thought have particularly developed this dimension of the larger tradition.[19]

One important direction has been pursued in the work of David Levine and colleagues. In the mid-1970s Levine was perhaps the foremost English-speaking exponent of Steindl's endogenous theory of capitalist growth (Levine 1975). He evolved quickly, however, in part by virtue of the seriousness with which he took what he understood to be the framework's most general principles.

Drawing from classical economics, classical social theory, Marx, and Hegel, Levine seeks to reconstruct economic theory as a whole on the principle that capitalism is an internally self-determining system structured by the principle of expansion (Levine 1977; 1978; 1981). He takes as a starting point the contention that the concept of wealth provides the basis for an understanding of capitalist development. Capital accumulation—the unceasing expansion of value implied by generalized commodity exchange—is then one implication of that concept, and indeed Levine holds tightly to the convention that units of capital are informed by an expansion-seeking nature which expresses itself in every aspect of their behavior. In that sense, Levine builds upon and activates the "accumulation for accumulation's sake" principle which, as stressed above, functions as a first principle in Steindl's framework perhaps more directly and palpably than in other Marxian traditions.[20]

But if the concept of wealth implies accumulation, Levine brings out another side which Steindl did not see—the evolving system of needs, or "needy individuals" who also (along with units of capital) shape and are shaped by the evolving system of commodity exchange as a whole. Moreover, Levine breaks from Steindl's framework in a second, equally fundamental way: citing Hegel, he adopts a rationalist approach to theory construction, one seen as the only alternative to empiricism's acceptance of the immediately given at face value. While abstract concepts bear determinate general implications, for Levine neither firms nor people are simple expressions of abstract principles; hence, firm behavior in particular is not structured by the sort of fixed quantitative relationships representable in an economic model. While wealth's inner determinations shape economic life, the way in which they do so can only be established through a process of theory elaboration, gradual construction of a "system in which the complex structure of relations discovers its own full determination" (1978, 22). Levine (1981) proceeds on that basis, fruitfully constructing pricing, product cycle, and investment phenomena in the context of the whole formed by interacting aspects of accumulation and its associated system of commodity circulation and need formation.

As a consequence, Levine's "economic science" no longer views stagnation as a dominant tendency of contemporary capitalism. Active agents of expansion (pursuing advertising, market research, product innovation, etc.), firms are not systematically left with unspent funds in their treasuries. Active agents in commodity circulation, consumers exhibit specific and evolving consumption patterns which may, depending on conditions investigated in Levine (1981), also stimulate commodity circulation and accumulation, even in oligopolistic conditions. In moving toward an ever more systematic elaboration of accumulation as a self-determining process structured by the principle of expansion, Levine has moved away from the kind of crisis analysis which Steindl linked to his version of such a theory.[21]

Donald Harris's analyses of Marxian, classical and Sraffian theory bring to bear basic suppositions which are in principle similar to Levine's, though perhaps in specifics remaining somewhat closer to Steindl's original vision. Harris calls for theory which fits "within the Marxian conception of the accumulation process as a whole" (1983, 312). He proposes the project of "conceiving the process of accumulation and development of capital as a total and unified process moving through qualitatively distinct phases as a result of its own inner logic" (1983, 328). He has recently promoted a tentative general conception of "uneven development," viewing monopoly capital theory (which "supposes that the structural conditions of capitalism are themselves subject to a process of ongoing development and change derived from the internal dynamics of the accumulation process itself") as an attempt to move in the same direction (1988, 160–61). Clearly he endorses the general principle that the accumulation process betrays a structuring logic which transforms itself over time, along with the more specific view that one must take "seriously the argument that there exist powerful stagnationist tendencies within capitalist economies" (1988, 158). Harris has used these principles to criticize the thesis of an automatically rising organic composition of capital (1983; Rowthorn and Harris 1985) and, more generally, to challenge those Marxian and Sraffian traditions which construe the rate of profit as determined by conditions in the realm of production alone (1988).

Keith Cowling brings to the tradition contemporary techniques and research findings from industrial organization. He promotes the "strong" version of monopoly capital theory, directly promoting its basic thesis that monopolization produces a dominant tendency to stagnation (Cowling 1982). This time, however, the focus is contemporary Britain, and the argument specifically concerns an increase of monopoly power rather than simply its existence. The British merger wave of the mid-1960s raised the degree of monopoly in major industries, he contends, thereby raising profit margins per unit sold and initiating forces which ultimately produced long term stagnation in the 1970s. Since the increased profits were not immediately translated into spending and other types of expenditures did not fill the gap, shortfalls of demand set in, raising excess capacity and launching the familiar oligopolistic cycle of investment decline.

In the process, Cowling brings considerable technical prowess to bear on questions which are pressing if the framework is to hold its own, from the demand-side effects of growing unproductive managerial expenses to the role of exports and government budget deficits.[22] As is evident from his specific arguments, he relies on a general supposition that giant oligopolistic firms are readily able to control their environment (from consumer taste formation to the progress of international trade) in every dimension except aggregate demand. Thus, while Cowling does not anchor his propositions on accumulation's "inner logic," the premise that giant firms can control aspects of their economic and social environment echoes Baran and Sweezy.

Meanwhile "structuralist" macroeconomists are putting ideas and method from the tradition to use in still other theoretical and historical contexts. Taylor (1985) and Dutt (1984; 1987a; 1987b) suggest that Latin America and India may be well approached through "stagnationist" categories: markup pricing enabled by oligopoly, excess capacity as an influence on investment spending, consumption behavior definable on the basis of income-based class categories, and so on. Like Steindl, they suggest that a rise in the markup of price over unit labor cost may lead to a rise in excess capacity rates and hence a fall in investment spending—depending, as Taylor in particular elaborates, on conditions in asset markets, fiscal and monetary policy, trade, "supply side" forces, and so on. Thus an improvement in the distribution of income may increase growth. Taylor and Dutt have pushed stagnationist theory in a new and macro-oriented direction, one at once more conditional and more conventional than the arguments of the tradition's founders.

There is, I think, something of a pattern in the concerns of contemporary authors influenced by the monopoly capital tradition. Interestingly, the view that contemporary capitalism has a stagnationist inner logic has provoked renewed interest in the forces which nevertheless nourish growth, particularly the dynamics of consumer spending. As noted, Levine eventually dropped the generalized stagnation thesis altogether, moving to a terrain in which the stimulating influence of new products meets on equal footing any possible demand-dampening effects of maturation. Similarly, although Nell (1987) retains the stagnationist framework as a whole, he supplements it with an extensive depiction of "transformations" in living conditions which have offset the tendency. As he suggests, paralleling Mandel (1978), new products such as the internal combustion engine can alter living and purchasing habits so extensively as to fuel prolonged booms during which old industries are replaced and old consumer habits destroyed. To some extent, analyses such as Nell's highlight an aspect of monopoly capital theory different from those I have emphasized—the concern to elaborate the rich array of historically changing forces, from international linkages to credit conditions, which may offset and counteract the stagnationist inner logic in particular periods.

POSTWAR PROFIT SQUEEZE AND RECENTLY EMERGING ACCUMULATION THEORIES

Many of the early works in what is here termed the profit squeeze analysis of advanced capitalist accumulation—Glyn and Sutcliffe (1972), Boddy and Crotty (1974; 1975), and Weisskopf (1979)—were pointedly empirical in presentation. The same is true of subsequent landmarks such as Bowles, Gordon and Weisskopf's *Beyond the Waste Land* (1983) and Armstrong, Glyn and Harrison's *Capitalism Since World War II* (1984). Theory is of course developed and applied in these works, but always as part of an argument about specificities of postwar growth developed using extensive data analysis. Conspicuously absent from these works are theoretical efforts like those noted above, in which analysis is derived from overt theses about capitalism's fundamental nature or the foremost features of the contemporary accumulation epoch.

The basic growth pattern in question is simple in outline: in the postwar period prolonged capitalist growth eventually engenders a fall in the average rate of profit. Glyn and Sutcliffe show that the profit share of British national income fell abruptly after 1964. In explanation, they point to an appealingly simple thesis. Pushed by strong trade unions, substantial money wage increases accompanied British growth from 1950 on. Wages began to seriously erode the share and rate of profit when international competition, worsening for British capitalists after the mid-1960s, prevented them from raising prices in response. The "crisis has developed," they conclude, "because mounting demands from the working class for a faster growth in living standards have coincided with growing competition between capitalist countries" (1972, 10, 58–59).

Boddy and Crotty's cyclical analysis was slightly different. Postwar business cycles follow a pattern in which unit labor costs rise more rapidly than output prices toward the end of each boom. They rise both because wages increase more rapidly and labor productivity tends to grow more slowly than in the early part of the boom, both for reasons related to the types of new investment put in place in this stage of the boom and because labor's improved bargaining position appears to allow a reduction in work intensity (1975, 8). When the reserve army of the unemployed falls, both wage pressures and productivity problems mount. Hence, contrary to Keynesian notions (and the theory of Steindl), prolonged growth is neither desirable for individual capitalists nor sustainable for the system as a whole. Whatever the case for prewar conditions, in the postwar period the thesis of Steindl and Baran and Sweezy that capitalists simply mark up labor costs to maintain their desired profit rate is wrong. The later part of business cycle expansions demonstrates their inability to keep pace with rising labor costs.

This was a powerful observation, the more so for its applicability to both the cyclical and secular dynamics of postwar growth. Placing class conflict in a clearly visible role regulating events explained in quite different terms in the newspapers, it had a direct political appeal. It seemed to imply a related, more general political critique as well: despite the illusions of economists and the deceptions of policymakers, contemporary capitalism is incapable of operating at full employment.

An empirical study solidified the position in 1979, when Weisskopf attempted to test the plausibility of three main variants of Marxian crisis theory. He differentiated the approaches in terms of which primary factor—rising organic composition of capital, demand shortfall, or the "rising strength of labor"—each expects to associate most clearly with declines in the rate of profit (both cyclical and postwar trend). Weisskopf formulated the profit rate of U.S. non-financial corporate business as the product of three variables: the share of profit in income (income minus wages and salaries), the capacity utilization rate, and the capacity/capital ratio. Roughly speaking, in the "rising strength of labor" theory, cyclical declines in profit rates should associate with declining profit shares; underconsumption theories stress falling capacity utilization rates, while rising organic composition theories emphasize declines in the capacity/capital ratio. Similar associations ought to be observable in the long term as well, over the entire postwar period.

Weisskopf found the reserve army approach to be superior: the profit share is closely associated with profit rate changes, declining along with the profit rate in the later part of every expansion, as well as over the trend. The other two variables did not perform well. Nor is the matter substantially different when the profit share variable is adjusted for its correlation with capacity utilization rates. Thus standardized, the profit share variable still "accounts for" the great bulk of the decline in the profit rate over time, and while in some individual cycles the other two variables also moved to dampen the rate of profit, on average the profit rate declines in the late expansion phases of postwar U.S. business cycles "appear mainly attributable to a corresponding rise in the strength of labor" (Weisskopf 1979, 364–65). As might be expected, Weisskopf's definitions and measurements drew substantive criticism from advocates of other frameworks;[23] nevertheless the study lent important support to the profit squeeze analysis.

But what was the analysis to be? While both Boddy and Crotty and Glyn and Sutcliffe linked their analyses closely to Marx's own, it became clear fairly quickly that profit squeeze theory was not going to develop within any existing radical tradition. For many contributors it was conflict which was of central interest, but this was not the sort of conflict envisioned in productionist theory—conflict embodied in determinate inner laws of motion and enforced by fixed necessities of technical change. Nor was Marxian value theory embraced, which ruled out incorporation within such relatively flexible value-theoretic analyses as Dobb's (1972). Broadly speaking, this left the monopoly capital tradition as a possible framework within which profit squeeze analysis might develop. But while writers like Gordon and Edwards began with a loose affiliation with this theory, this also was to be short-lived.[24]

Given the stage-theoretic bent of several radical traditions, one general theoretical alternative was to construe the postwar period or some portion of it as a new epoch marked by new and different "laws of motion." Several influential authors presented such arguments. Relying heavily on Hegelian principles, Lebowitz (1976) constructs accumulation as a process shaped by an urge to grow, on one hand, confronting various barriers to growth, on the other. Responding to each dominant barrier, capital's expansion process changes over time in a characteristically Hegelian way: the solution to one contradiction forms a new contradiction in the following period. Wright (1978, 112, 166–70) deploys a similar principle of epochal succession with generally similar results, though his framework differs from Lebowitz's in particulars. For Wright, "systemic solutions to the dominant impediments at a given stage of capitalist development generate the new impediments which constrain the accumulation process in the subsequent stage," a thesis he ultimately traces to the contention that "inherent class antagonisms of capitalism" underlie capitalist historical processes (1978, 112, 166 fn., 167–70 fn.).[25] Wright presents the cost pressures on profits stressed in profit squeeze theory as in part the product of past state efforts to overcome stagnation; these have increased both the state's unproductive claims on surplus value and the political and economic power of the working class.

O'Connor (1984) has contributed to such a stage analysis from a substantially different angle. He charges dominant traditions in crisis theory with economic determinist reasoning and, more specifically, failure to understand the constitutive role of "dominant ideologies"—for the U.S., a cultural formation O'Connor terms "individualism"—in shaping economic and social crisis tendencies. Affirming a fundamentally historical, as opposed to deductionist, approch to crisis theory, O'Connor distinguishes prewar and postwar patterns of articulation between the accumulation process and a U.S. working class and "salariat" whose self-organizing capacities and outlooks were shaped by individualism (1984, 55–58).[26] Whereas before the Depression working class resistance stimulated accumulation by hastening its reorganization, the more recent success of the now stronger and larger proletariat and "salariat" in pursuing special interest goals, as well as the state's reactions to prior crises, have progressively cut into the rate of surplus value and produced the "accumulation crisis" of the book's title.

While O'Connor opposes the abstract determinism of traditional Marxian crisis theories (see especially O'Connor 1987), a notable effect of his approach is to move the postwar "crisis" away from the conjunctural framework in which Glyn, Sutcliffe, and others had placed it, and into a position in which, much as for Lebowitz and Wright, it appears as a logical, (almost-)necessary outcome of long historical processes. For O'Connor, crisis is not simply the effect of prolonged growth which exhausted the reserve army, though that was important. It stems more generally from basic tendencies of the "full capitalism" established once concentration occurred, industrial unionism took hold, and the state reacted to the Depression by broadening social welfare programs—all in the context of an individualist culture (cf. 1984, 68–74, 106). At that point, he argues, "the working class/salariat became a seemingly insurmountable barrier to capitalist accumulation" (1984, 106). And at that point both traditional forms of capitalist crisis and the economic-determinist traditions of Marxian crisis theory lost their force. Thus, while undermining traditional stage theories of accumulation, O'Connor's insertion of cultural processes into crisis theory seems to substitute another kind of "logic" to capitalist development, a seemingly inevitable chain of events in which the very nature of accumulation eventually undermines its own necessary conditions for success (cf. Lebowitz 1976, 249–50).

While equally eager to distinguish and theorize long periods of capitalist growth, profit squeeze theorists in the U.S. and U.K. economics profession took the analysis in a substantially different direction.[27] The period of reduced profitability and high unemployment beginning around 1970 was not to be conceived as the denouement of an inevitably unfolding linear plot. It represented instead a long-wave downturn, one of a series of generation-spanning periods of turmoil which have wracked capitalist economies since the mid-nineteenth century.

In itself, of course, a long-wave analysis need not substantially transform traditional accumulation theory. Indeed, Mandel (1978; 1980) and Shaikh had already both conceived long-wave downturns as the form in which the falling rate of profit logic inherent in accumulation finds periodic expression. While Mandel added a richly multidimensional conception of the modalities of long-period capitalist *growth*, his analysis remains a flexible and multi-causal substantiation of precisely traditional general theses. However normal to capitalist functioning, long-wave upturns cannot continue forever, for eventually "the inner logic of capitalism (i.e., the laws of motion of the system)" must lower profitability and turn the long-wave upturn into contraction. If changing historical conditions were to render such "laws" indeterminate, "one rejects out of hand Marx's entire economic analysis" (1980, 29).

But the long-wave analysis elaborated by authors such as Gordon in the U.S. (and, somewhat differently, by Glyn, Sutcliffe, and others in the U.K.)[28] jettisoned the productionist stress on the "inner logic" of capitalism. The new direction began to materialize in Gordon (1978; 1980) and Gordon, Edwards, and Reich (1982), which set out an initial statement of what is now known as "social structures of accumulation" (SSA) theory. The latter work overtly breaks from prior traditions on a fundamental matter of general theory. Long waves of economic activity, Gordon et al. argue, are not results of a dynamic "internal" to accumulation per se. Accumulation does not produce and reproduce its own dynamic through the necessities of a regulating inner logic. Rather it "is mediated fundamentally by social (or institutional) forces . . . factors external to individual capitalists that are determined by collective social activities" (1982, 26, cf. 23). To understand long swings one must thus turn to the interacting set of institutions which form the environment, or SSA, within which capitalist growth takes place.

The immediate issue is profitability. For SSA theorists, like production theorists, accumulation itself—more generally, the allocation of gross profit income—is not the direct focus of the theory. Investment is thought to occur naturally in response to profitability conditions (and capacity utilization), and it is then primarily changes in the profit rate (and utilization) which must be understood (cf. Bowles, Gordon, and Weisskopf 1989).

In terms of basic principle, SSA theory is at this point again relatively "open." Profitability is shaped by conditions in each of the circuits constituting accumulation: purchase of inputs, production, and sale of outputs. Priority is not given to one or another sphere on general principle (as in productionist theory) or because one sphere is thought to function smoothly and automatically (as in extreme versions of the monopoly capital framework). The state, credit and financial processes, institutions shaping labor-capital relations, and so on, may all be fundamentally important to long-term growth patterns, as is, in principle, any aspect of social life impinging on any of the circuits constituting accumulation (Gordon et al. 1982, 25)

The "circuits of capital analysis" which informs these theorists' understanding of accumulation is certainly not new to Marxian-influenced frameworks, but as a first principle it has come to new prominence in recent years.[29] Non-SSA theorists such as Foley (1986) have also contributed fruitfully to a somewhat different version of a "circuits of capital framework." In effect removing both "production" and the firm's reinvestment urge as the theoretical starting point, it tends to rule out assigning casual priority in advance to any of the spheres through which capital passes.

However, the SSA framework's architects sought not openness but closure in a further set of propositions which, in effect, extend the profit-squeeze theorists' linkage between rapid growth and rising cost to the realm of general social theory. Rapid growth occurs when a set of institutions coheres so as to promote profitable capital accumulation. Eventually though, such growth is itself "likely to set off forces that undermine the institutional basis of the expansion. . . . at some point barriers to accumulation begin to appear" (Gordon et al. 1982, 28–29). A period of slow growth ensues, during which political conflict—particularly conflict over class interest—grows. Out of this conflict, but only after prolonged experimentation and political jockeying, come new institutions capable of nourishing a long swing upturn, a new SSA, and the long-wave cycle begins anew.

If one seeks to avoid the abstract determinacy of the productionist and monopoly capital traditions, then the general SSA approach has certain advantages. But even granting these comparative advantages, a further question arises: what is radical about this school of radical economics? Eschewing the general critiques of capitalism inherent in productionist and monopoly capital theory, this school also eschews class concepts and thus the critique of "equal exchange" conceptions of labor market processes such concepts enable. As developed so far, one is left with a long swing view of capitalist dynamics. One might conclude simply that the framework links an appreciation of social structure to a Keynesian sort of instability hypothesis, thereby producing an interesting but not necessarily radical approach to economic theory.

The variant of SSA theory developed in a recent series of works by Bowles, Gordon, and Weisskopf in effect offers one answer to this question. Here a theme which animated the approach from its inception—the concern to theorize *conflict* —is rigorously placed at the heart of the analysis. In the process, however, as I shall argue, these SSA theorists repeat the thrust of productionist and monopoly capital theories by founding their political critique on an essentialist conception of the accumulation process.

Capitalism is not only unstable, say Bowles et al., it is unjust. The accumulation process rests upon and functions through a coercive system of power relations. While it is a nominally diverse set of institutions which constitutes an SSA, as

Bowles et al. argue, there is ultimately but a single channel through which these varied institutions impact on the rate of profit and accumulation: their ability to modulate the level of power domestic capitalists wield over other actors in economic life. To show this, the authors first elaborate a "representation of profits as the money measure of the power of capital," a formulation seen as applicable to any capitalist economy (Bowles et al. 1986, 137). Domestic capitalists are said to confront three other kinds of agents: workers who produce goods, "citizens" who elect officials and press for legislative acts, and foreign capitalists with whom they exchange goods. Capitalist reap profit when their transactions with each of these actors are on favorable terms: when workers work intensely for low real wages, when exchange with foreign capitalists yields favorable terms of trade, or when taxes on profits are low and government regulations on business behavior limited.

For Bowles et al., it is capitalist power which effects favorable conditions on all these fronts. And it is a stable and functional set of social institutitions, a viable SSA, which in turn buttresses and reinforces capitalist power. Moreover, this can be shown econometrically, or at least the argument can be so elaborated, once the basic features constituting a particular SSA have been theorized. From the general power-theoretic analysis of profits one can deduce certain observable variables which measure the state of capitalist power vis-à-vis other actors. If one can then link the existence of an SSA, its specific institutions conducive to profitability, to favorable values taken by these variables in particular years, values signifying a high degree of capitalist power, then one has translated qualitative social structural analysis directly into quantitative terms. What remains is to statistically link changes in the rate of profit over time to changes in the variables representing capitalist "power," and this the authors do through regression analysis. In short, in this framework accumulation is rapid in certain decades because key variables took values favorable to the rate of profit, and these variables behaved as they did because the institutional environment molding accumulation supported and reinforced that outcome by sustaining capitalist power. A "unified theory of the social determination of profits and accumulation" is forged.

The analytical results provide a generalization of Glyn and Sutcliffe's original vision of the contours of postwar dynamics. Between 1966 and 1973, rapid and prolonged accumulation and associated social changes began to undermine the bases of profitability in the U.S. In particular, one key measure of capitalist power took a decided turn for the worse: the "cost of job loss," a measure of the yearly loss of income suffered by a representative worker upon job termination, fell substantially, in response to both rising availability of income substitutes such as unemployment compensation and lower average duration of unemployment. Workers reacted, the authors suggest, by laboring less intensively and demanding higher wages. On other fronts capitalists suffered likewise, as citizens sought and won increased levels of regulatory legislation while foreign capitalists won more favorable terms of trade. The postwar American SSA crumbled under the pressure of prolonged growth and prosperity. And behind the diversity of particular contributing factors lies one moral: too much growth undermined capitalist power.[30]

Bowles et al. link this SSA/power analysis of accumulation to a generalized theory of long waves, thereby continuing the line of thought in Gordon (1978) and Gordon et al. (1982). Capitalist economies are capable of prolonged periods of rapid growth when institutional conditions are favorable, but eventually growth will undermines itself (cf. Crotty 1986, 314–15). For Bowles et al., this may happen in either of two different general ways: crisis may occur either because the capitalist class is "too strong" or because it is "too weak" (Weisskopf et al. 1985, 259). Thus in the 1930s excessive capitalist power may have undermined the conditions for demand-side stability, as monopoly capital theorists suggest. After World War II though, social conditions changed and the problem potentially jeopardizing accumulation was an insufficiency of capitalist power (Weisskopf et al. 1985, 259). In any case, sooner or later the shifting modalities of power cause accumulation to undermine itself and precipitate secular crisis, or long-wave decline.[31]

In light of the other radical accumulation theories considered above, it is striking that SSA theory seems also to rely upon the general kind of causal reasoning informing both productionist and monopoly capital theories.[32] In that reasoning, *every* capitalist crisis *expresses* a given and fixed underlying contradiction rooted in the very essence of capitalism, the social relations thought to define it. For Bowles, Gordon, and Weisskopf, as for the others, to understand capitalist crisis is to explain it as an expression of an underlying essential root, a general problem built into and coterminous with capitalism itself. The whole (accumulation) is structured so as to necessarily express its essential core, the contradiction which ultimately produces recurrent crisis as each tradition defines it.

We saw earlier that for productionist and monopoly capital theorists their particular conception of science helped enforce and define this reasoning. Productionists proceed through levels of abstraction, tracing out the expression of a general and abstract logic in the more concrete analyses which successively approach conceptions of the actual world. Monopoly capital theorists, on the other hand, construct their logic in the form of an abstractly determinate model of the system's inner logic. In like manner, Bowles et al. act within a conception of science which, while partly implicit, visibly animates their entire recent project. Radical economics must translate its analyses into quantitatively "precise" form, a form which, as it turns out, involves well-specified models built from simple behavioral postulates of the sort representable in and estimatable through standard econometrics.

The conflict approach to accumulation and this implicit epistemology intertwine with and sustain one another. For if it is the exertion of power in situations structured by conflict which produces profits, it is also the contest over conflicting, abstractly defined intentions which provides the simple behavioral hypotheses amenable to representation in the form of models.[33] Simultaneously, the reassuring notion that precise quantitative techniques underpin the analysis supports the authors' attempt to establish power as the crucial underpinning of capitalism.

Potentially lost in this, I suggest, is the framework's ability to fully recognize those diverse forces shaping capitalist economies which are not readily conceived in terms of transactions involving conflict between agents with well defined interests. Commodity circulation processes are not so amenable, and are not developed. But what sort of theory of capitalist dynamics fails to puzzle over the ways in which the struggle to speed up commodity realization has reshaped corporate structures, geographical patterns, and social life as a whole?[34] Or consider cultural processes: do they not shape behaviors in production and consumption, and thus help to determine the aggregate rate of profit? Such a possibility is ruled out by the effort to construe profit as the product of power; if agents' behaviors are shaped by cultural processes rather than "interests" specified by economic theory, outcomes are not construable as products of one agent's superior ability to work its will. Again, patterns of technological change (whether Fordist mass production or Mandel's transformations in motive power) may inform and shape periods of capitalist development in ways not necessarily closely tied to capitalists' intentions. They have a "power" just as cultural processes have a power—the power to help shape and reconstitute social life.[35] But that is not the sort of power theorized in this framework, for it is not representable in terms of inter-agent conflict.

The loose but influential new tradition known as "regulation theory" offers an instructive contrast. Paralleling SSA theory both in concern to transcend unilinear conceptions of capitalist epochal growth and in emphasis on the constitutive role of the social environment within which accumulation takes place (here termed the "mode of regulation"), regulation theorists diverge somewhat by conceiving accumulation dynamics not first of all in terms of power but rather as a "regime of accumulation" defined as a system of interactions between producer and consumer goods industries. For example, a hypothesis fundamental in the emergence of this framework (Aglietta 1979) is that the Depression in the U.S. was precipitated by a mismatch between its regulation mode (a social environment prohibiting industrial unionization and growth in state social spending, thus failing to support rapid growth in semi-skilled workers' consumption spending) and an accumulation dynamic now dependent on expansion in consumption goods industries rather than, as in the late nineteenth century, expansion of plant, equipment, and railroads. After World War II, on the other hand, "Fordism" flourished: rapid productivity growth in mass-production consumer goods industries was now matched by equal growth in wages, allowing balanced expansion in consumer and producer goods industries. Analyzing postwar capitalism within this framework, authors such as Aglietta and Lipietz (1986; 1987) place more stress on breakthroughs in mass production technology than does the "over-accumulation" logic in works such as Bowles et al. (1983) and Armstrong et al. (1984).[36] At the same time, in regulation theory as in Levine (1981) and Levine-influenced works like Bernstein (1987) and Matthaei (1982), specific and historically evolving patterns of *consumption* behavior come to equal prominence as fundamental starting points for analyses of capital accumulation, an approach which also points accumulation theory decisively away from any narrowly reductionist focus.

A further effect of SSA theory's formalized power approach to capitalist dynamics, related to the relative lack of concern about commodity circulation processes noted above, is in my view ironic in the context of radical theory. Conceiving profitability as the product of capitalist/worker power dynamics, the framework seems to repress theorization of the great growth of jobs which involve neither directly producing commodities nor directly supervising those who do. In other words, like productionist theory, the SSA approach fails to pursue the non-accumulation expenditures out of surplus value made at step (1′) in the circuits of capital diagram, presuming simply that investment spending follows profit rates. This absence may well obscure rather than contribute to a class understanding of the contemporary United States.

CONCLUSIONS

An initial conclusion is readily drawn from the analyses above. Fragmentation will continue to mark radical theories of accumulation and crisis, since presumably all of the frameworks traced above will persist and grow. We have seen that the arguments tend to be resilient; they appeal to their proponents on various grounds, and in general can readily withstand the criticisms of others. Each finds textual support in particular works of Marx (or Kalecki and Steindl, or still others). Each presents a particular understanding of the nature of scientific inquiry, and uses that both to develop its own theses and criticize those of others. Political conceptions also shape as well as respond to theoretical preferences, so proponents of each analysis generally find their standpoints more palatable in political implication. In many cases, moreover, attachments between particular writers and general frameworks are further cemented by facility with the theoretical techniques appropriate for that particular approach, some tending to make macroeconomic growth models important, others Marxian value theory, or aggregate data analysis, or mathematical modelling in general, and so on.

In any case, these considerations suggest a need to confront and reconsider a defining characteristic of what many radical economists have understood as the project of accumulation and crisis theory: the widely shared premise that an adequate theory must explain crises as expressions of a given inner logic of accumulation, and hence of capitalism itself. We have seen how several traditions explicitly present this as a political necessity, a requirement for the argument to be specifically radical rather than reformist. In others it is simply assumed that radical theory traces essences to their expressions in economic phenomena, just as, for example, neoclassical economics does. That, indeed, is presented as a criterion of rigor.

This project imposes several requirements and constraints on radical economic theory, most obviously the assumption that the world works in a particular way. On the one hand, capitalism must have an essential core of an abstractly determinate sort, adequate to structure "the accumulation process" in an epochally fixed way. On the other hand, the important phenomena of economic life, the growth rates of various macroeconomic variables (productivity, profit rates, fixed capital investment, etc.) must be regarded as responding to and expressing that core. The first reason to reevaluate these assumptions may then be simply the plausible suspicion that the world does not work in this fashion.[37]

It is also possible that reconsideration of this aspect of accumulation theory might constructively interact with, and indeed facilitate, other desirable reformulations. Certainly radical accumulation theories need to theorize in more satisfactory terms race and gender processes and oppressions in relation to accumulation, and not by conceiving them as expressions of an inner logic rooted elsewhere. Perhaps various fundamental concerns recently raised about basic conceptual building blocks of accumulation theory—its failure to incorporate fully constitutive processes of spatial definition (Soja 1989), of finance (Crotty 1985; Roche 1985), or of culture (O'Connor 1984; 1987), and its tendency toward functionalist forms of explanation (Lipietz 1987)—might be more readily responded to if the totalizing vision within which accumulation theories are developed were subject to explicit consideration and criticism. As Soja emphasizes, to incorporate spatial dimensions adequately into Marxian accumulation theory would be to thoroughly transform that theory's very basis. As O'Connor has underlined, the same is true of culture.

And whether or not one turns away from efforts to trace capitalist crises to capitalism's "inner logic," the task of clarifying evolving class processes—and, using the rich diversity of insights reviewed above, linking this evolution to accumulation and crisis—looms larger than ever. For if not an inner logic, class processes remain hidden. They are obscure, not as an essence beneath the surface of appearance, but as processes which, ignored or unrecognized in dominant forms of discourse, remain lodged in minority analyses, even there only haltingly conceived.

NOTES

1. While most of Grossman's work is not readily available in English, several accounts provide a general outline (see Sweezy 1942; Jacoby 1975; Rosdolsky 1977; Itoh 1980; Mattick 1981; Howard and King 1988).

2. Grossman sought to rebut both reformism and the underconsumptionist and

disproportionality crisis theories prominent before his time. See Jacoby (1975) on the political dimensions of Grossman's work.

3. I use this expression for illustrative purposes; a more precise formulation would incorporate turnover times and varying compositions of capital among industries, and would elaborate the stock/flow distinction relevant to fixed capital. Among other sources, see Shaikh (1987a; 1987b), Harvey (1982), Harris (1983), and Resnick and Wolff (1987).

4. See, e.g., Alberro and Persky (1978), Roemer (1979; 1981), van Parijs (1980), and Bowles (1981), as well as Okishio (1977). Howard and King (1985, ch. 12) regard the theorem as a refutation of Marx's thinking, but the predominant view seems to be that its limited application makes it of severely limited interest; see Roemer (1981, 132–33) and Foley (1986, 42–47). Lipietz (1986) offers a stronger critique of the Okishio argument.

5. With $L = (V+S)$, then $C/V = (C/L)(L/V) = (C/L)[(V+S)/V] = (C/L)[1+(S/V)]$. Since the second term should rise over time, a secularly rising C/L should also raise C/V. See Shaikh (1987a; 1987b).

6. Presumably, none of these arguments satisfied Shaikh's critics; for the pointed debate provoked by Shaikh's thesis, see Roemer (1979) and the various comments published in connection with Shaikh (1980); see also Fine (1982, ch. 8), Cullenberg (1988).

7. Yaffe, in fact, *defines* accumulation in a way which lumps valorization, or expansion of value in capitalist production, together with accumulation itself, or reinvestment of surplus value in productive capital (1973a, 188).

8. Yaffe carries this to its logical conclusion, arguing, for example, that a cheapening of constant capital would raise the rate of profit, thus accelerating accumulation and the pressure for a rising organic composition (1973a, 198). In this light, anything which raises the rate of profit serves only to lower it shortly thereafter, a thesis exemplifying the closure to accumulation which the productionist logic tends to produce.

9. See Jacoby (1975). Shaikh rebuts suggestions that conceptions of necessary "laws of motion" might lead to political fatalism: " it is precisely *from* Marx's theoretical framework that revolutionary politics flow" (1978b, 236). Cf. Weeks (1981, 10).

10. Weeks writes: "the accumulation process is essentially a production process carried out under specific relations of production" (1981, 156).

11. Harvey sets out to uncover the essence from the world of appearances, "the fount of all forms of capitalist crisis" (1982, 176), and finds it grounded in the ultimately determinative world of production, specifically the contradiction between the forces and relations of production. In Harvey's analysis capitalism has an innate propensity toward "overaccumulation," and crisis phenomena of all sorts "are surface forms of appearance of overaccumulation " (1982, 192–96).

12. Sweezy writes that "the internal logic of the accumulation process . . . cannot but be abstract in the sense of focusing on a small number of variables" (1979). What is at stake here, though, is the additional assumption, on which the theory of monopoly capitalism hinges, that such "abstract" relationships can be thought quantitatively fixed in tendency prior to consideration at a "less abstract" level.

13. Marx uses the expression "independent variable" and other constantly quoted phrases (e.g., "accumulation for accumulation's sake" and "Accumulate, accumulate! that is Moses and the Prophets!")(1976, 742, 770). Norton (1983) argues that these expressions do not adequately represent the kind of reasoning Marx elaborates in the passages and arguments in which they occur.

14. An earlier stage is also suggested, though very sketchily (Steindl 1976, 134–37).

Levine (1975) elaborated more fully a conception of this stage and stressed that, as in later capitalist development, the stage itself produces the transition to the next stage of capitalist development.

15. This conclusion represents a key linkage. For Steindl, price competition has a single, unique cause: it occurs only during the process of absolute concentration, as leading firms squeeze out smaller high-cost firms, and "the cause of both is the competitive pressure of the internal accumulation of funds" (1976, 51–52).

16. This presentation of consumption out of dividends and investment as the exclusive "normal" spending outlets perhaps loosely corresponds to the view that capitalism's essence is accumulation, but it leaves certain questions unresolved. Why, for example, is spending funded by interest payments from profit income not considered an equally "normal" part of the system? For a contrasting approach, see Resnick and Wolff (1987).

17. Baran and Sweezy's critique involves several linkages which are difficult to accept outside the critical theory framework which appears to sustain them. Thus workers' consumption plus "normal" spending out of surplus are thought qualitatively different from other expenditures out of surplus: the former are "rational" and the latter are "irrational" and wasteful. Accumulation per se is, in effect, endowed with superior claims to rationality by this logic (Wolff's (1987) study of unproductive activity makes a similar conceptual linkage.) Their extension of concepts of "waste" and "irrationality" to U.S. culture as a whole appears related to themes advanced by critical theorists such as Horkheimer (see Arato's introduction to Arato and Gebhardt 1982).

18. The most immediate political question in *Monopoly Capital*'s perspective is who it is who will seek to change the system. Here the implications of the entire approach must be reckoned with. If every aspect of the society is undermined by monopoly capitalism's essential contradiction, who is going to resist, and why? Baran and Sweezy point to the system's "special victims," groups such as the unemployed and unemployable, migrant farm workers, the elderly poor, and the residents of urban ghettos. But these are precisely society's most scattered people, and the "oligarchy," in any case, "knows how, through doles and handouts, to keep them divided" (1966, 363–64). Indeed, if the analysis is pushed to the extreme, we are left without a site within the society capable of nurturing a positive political movement. All that is left for political guidance are Third World rebellions (1966, 365–67) or diverse social movements against waste and irrationality.

19. Other authors continue to work largely within the original theoretical framework. Foster (1986), for example, remains closely in the Baran and Sweezy tradition.

20. See also Levine (1988; 1989). For criticism of the framework, see Norton (1986).

21. Recent works influenced by Levine's evolving framework include Matthaei (1982), Heim (1986), and especially Bernstein (1987), who approaches the Depression as a period shaped by secular changes in accumulation which had created new consumption and demand patterns requiring a shift in the composition of output.

22. Cowling also borrows from Kalecki, seeming to integrate conceptions of class struggle over distribution more readily associated with the "wage squeeze" tradition of crisis theory into "a world where monopoly or oligopoly capitalism dominates" (Cowling 1982).

23. Among the critical responses were some stressing realization difficulties (Hahnel and Sherman 1982; Sherman 1986) and some the distinction between productive and unproductive labor (Moseley 1985; 1987). Indeed, Moseley argues that, by ignoring this distinction, Weisskopf fails to adequately measure either the rate of surplus value (which Moseley's figures indicate rises over the period, once payments to unproductive workers are

deleted from variable capital) or the value composition of capital (which similarly rises).

24. In a cyclical, though presumably not secular, context, it is possible to theorize a profit squeeze mechanism in a monopoly capital type model; see Taylor (1985), Sherman (1987), and Harris (1978, 273–76).

25. Wright's recent endorsement of "analytical Marxism," based in part on its "commitment to *conventional scientific norms* in the elaboration of theory and the conduct of research" (1989, 38), is perhaps understandable in the context of this earlier direction.

26. In my view, O'Connor's particular construction of individualism as a dominant ideology in the U.S. suffers from its reliance on critical theory; he juxtaposes the reified roles of modern life, in which there can be no satisfactory "self," to the prospect of an emancipatory "cooperative world based on mastering the relationships between human beings and history and nature" (1984, 23). Nevertheless, associated with these humanist aspects are his powerful critiques of economic determinism and "capital-as-subject-of-history" accumulation theories.

27. Several other theorists have placed profit squeeze dynamics firmly within more traditional conceptions of Marxian theory. Itoh (1980) brings to bear concepts from Japan's Uno school in maintaining that crises are the inevitable and "logical" result of basic principles of capitalist economies. Dumenil, Glick, and Rangel (1984–85; 1987) link episodes of rapid wage growth to pressures for technical change in a new interpretation of Marx's tendency for the rate of profit to fall.

28. Armstrong, Glyn and Harrison (1984) and Green and Sutcliffe (1987) stress the high rate of accumulation as the most fundamental factor behind the decline in profitability after 1968–1973. (1984, 257).

29. See, in particular, Armstrong et al. (1984), Green and Sutcliffe (1987), and Crotty (1986).

30. After 1973, government demand-management policy reinforced this dynamic. With costs rising due to the overheating of the prior six years, the govenment reacted with a "cold bath" approach, regulating the system so that high levels of unemployment reinforced capitalist power.

31. Although eventually political developments may presumably enable consolidation of a new SSA, the authors' recent investigation of data from the 1980s suggests that this has not yet happened. So far their measures of "structural" power reveal no new alignment of the forces precipitating the decline after 1966. See Bowles et al. (1989).

32. Norton (1988b) analyzes the framework in some detail, questioning particularly a concept of power which entails as a necessary condition the definition of behaviorally structuring "interests" imputed to economic agents on the basis of abstractly depicted economic roles. A related theme builds on Amariglio (1987) in questioning the singular conception of "science" which, as argued, informs the authors' struggle to translate radical theses into the sorts of equational expressions accepted as economic discourse under the neoclassical standards which now define that discourse.

33. Thus domestic capitalists seek high levels of work effort and low real wages; workers seek to work less for more. Domestic capitalist seek to sell at high export prices relative to import prices; foreign capitalists seek the reverse. Capitalists seek less government intervention in economic affairs; citizens seek more. Incentives and behaviors are thought determined by economic roles, apart from cultural processes. Hence they can be readily captured in model form.

34. These forces are stressed in Harvey's reading of Marx (Harvey 1982, chs. 3, 5),

which in this respect nicely complements the historical analysis of Chandler (1977).

35. Willoughby (1989) suggests that a "power" of another sort has undergirded the entire postwar era so as to prevent any real capitalist crisis: the stability of international agreements enforcing liberal trade and capital flows.

36. Indeed, Lipietz disputes the view that real wage growth accelerated in the early 1970s (except for Germany and Japan). "The few cases in which purchasing power did rise faster than productivity," he concludes, "can be better explained in terms of a slowdown of productivity growth" (1987, 42; cf. Lipietz 1986, 19–22) which is itself linked to "the limitations of Taylorist and Fordist work-organization principles" (1987, 43–44). Aglietta's (1979) analysis agrees with this general explanation of the "crisis of Fordism," stressing in addition the role of rising "indirect wages" and "unproductive" expenditures for services provided by the state. For a summary of his analysis of the causes of recent crisis, see Aglietta (1979, 162–69)

37. For examples of relatively developed theoretical elaborations of such a position within Marxian theory, see Resnick and Wolff (1987) and Wolff and Resnick (1987).

REFERENCES

Abramowitz, M., and David, P. 1973. "Reinterpreting American Economic Growth." *American Economic Review* 63 (2).

Aglietta, M. 1979. A Theory *of Capitalist Regulation: The U.S. Exprerience*. Trans. D. Fernbach. London: New Left Books.

Alberro, J., and Persky, J. 1978. "The Simple Analytics of Falling Profit Rates, Oskshio's Theorem and Fixed Capital." *Review of Radical Political Economics* 10: 37–41.

Alcaly, R. 1978. "An Introduction to Marxian Crisis Theory." In *U.S. Capitalism in Crisis*, ed. Crisis Reader Editorial Committee, 15–22. New York: URPE.

Amariglio, J. 1987. "Marxism Against Economic Science: Althusser's Legacy." In *Research in Political Economy* 10, ed. P. Zarembka. Greenwich, CT: JAI Press.

Arato, A., and Gebhard, E. 1982. *The Essential Frankfurt School Reader*. New York: Continuum Publishing Co.

Armstrong, P.; Glyn, A.; and Harrison, J. 1984. *Capitalism Since World War II: The Making and Breakup of the Great Boom*. London: Fontana Paperbacks.

Baran, P. A., and Sweezy, P. M. 1966. *Monopoly Capital: An Essay on the American Economic and Social Order*. New York: Monthly Review Press.

Bernstein, M. A. 1987. *The Great Depression: Delayed Recovery and Economic Change in America, 1929–1939*. New York: Cambridge University Press.

Boddy R., and Crotty, J. 1974. "Class Conflict, Keynesian Policies, and the Business Cycle." *Monthly Review* (October): 1–17.

———. 1975. "Class Conflict and Macro Policy: The Political Business Cycle." *Review of Radical Political Economics* 7 (1).

Bowles, S. 1981. "Technical Change and the Rate of Profit: A Simple Proof of the Okishio Theorem." *Cambridge Journal of Economics* 5: 183–86.

Bowles, S.; Gordon, D. M.; and Weisskopf, T. 1983. *Beyond the Waste Land*. New York: Anchor Press/Doubleday.

——.1986. "Power and Profits: The Social Structure of Accumulation and the Profitability of the Postwar Economy." *Review of Radical Political Economics* 18 (1&2): 132–67.

——. 1989. "Business Ascendancy and Economic Impasse: A Structural Retrospective on Conservative Economics, 1979-87." *Journal of Economic Perspectives* 3: 107–34.

Chandler, A. 1977. *The Visible Hand*. Cambridge: Harvard University Press.

Cogoy, M. 1973. "The Fall of the Rate of Profit and the Theory of Accumulation: A Reply to Paul Sweezy." *Bulletin of the Conference of Socialist Economists* (Winter): 522–67.

Cowling, K. 1982. *Monopoly Capitalism*. New York: John Wiley and Sons.

Crotty, J. 1985. "The Centrality of Money, Credit and Financial Intermediation in Marx's Crisis Theory: An Interpretation of Marx's Methodology." In *Rethinking Marxism: Struggles in Marxist Theory*, ed. S. Resnick and R. Wolff, 45–81. New York: Autonomedia.

——. 1986. "Marx, Keynes, and Minsky on the Instability of the Capitalist Growth Process and the Nature of Government Economic Policy." In *Marx, Schumpeter and Keynes: A Centenary Celebration of Dissent*, ed. S. W. Helburn and D. F. Bramhall. Armonk, NY: M.E. Sharpe.

Cullenberg, S. 1988. "Theories of Social Totality, the Okishio Theorem, and the Marxian Theory of the Tendency of the Rate of Profit to Fall." Ph.D Diss., University of Massachusetts, Amherst.

Dobb, M. 1972. *Political Economy and Capitalism*. Westport, CT: Greenwood Press.

Dumenil, G.; Glick, M.; and Rangel, J. 1984–85. "The Tendency of the Rate of Profit to Fall in the United States." Parts I, II. *Contemporary Marxism* 9: 148–64; 11: 138–52.

——. 1987. "The Rate of Profit in the United States." *Cambridge Journal of Economics* 11: 331–59.

Dutt, A. 1984. "Stagnation, Income Distribution and Monopoly Power." *Cambridge Journal of Economics* 8.

——. 1987a. "Alternative Closures Again: A Comment on 'Growth, Distribution and Inflation'." *Cambridge Journal of Economics* 11: 75–82.

——. 1987b. "Competition, Monopoly Power and the Uniform Rate of Profit." *Review of Radical Political Economics* 19 (4): 55-72.

Fine, B. 1982. *Theories of the Capitalist Economy*. New York: Holmes and Meier.

——. 1983. "Accumulation." In *Dictionary of Marxist Thought*, ed. T. Bottomore, 3–4. Cambridge: Harvard University Press.

Fine, B., and Harris, L. 1976. "Controversial Issues in Marxist Economic Theory." In *The Socialist Register*, ed. R.Miliband and J. Saville, 141–78. London: Merlin Press.

Fine, B., and Harris, L. 1977. "Surveying the Foundations." In *The Socialist Register*, ed. R. Miliband and J. Saville, 106–20. London: Merlin Press.
———. 1979. *Rereading Capital*. New York: Columbia University Press.
Foley, D. K. 1986. *Money, Accumulation and Crisis*. London: Harwood Academic Publishers.
Foster, J. B. 1986. *The Theory of Monopoly Capitalism*. New York: Monthly Review Press.
Glyn, A., and Sutcliffe, B. 1972. *Capitalism in Crisis*. New York: Pantheon Books.
Gordon, D. M. 1978. "Up and Down the Long Roller Coaster." In *U.S. Capitalism in Crisis*, ed. URPE Crisis Reader Editorial Collective, 22–35. New York: URPE.
———. 1980. "Stages of Accumulation and Long Economic Cycles." In *Processes of the World System*, ed. T. Hopkins and I.Wallerstein. Beverley Hills: Sage.
Gordon, D. M.; Edwards, R.; and Reich, M. 1982. *Segmented Work, Divided Workers*. Cambridge: Cambridge University Press.
Green, F., and Sutcliffe, B. 1987. *The Profit System: The Economics of Capitalism*. Harmondsworth: Penguin Books.
Hahnel, R., and Sherman, H. 1982. "The Rate of Profit Over the Business Cycle." *Cambridge Journal of Economics* 6: 185–94.
Harris, D. J. 1978. *Capital Accumulation and Income Distribution*. Stanford: Stanford University Press.
———. 1983. "Accumulation of Capital and the Rate of Profit in Marxian Theory." *Cambridge Journal of Economics* 7: 311–30.
———. 1988. "On the Classical Theory of Competition." *Cambridge Journal of Economics* 12: 139–67.
Harvey, D. 1982. *The Limits to Capital*. Chicago: University of Chicago Press.
Heim, C. 1986. "External Spheres and the Theory of Capitalist Development." *Social Concept* 3 (2): 3–42.
Howard, M. C., and King, J. E. 1985. *The Political Economy of Marx*. 2d ed. New York: New York University Press.
———. 1988. "Henryk Grossman and the Breakdown of Capitalism." *Science & Society* 52 (3): 290–309.
Itoh, M. 1980. *Value and Crisis*. London: Pluto Press.
Jacoby, R. 1975. "The Politics of the Crisis Theory: Toward the Critique of Automatic Marxism II." *Telos* 23: 2–52.
Kenway, P. 1980. "Marx, Keynes, and the Possibility of Crisis." *Cambridge Journal of Economics* 4: 23–36.
Lebowitz, M. A. 1976. "Marx's Falling Rate of Profit: A Dialectial View." *Canadian Journal of Economics* 9: 232–54.
Levine, D. P. 1975. "The Theory of the Growth of the Capitalist Economy." *Economic Development and Cultural Change* 24: 47–74.
———. 1977. *Economic Studies: Contributions to the Critique of Economic Theory*. London: Routledge and Kegan Paul.

——. 1978–81. *Economic Theory*. 2 vols. London: Routledge and Kegan Paul.
——. 1988. *Needs, Rights, and the Market*. Boulder, CO: Lynne Rienner.
——. 1989. "The Sense of Theory in Political Economy." *Rethinking Marxism* 2 (1): 29–48.
Lipietz, A. 1986. "Behind the Crisis: The Exhaustion of a Regime of Accumulation. A 'Regulation School' Perspective on Some French Empirical Works." *Review of Radical Political Economics* 18 (1&2): 13–32.
——. 1987. *Mirages and Miracles: The Crises of Global Fordism*. Trans. D. Macey. London: Verso.
Mandel, E. 1978. *Late Capitalism*. Trans. J. De Bres. London: Verso.
——. 1980. *Long Waves of Capitalist Development: The Marxist Interpretation*. Cambridge: Cambridge University Press.
Marx, K. 1967. *Capital*. Vol. 3. New York: International.
——. 1968. *Theories of Surplus Value*. Vol. 2. Moscow: Progress.
——. 1973. *Grundrisse*. Trans. M. Nicolaus. New York: Vintage.
——. 1976. *Capital*. Vol. 1. Trans. B. Fowkes. New York: Vintage.
Matthaei, J. 1982. *An Economic History of Women in America*. New York: Shocken Books.
Mattick, P. 1969. *Marx and Keynes: The Limits of the Mixed Economy*. Boston: Porter Sargent.
——. 1981. *Economic Crisis and Crisis Theory*. White Plains, NY: M.E. Sharpe.
Moseley, F. 1985. "The Rate of Surplus Value in the Postwar U.S. Economy: A Critique of Weisskopf's Estimates." *Cambridge Journal of Economics* 9: 57–79.
——. 1987. "Marxian Crisis Theory and the Postwar U.S. Economy." In *The Imperiled Economy: Book I*, ed. R. Cherry et al., 105–14. New York: URPE.
Nell, E. 1987. "Transformational Growth and Stagnation." In *The Imperiled Economy: Book I*, ed. R. Cherry et al., 93–102. New York: URPE.
Norton, B. 1983. "The Accumulation of Capital and Market Structure: A Critique of the Theory of Monopoly Capitalism." Ph.D. diss., University of Massachusetts, Amherst.
——. 1986. "Steindl, Levine and the Inner Logic of Accumulation: A Marxian Critique." *Social Concept* 3 (2): 43–66.
——. 1988b. "The Power Axis: Bowles, Gordon, and Weisskopf's Theory of Postwar U.S. Accumulation." *Rethinking Marxism* 1 (3): 6–43.
O'Connor, J. 1984. *Accumulation Crisis*. Oxford: Basil Blackwell.
——. 1987. *The Meaning of Crisis: A Theoretical Introduction*. Oxford: Basil Blackwell.
Okishio, N. 1961. "Technical Changes and the Rate of Profit." *Kobe University Economic Review* 7: 85–99.
——. 1977. "Notes on Technical Progress and Capitalist Society." *Cambridge Journal of Economics* 1: 93–100.

Resnick, S. A., and Wolff, R. D. 1987. *Knowledge and Class: A Marxian Critique of Political Economy*. Chicago and London: University of Chicago Press.

Roche, J. 1985. "Marx's Theory of Money: A Reinterpretation." *Review of Radical Political Economics* 17 (1&2): 201–11.

Roemer, J. E. 1979. "Continuing Controversy on the Falling Rate of Profit: Fixed Capital and Other Issues." *Cambridge Journal of Economics* 3: 379–98.

——· 1981. *Analytical Foundations of Marxian Economic Theory*. New York: Cambridge University Press.

Rosdolsky, R. 1977. *The Making of Marx's "Capital."* Trans. P. Burgess. London: Pluto Press.

Rowthorn, B., and Harris, D. J. 1985. "The Organic Composition of Capital and Capitalist Development." In *Rethinking Marxism: Struggles in Marxist Theory*, ed. S. Resnick and R.Wolff, 345–57. New York: Autonomedia.

Shaikh, A. 1978a. "An Introduction to the History of Crisis Theories." In *U.S. Capitalism in Crisis*, ed. URPE Crisis Reader Editorial Collective, 219–41. New York: URPE.

——. 1978b. "Political Economy and Capitalism: Notes on Dobb's Theory of Crisis." *Cambridge Journal of Economics* 2: 233–51.

——. 1980. "Marxian Competition Versus Perfect Competition: Further Comments on the So-Called Choice of Technique." *Cambridge Journal of Economics* 4: 75–83.

——. 1983. "Economic Crisis." In *Dictionary of Marxist Thought*, ed. T. Bottomore, 138–43. Cambridge: Harvard University Press.

——. 1987a. "Organic Composition of Capital" and "Capital as a Social Relation." In *The New Palgrave*, ed. J. Eatwell et al., 333–36, 755–57. London: Macmillan.

——. 1987b. "The Falling Rate of Profit and the Economic Crisis in the U.S." In *The Imperiled Economy: Book I*, ed. R. Cherry et al., 115–26. New York: URPE.

Sherman, H. 1986. "Changes in the Character of the U.S. Busines Cycle." *Review of Radical Political Economics* 18 (1&2): 190–203.

——. 1987. *Foundations of Radical Political Economy*. Armonk, NY: M. E. Sharpe.

Soja, E. W. 1989. *Postmodern Geographies: The Reassertion of Space in Critical Social Theory*. London: Verso.

Steindl, J. 1976. *Maturity and Stagnation in American Capitalism*. New York: Monthly Review Press.

Sweezy, P. M. 1968. *The Theory of Capitalist Development*. New York: Monthly Review Press.

——· 1974. "Some Problems in the Theory of Capital Accumulation." *Monthly Review* (5): 38-55.

——. 1979. "Marxian Value Theory and Crisis." *Monthly Review* 31 (3): 1–17.

Taylor, L. 1985. "A Stagnationist Model of Economic Growth." *Cambridge Journal of Economics* 9 (4).

van Parijs, P. 1980. "The Falling-Rate-of-Profit Theory of Crisis: A Rational Reconstruction by Way of Obituary." *Review of Radical Political Economics* 12 (1): 1–16.

Weeks, J. 1981. *Capital and Exploitation*. Princeton: Princeton University Press.

Weisskopf, T. 1979. "Marxian Crisis Theory and the Rate of Profit in the Postwar U.S. Economy." *Cambridge Journal of Economics* 3: 341–78.

Weisskopf, T.; Bowles, S.; and Gordon, D. 1985. "Two Views of Capitalist Stagnation: Underconsumption and Challenges to Capitalist Control." *Science and Society* 49 (3): 259–86.

Willoughby, J. 1989. "Is Global Capitalism in Crisis? A Critique of Postwar Crisis Theories." *Rethinking Marxism* 2 (2): 83–102.

Wolff, E. N. 1987a. *Growth, Accumulation, and Unproductive Activity: An Analysis of the Postwar U.S. Economy*. Cambridge: Cambridge University Press.

Wolff, R. D., and Resnick, S. A. 1987. *Economics: Marxian Versus Neoclassical*. Baltimore: Johns Hopkins University Press.

Wright, E. O. 1978. *Class, Crisis, and the State*. London: Verso.

———. 1989. "What is Analytical Marxism?" *Socialist Review* 19 (4): 35–56.

Yaffe, D. S. 1973a. "The Crisis of Profitability: A Critique of the Glyn-Sutcliffe Thesis." *New Left Review*, no. 80: 45–61.

———. 1973b. "The Marxian Theory of Crisis, Capital and the State." *Economy and Society* 2: 186–232.

RADICAL THEORIES OF ACCUMULATION AND CRISIS: A COMMENT ON NORTON

David P. Levine

Bruce Norton's survey of theories of accumulation provides, I think, a vivid picture of the diversity of approaches currently available to those interested in understanding and exploring the growth process of a capitalist economy. Beyond summarizing salient features of the theories, Norton provides a framework for thinking about them as a whole. I think this is a valuable contribution. In my comment, I will further explore the framework he proposes.

As I understand it, Norton's framework divides theories along two dimensions. The first involves the extent to which the theory attempts to develop an economic analysis of economic phenomena, thus assuming (at least to some significant degree) the separability of the economy from other social processes. Of the theories Norton considers, all in his estimation fall short of fully taking into account the dangers of pursuing an economic theory of the growth process of capitalist economies. But some fall further short than others. The second dimension distinguishes those theories that center on the production process as the locus of determination of long-run dynamics, which he refers to as production-dominated theories, from those that center on the market, which he refers to as stagnation theories. I will consider these two dimensions in turn, beginning with the second, which is the more concrete.

The law of the falling tendency of the rate of profit remains the centerpiece of the production-dominated theories. The analytical underpinnings of this law have been doubtful from the beginning (its weaknesses were pointed out forty years ago by Robinson, Steindl and Sweezy). The law itself is in the nature of an analytical error. Yet it is one of those errors, common in social and economic theory, that has deep roots in the overall theoretical construction it occupies. Much like Ricardo's search for the invariable measure of value, it is a mistake made for compelling reasons. These reasons are more interesting than either the law itself or its failings.

Of primary importance is a weakness in Marx's method, and especially in his application of it. Marx argues that the law of the falling tendency of the rate of profit demonstrates that the limits of the accumulation process are internal to it. Thus, for

Marx, the Law extends the notion of capital's self-determination to encompass its self-limitation. Accumulation encounters barriers that it itself creates. But, when Marx thinks about limits internal to capital, he thinks about limits internal to the production of surplus-value and profitability. Thus, he links capital's self-determination (self-limitation) to its material determination (limits in production), and he does so even though the Law emerges as part of his investigation of the system of capitalist production as a whole, which ostensibly includes the market system.

In the tradition of his classical predecessors, Marx's materialism led him to think of the material production process as the more general and fundamental of the processes that constitute a capitalist market economy. Production formed, so to speak, the determining moment. Those aspects of the economic system specifically involving exchange and the process of circulation of commodities were to be understood by connecting them to the production process, including the social relations of production. The law of the falling tendency of the rate of profit does this, since it can be formulated in abstraction from the dynamics of price formation and competition, even if the latter processes must at some point be reconciled with it.

Of equal importance, the law of the falling tendency of the rate of profit conceives the historical limits of capitalist accumulation as limits on the capacity of capital to produce an adequate level of profitability. I think it will prove helpful to formulate this point in more general terms. To Marx, the capitalist form of economic organization had a two-sided historical mission—revolutionizing the methods of production and creating the world market. The law of the falling tendency of the rate of profit formulates the completion of the first dimension of this mission, in the way it was experienced by capital. The industrial revolution provides a vivid historical metaphor for and illustration of that dimension. But note that this dimension of capital's mission requires only the transformation of the "forces of production" and is complete, so to speak, when those forces achieve a certain level of development. The creation of the world market is another matter. The law of the falling rate of profit is formulated in a way that leaves this second dimension out of account.

The stagnation theories begin to incorporate the second dimension, and I think they succeed, at least up to a point. They certainly demand none of the heroic assumptions of the earlier theory, while opening up the analysis to consideration of the active role of the market. In doing so, they modify the materialist method to a degree and have, because of this, met with mixed reviews among Marxist theorists. The stagnation theories locate the determinants of capital accumulation not within the process of production, but instead in the interaction between the production process and the market.

Stagnation theory is arguably less reductionist than its predecessor, since it includes two moments rather than one. Nonetheless, stagnation theory continues to explain the limits of capitalist accumulation in economic terms. That is, it treats the economy as a separable, if not independent, system within the larger social whole. Norton doubts the wisdom of this sort of undertaking. I think that the production and stagnation approaches do exhibit important methodological continuities, and that these are problematic. While modifying the materialist grounding of economic analysis, stagnation theories share an important characteristic of the production-dominated approach we associate with Marx. The link between them is the common attempt to analyze the dynamics of capitalist economy on the assumption that the composition of output remains unchanged.

This assumption directly connects stagnation theories to the classical manner of treating consumption. The classical notion of subsistence tended to sever the link between what was consumed and the manner in which the means of consumption were acquired. This made the market a mechanism for providing subsistence rather than an active determinant of the nature of the consumption basket itself. Growth then appears as the expansion of a fixed structure of output rather than a process of change in that structure. The stagnation theories retain this way of thinking; indeed, it plays a central role in leading to their conclusion that the growth process tends to stagnate.

The assumption of a fixed composition of output protects the theory from the possible incursion of the neoclassical conception of the dynamics of product demand. But it also prevents the theory from taking into account the role of the market in advancing individual welfare and qualitatively transforming modes of life. The historical mission of a market economy still appears as the quantitative expansion of the producing apparatus and of output, not the transformation of modes of life and consumption. Thus, that mission might be thought to be complete when there is, so to speak, "enough to go around." Exactly what there is enough of is not considered a central concern. Missing in all of this is a broader and more compelling vision of the historical mission of capitalist economic organization, one that incorporates the transformative significance of the market economy for the ways of life of those caught up in it. Only within such a vision can the outlines of the accumulation process be meaningfully drawn. The rearticulation of this overall vision remains on the agenda. In its absence, we are severely limited in our attempts to evaluate concrete analytical arguments.

The theories Norton summarizes under the heading "Recently Emerging Accumulation Theories" break with what he refers to as the abstract determinancy of the more traditional production-dominated and stagnation theories. Evidently the break is not sharp enough to satisfy Norton. It nonetheless signals a change he favors in the method and objectives of the investigation of capitalist expansion.

The "social structures of accumulation" approach embodies a skepticism regarding theory, which Norton takes a step further. Given the identification between "theory" and "model" in economics, this skepticism of theorizing carries some weight. If theorizing means building models, then it does tend to isolate elements of the whole one from the other, in arbitrary ways. It is not unreasonable to argue against the "abstract determination" implied in this methodology. Yet Norton's argument implicitly and explicitly goes beyond criticism of modeling to cast doubt on the very effort to think abstractly about the determination of the expansion process. This sort of skepticism, I think, misconstrues the nature of theoretical work and what can be accomplished by it.

Genuine theory searches for meaning, order, and sense. It assumes that these can exist within our thinking, but recognizes that a specific effort is demanded for them to be made known to us. This effort is the effort to think abstractly, and by abstracting to isolate what is real from what is not. Theory helps us recognize that what we think things are (the way they appear to us) is not what they really are. Their truth can elude us in their appearance. This distinction, between appearance and underlying truth (or essence, if you like), should be understood as an insight about our thinking. We can think in different ways; some obscure and some clarify. One way we can think about things leads us to their appearance, another to their essence or truth. We express this distinction when we say that the way things appear is the way we think they are. More accurately, though, appearance refers to the way we think things are before we have really expended the effort to think systematically about them. This more systematic effort is theorizing; done well, it takes us from the appearance of things to the way they really are. Good theory is thus a process of rethinking our world. If we (perhaps incorrectly) identify the concrete with the way things appear to us, then theoretical thinking corresponds to the abstractness of things.

Consider an example. One way to think about price, one favored prior to the rise of the classical school, emphasized the variety of concrete factors that might affect the price of any given commodity. This approach corresponds to one of the ways price determination appears to us as actors within the framework of a market. But it is not the only way we can think about price determination within more or less competitive markets. We can reorganize the various factors in different ways, thereby diminishing their variety and imposing unity where previously only diversity was apparent. Thus, for example, classification of the relevant variables into cost and demand determinants transforms our interpretation of what we see and makes possible a different understanding of price formation. Theorizing is this process of rethinking, which is also a process of reorganizing. We can identify the original way of thinking with appearance, and the way we think as a result of the effort to theorize with the essence. The latter has a different order of reality than the former.

Theoretical thinking reorganizes our ideas in part by drawing distinctions and identifying the fault lines that separate the moments of the whole. These distinctions and fault lines delineate a structure with a determinate form, a structure we understand by grasping both the inner distinctions and the principle that integrates them. The latter is especially important in responding to Norton's critique. Theorizing requires us both to distinguish and to integrate, and to integrate we must find a common theme that runs through the different moments of the structure as a whole.

These general considerations concerning theory are at the heart of what I think is the central question raised by Norton's critique: does theory seek to identify an integrating theme or principle that animates and gives meaning to the system as a whole? If, as argued, theorizing demands the identification of such a theme, then theoretical work is the work of uncovering how that theme animates the more concrete relations and structures. Such work does involve a kind of abstract determination, since (1) insofar as concrete phenomena take their meaning from their relation to the integrating theme, they are determined by that relation, and (2) the theme must be understood abstractly before it can be concretely applied.

The various radical theories of accumulation all refer us back to the classical-Marxian theme of capital as self-expanding value. That they do so is not arbitrary. I think Marx had it in mind to argue that the self-expansion of value is deeply rooted in the logic of economic relations, once the economy has been set loose (or, in Karl Polanyi's phrase, "disembedded") from its determination as part of the family or the state. While the matter of embeddedness or disembeddedness may appear complex historically, economic theory cuts through this complexity by assuming a disembedded economy as its subject matter. By disembedded, the theory does not mean disconnected or independent. Rather, it means that the economy is not immediately the subject of family or state; its logic is not a political or familial logic. It is only by assuming that the economy is disembedded in this sense that economic theory becomes possible.

It is, then, not surprising that the theories of accumulation are economic theories of an economic process. Norton's critique is essentially a critique of the possibility or meaningfulness of economic theory rather than a call for an alternative. His critique questions the project of identifying the fault lines that distinguish the moments of the social order considered as a whole. Identifying those fault lines can lead us to economic theory understood as a part of a larger social theory.

Having said this much, I would emphasize that the pursuit of an economic theory need not imply that understanding the economy requires no reference to anything not strictly economic. When economists do economic theory they need make no claims about the autonomy of their subject matter. Demand depends on personal life, which is not determined by the economy. The economy consists of a system of property rights, whose meaning is only partly "economic." Acceptance or denial of links of this sort does not separate the theories Norton favors from those he criticizes. The relevant distinction has to do instead with theorizing itself. Without the distinction between essence and appearance considered above, without the effort to think abstractly and therefore to organize our thinking and categories of thought, and finally, without identifying the fault lines and thus the distinct moments of the whole, how could we begin to understand the economy and its place in the system of social relations as a whole?

6 POWER AND CLASS: THE CONTRIBUTION OF RADICAL APPROACHES TO DEBT AND DEVELOPMENT

David F. Ruccio

> The individual capitalist who sends his money abroad and receives 10 per cent interest for it, whereas by keeping it at home he could employ a mass of surplus people, deserves from the standpoint of capitalism to be crowned king of the bourgeoisie.
>
> –Marx, *Capital*, Vol. 1

THE CRISES OF DEBT AND DEVELOPMENT

The total external debt of the developing countries at the end of 1990 was estimated at $1,246 billion, an amount equivalent to 123 percent of their total exports of goods and services.[1] Debt service (amortization plus interest payments) alone consumed 17.3 percent of their export earnings. Of the long-term guaranteed component of these debts ($949 billion), some 45 percent was owed to international private banks and other private creditors located in the advanced industrial nations of the West.

The increased importance of external borrowing during the decade of the 1970s reflected in these figures was more than matched by a decline in the quantitative

---

I wish to acknowledge the comments and suggestions of Robert Devlin, Manuel Pastor, the members of the University of Notre Dame Economic Development Workshop, and the editors of this volume. Earlier versions of parts of this paper were presented at the annual meetings of the Association for Economic and Social Analysis (1985), the Eastern Economic Association (1986), and the Union for Radical Political Economics (1987).

significance of foreign direct investment in the total capital movements to developing countries. In 1960, for all developing countries, net direct foreign investment represented 47.9 percent of annual net long-term capital flows (World Bank 1980). The 1970 figure declined somewhat to 34.2 percent but by 1977 it had fallen to 19.3 percent. Official lending suffered a similar relative decline during the same period. The share lost by those two items was taken over by debt-creating flows of capital on commercial terms, especially private bank lending.

Recent controversial debt repayment schemes, in turn, have focused attention on the sharp decline in economic growth rates and in most, if not all, indicators of standards of living in the developing countries. The abrupt end of relatively high "golden age" growth rates in the Third World—from 5.2 percent in the 1960s and 5.4 percent in the 1970s, to 3.2 percent in the first half of the 1980s (World Bank 1988)—has been accompanied by widespread environmental destruction, growing poverty, and deteriorating conditions in health, nutrition, and education (Bell and Reich 1988; Cornia et al. 1988).

Faced with such information, few would deny that the international economic relations of developing countries have changed dramatically in the past decade, or that the external debt situation of those countries—in Africa, Asia, and especially Latin America—reached crisis proportions during the same period. However, it is not enough to cite shocking statistics on levels of external debt or income inequality—or, on the other hand, to report on successful cases of economic stabilization and structural adjustment—as if the facts could speak for themselves (cf. Bacha and Diaz Alejandro 1982, 14). Rather, all economic "facts" are theoretical, in the sense that they only exist and make sense within theoretical frameworks. Different economic theories produce different sets of facts, and each, in turn, understands its facts—and those of other frameworks—differently, depending on the concepts used to produce and interpret them.

External debt is one case in point. The analysis of external debt and the recent debt crisis has been dominated by work within the "orthodox" or neoclassical/Keynesian tradition. Even the data collected, as I show below, are beholden to the categories that make up this particular analytical framework. The orthodox tradition tends to view international flows of capital and commodities in terms of individual decision-making and, in the aggregate, in terms of the ability of these flows to satisfy national development requirements. External debt is aggregated together with other foreign capital flows and analyzed as a means to finance the so-called "foreign-exchange" and "savings" gaps, enhancing allocative efficiency. Alongside this orthodox tradition, an alternative "radical" analysis has emerged focusing on unequal power relations among and within the various nations in the international economy. International economic relations, radicals argue, create and reproduce relations of dependency between developed and developing nations. External debt, in particular, is seen to involve a form of "debt-peonage" between developing nations and their creditors, especially private banks, in the developed nations.

Of course, such different perspectives on external debt, as well as on the other international aid, trade, and investment activities among nations, have provoked an extended debate about the role of developing countries in the world economy. Does international financial intermediation involve capital flows that directly or indirecly benefit individuals in both the advanced industrial nations and the less-developed Third World? Or do international loans to developing nations trap them in an exploitative web of financial commitments that distort their short-term development prospects and undermine the possibility of development in the long run?

A parallel debate concerns alternative "solutions" to the debt crisis. Some economists, especially the orthodox ones who dominate the discussion, debate the relative merits of domestic stabilization and adjustment policies, increased foreign aid and bank lending, and the resumption of world economic growth as means to the end of alleviating the developing countries' heavy burden of external debt-service payments. The radical response is that such measures are inadequate, that the burden in any case falls disproportionately on the debtor countries (and on the poorer sectors within those countries), and that debt cancellation and other fundamental changes in the world economy are necessary for development to occur in the Third World.

This essay both critically analyzes and participates in this debate concerning the nature and effects of international economic relations. External debt is a way of focusing on, and entering into, the larger debate concerning economic development. My critical review of orthodox and radical approaches to debt and development leads, in turn, to an extension of the radical analysis of external debt. While radical political economists have been remarkably successful in challenging many of the theoretical presumptions and policy prescriptions of neoclassical and Keynesian economists, they have been less successful in elaborating an alternative approach. In particular, they have missed the opportunity to develop and extend the radical insights that can be gained by placing class at the center of the analysis. To begin the process of filling this gap, I present a class analysis of external debt, one which focuses on exactly those class aspects of the "debt crisis" that have been downplayed or left out by existing treatments. The specific implications of this class-theoretic approach to external debt are suggestive of some of the remaining problems and issues which the radical literature on economic development needs to address.

ALTERNATIVE APPROACHES TO DEBT AND DEVELOPMENT

The two basic approaches to external debt can be roughly grouped under the convenient shorthand terms "orthodox" and "radical." A brief discussion of the main elements of the orthodox approach helps to highlight the particular contributions of a radical approach to debt and development.

The Orthodox Approach. It is typically argued that borrowing from foreign sources by Third World countries is one component of a larger transfer of resources from developed to less-developed nations. The purpose of foreign credit, together with private investment and (multilateral and bilateral) aid, is to finance the aggregate foreign capital requirement of developing countries. This requirement may take the form of a "savings gap" and/or a "foreign-exchange gap" (Chenery and Strout 1966). In the former case, the supply of domestic savings from all sources falls short of the demand for savings for investment purposes. An inflow of foreign capital can serve to bridge this domestic savings gap. The latter, foreign-exchange gap is understood as the outcome of a shortage of foreign funds to finance the external balance of the national economy: a shortfall of foreign-exchange earnings (from exports of goods and services, etc.) with respect to foreign-exchange requirements (for imports, etc.). In both cases, foreign capital is understood to overcome "bottlenecks" that arise in the course of development, thereby contributing to further development.

The fact that foreign capital (whether as direct and portfolio investment, government aid, or loans) enters into the credit column of official national balance of payments statements lends support to the idea that such foreign capital represents a resource transfer to and, therefore, a form of "national investment" for developing countries. This is certainly the case, according to the orthodox perspective, when capital inflows and outflows are kept within certain "limitations" (no balance of payments crisis arises) and repayment (debt service) is not "excessive." In addition, international economic relations are understood to be structured in such a way that this flow of capital from developed to less-developed nations occurs more or less automatically. Orthodox economists start from the premise that "in the normal course of world development, capital should flow from advanced countries, where it is abundant and its return is relatively low, to developing countries, where capital is scarce and its return high" (Cline 1983, 9). Apart from the existence of market imperfections, developing nations should be able to attract the foreign capital necessary to promote economic growth through the normal functioning of the institutions of international financial intermediation.

This orthodox approach insists, finally, that international capital flows not only directly promote the development of Third World countries but also indirectly promote growth and development throughout the world. Overcoming the foreign capital bottlenecks of developing countries increases international trade and thereby promotes growth and efficiency of the world economy. Thus, it is said, the availability of foreign credits for developing countries during the 1970s, especially after the first "oil shock," averted a world recession even deeper than that which in fact occurred.

To summarize briefly, the orthodox approach views foreign loans and other foreign capital flows as (*a*) mutually beneficial to both developed and less-developed nations within the world economy and (*b*) a product of the more or less normal functioning of contemporary international economic relations.

This orthodox approach to foreign debt is, of course, linked to a more general theory of development that emerged in the early 1950s.[2] The aim of development, according to this approach, is to transform the small "modern sector" of developing countries into an "engine of growth." Orthodox development economists support the transfer of capital and technology through direct investment, aid, and credit from developed nations to this modern sector (with the goal in some cases of transforming the traditional sector itself). Growth then ensues, at least partly in response to this transfer, allowing the developing nations to pay back their benefactors, both directly and indirectly, especially through the acceleration of world trade. There have been differences, to be sure, concerning whether these capital flows would have to be concentrated and short-lived or a long-term necessity but, in either case, self-sustaining growth is said to be the result. Obstacles to this untrammeled flow of capital on either side—for example, through nationalizations or a decline in aid-giving—are understood to curtail world economic growth.

Certainly there has never been a consensus among orthodox economists on the myriad issues associated with international capital flows.[3] And the emergence of the debt crisis in the 1980s, especially in the aftermath of the Mexican difficulties in 1982, only served to exacerbate these differences, especially regarding the origins of the debt crisis and proposed solutions. With respect to the origins of the crisis, debate continues over whether recent problems of repayment can be attributed to debtor countries living "beyond their means" (for example, in using foreign loans to augment consumption instead of investment), to policy "errors" (such as maintaining overvalued exchange-rates for too long), or to externally-induced terms of trade, recession, and oil-price shocks.[4] Proposed policy measures, especially considering the role of International Monetary Fund (IMF) "conditionality" in many recent refinancing and rescheduling agreements, have produced even more diversity among proponents of the orthodox approach.[5] However, notwithstanding these specific differences, the orthodox approach to external debt remains committed to the view that loans and other foreign capital flows represent a positive resource transfer from capital-rich to capital-poor countries and, as such, a source of mutually beneficial economic growth.

The Radical Approach. Both of these points are contested by radicals. According to this alternative approach, external debt takes its place alongside other flows of capital from advanced industrial, "core" nations to less-developed, "peripheral" nations as a source of dependency of the latter on the former. Through these international capital flows, power is exercised by the core over the periphery. The result of these unequal power relations is that a surplus is extracted by the developed nations from the less-developed nations; development in the core on the basis of this surplus transfer, then, results in either underdevelopment or dependent and distorted development in the periphery.

This radical approach became prominent in the late 1960s and early 1970s as a critique of foreign aid and foreign direct private investment in the Third World. Such aid and investment were seen as mechanisms whereby development in the Third World was shaped and guided to benefit development elsewhere, in the nations where the aid and investment originated (see, e.g., Richards 1977). Multinational corporate investment also resulted in profit repatriations and thus in the "foreign exploitation" of the periphery by the core. Supranational lending agencies (especially the World Bank and the IMF) were seen as partners in this exploitation (Payer 1974; 1982). Finally, the "unequal exchange" of commodities and the decline of the external terms of trade of peripheral countries were additional mechanisms for the exercise of power over and the "exploitation" of Third World countries.[6]

During the late 1970s and early 1980s, with the relative decline of both the aid and investment components of total foreign capital flows to developing countries, external debt assumed, in the radical framework, the role of previous mechanisms as the primary means of foreign exploitation of the periphery by the core.[7] In the new situation, interest payments to private creditors in the dollar and Eurodollar markets take the place of profit repatriations in transfering a surplus from the periphery to the core and creating a form of "debt-peonage" (see DeWitt and Petras 1979; cf. Hawley 1979). And, in the case where countries fall behind on repayment of the debt, the conditions established by the IMF or by private bank creditors themselves are such that the "poor" are eventually forced to shoulder the debt burden. Whereas in the orthodox view external debt is a mechanism for increasing international wealth through resource transfers from developed to developing nations, for radicals it is a means by which core countries extract wealth from peripheral countries and, ultimately, from the "super-exploited" poor within the periphery.

This radical approach to external debt is, like its orthodox opposite, rooted in a more general theory of development and international economic relations. According to the radical framework, capitalist international economic relations are ruled by unequal power relations among and between countries within the world economy; indeed, capitalism itself is defined as a "deeply unequal system of domination of one class by another, of one nation by the ruling class of another" (Bagchi 1982, 39). In this view, then, global economic relations are structured such that international flows of resources have differential effects on the nations involved. Where proponents of the orthodox approach see mutual benefit as the result of international economic relations, radicals see the exploitation of one group of nations by another. This exploitation, in turn, serves as the basis for complementarily opposite effects: development and social stability in the core, and underdevelopment (and/or dependent development) and instability in the periphery. These effects serve, finally, to reproduce conditions for these unequal power relations, as a low-wage, "extraverted" structure of accumulation and a high-wage, "autocentric" structure of accumulation emerge in the periphery and core, respectively (Amin 1974; 1988; cf. Ruccio and Simon 1987). The result is that the free flow of capital and commodities in international markets, instead of leading to global economic growth as in the orthodox approach, serves to drive a deeper wedge between developed and underdeveloped, core and periphery nations. External debt represents merely the most recent form of this foreign exploitation of the periphery (see, e.g., MacEwan 1985).[8]

We have, then, two diametrically opposite approaches to external debt based, in turn, on different theories of development in general. According to the orthodox approach, foreign loans represent one means for developing countries to close their savings and/or foreign-exchange gaps, a tool which, if "responsibly" used, serves to enhance development throughout the world economy. This view of external debt ultimately assumes that capitalist international economic relations provide an appropriate environment within which individual rational decision-making—individual choice—operates to secure growth and development for all nations. Developing countries benefit directly from the freedom of individuals to buy/sell commodities and borrow/loan capital in international markets, but ultimately all nations are beneficiaries of this free international flow of capital and commodities.[9]

The radical story is, of course, quite different. External debt instead ties developing countries into an unequally structured world economy and in the end leads to a net capital outflow. This exploitative transfer of surplus in the form of interest payments enhances development in the advanced industrial countries but worsens the possibility for development in the Third World. Therefore, external debt, along with foreign aid, foreign direct private investment, and unequal commodity exchange, is a product of unequal power relations and a mechanism through which unequal power is exercised to produce an unequal international distribution of the gains from the world accumulation of wealth.

Debates within the Radical Approach. Radical political economists have succeeded in challenging many of the most cherished propositions of orthodox economists. Their approach, to borrow Evans's (1985, 149) phrase, is "no longer an upstart challenger from the periphery." In fact, the thesis that the metropolis is the "prime mover" behind poverty and underdevelopment in the periphery is no longer the sole province of dependency theorists; Taylor (1988, 20), for one, has argued that "at root, the poor growth performance of the developing countries is caused by the economic slump of the industrialized world" (see also Singh 1986). There is, however, much debate among radicals about the appropriate framework for their alternative analysis of international relations and Third World development.[10]

The debate has surfaced most recently in the radical attempt to analyze the emergence of the so-called newly industrializing countries (Brazil, South Korea, etc.) during the past decade (Chakravarty 1987). Alternative radical analyses have used these various country experiences as examples of either "dependent development" (Landsberg 1979; Hart-Landsberg 1984) or of the possibility of successful capitalist development in the Third World (Barone 1983; 1984). Warren (1973; 1980), in fact, provoked considerable consternation when he argued that imperialism had created the conditions, not for underdevelopment, but for successful capitalist development in the Third World.

This debate, however, has existed within the radical approach almost from the beginning. Much discussion has focused on the relationship between power and class, with critics maintaining that class has been subordinated to power in radical analyses of development and international economic relations. Jenkins, for example, takes Warren to task on the grounds that "the specific class structures and modes of surplus appropriation which have permitted rapid capital accumulation in certain Third World countries (particularly the newly industrializing countries) are not analyzed" (1984, 38). This critique echoes points raised in the earlier "modes of production controversy," which emerged from Laclau's (1971) critique of Frank's version of dependency theory.[11] According to Laclau, early dependency theorists such as Frank focused on unequal power relations within homogeneous capitalist markets and failed to analyze the combination of capitalist and non-capitalist modes of production present in Third World settings. This criticism has led some (e.g., the various contributions to Wolpe 1980; Taylor 1979) to reformulate the radical development approach on the basis of the "articulation of modes of production" or other versions (e.g., that of "peripheral modes of production") in which the mode of production played a central role in the analysis of world capitalist development.[12] This work was successful in bringing classes back into analytical focus within the radical approach. However, it ended up overemphasizing the external relations of dominance of the capitalist mode of production over other, non-capitalist modes of production. As a result, modes of production theorists downplayed the dynamics and complexity of the class processes within the various modes of production.

Another major debate within the radical approach was initiated by Brenner's (1977) critique of the emerging "world-systems" theory associated with the work of Wallerstein (1974; 1980; Hopkins and Wallerstein et al. 1982), Frank, and other radical development theorists. Brenner took issue with the world-systems theorists' definition of capitalism as a system of power exercised through exchange relations and involving production oriented toward profit in the market. Their definition led, in turn, to a type of analysis in which the emergence of a capitalist class structure was determined by market relations. According to Brenner, market opportunities could not determine class, as in the Wallerstein-Frank view. Rather, he argued, the origins of capitalist market relations had to be sought in the prior emergence of a specifically capitalist class structure.[13]

Gourevitch (1978) echoed Brenner's theme in observing that, according to the world-systems theorists, international market forces rely upon and accentuate inequality. Unequal power relations confine weak peripheral states to a subservient role, perpetuating their weakness. In this sense, Wallerstein and the other world-systems theorists reduce the various socio-economic (including class) structures within the world economy to unequal world market opportunities (Skocpol 1977).

More recently, Lipietz (1987) has criticized radical approaches that start with or presume a hierarchically structured world system, thereby emphasizing an unchanging structure of core-periphery relations. Because such approaches pay scant attention to the "concrete conditions of capital accumulation in the centre or on the periphery" (1987, 2), they have missed important changes, in center-periphery relations and within the periphery itself, over the course of the last century, and especially in the last twenty years.

Lipietz's observation strikes to the heart of the dilemma posed for radical development thought by the newly industrializing countries and other "unexpected" events in the Third World.[14] It coincides with the critical comments of others like Gunnarsson (1985) and Willoughby (1986), who argue that the various forms of capitalism recently emerging in the Third World require a framework of analysis different from existing radical approaches—one more sensitive to the *variety* of political and economic processes which integrate the different Third World social formations into the world capitalist system.

In response to this requirement, Evans has called for a "dependency approach but without the dependency label" (1985, 157). Others (such as Becker et al. 1987) have proposed a "postimperialist" framework of analysis. In general, they argue that radical development theory needs to be modified and extended by focusing on the class aspects of relations within and between the Third World and the advanced capitalist countries. This suggestion deserves to be taken seriously and, in the next section, I sketch the outlines of a specifically class-theoretic approach to development issues, focusing on the concrete problem of external debt.

A CLASS ANALYSIS OF EXTERNAL DEBT

A class analysis obviously requires clarity on the meaning of the term "class." Not surprisingly, Marx's writings are the most important example of class analysis for the radical tradition in development economics, but there are, of course, different possible readings of Marx's contributions. Richards (1986), for example, recognizes at least two interpretations of Marx's concept of class: one focusing on property endowments in a context of individual choice, and another defining class as a process of appropriation of surplus labor. Here, I adopt the latter approach.[15]

Class Processes. The heart of Marx's approach to class was the distinction between necessary labor (labor necessary to reproduce the social existence of the direct producers) and surplus labor (labor performed above and beyond necessary labor). According to the present interpretation, Marx built on this distinction, defining the class process as the particular social process in which surplus labor is appropriated from the direct producers, the performers of that surplus labor.[16] This process of surplus labor appropriation is, in turn, complexly determined by the other economic, political, and cultural processes that make up social life. The various modes of surplus labor appropriation or class processes designated by Marx (primitive communal, feudal, slave, capitalist, etc.) are then produced by differing configurations of such non-class social processes. Each particular class process is understood to exist only as an effect of its own uniquely constituted social context.

The capitalist class process, in particular, is defined as the appropriation of surplus labor in the form of surplus value.[17] The source of this surplus value is, as discussed at length in *Capital* 1, the extraction of labor from labor power. Assuming that the commodity labor power is purchased at its value (the value of the commodities necessary to reproduce the social existence of the sellers of labor power), capitalists gain income only if the labor performed in the course of production creates new value greater than the value of labor power. This extra value, Marx's surplus value, is realized in the sale of the commodities and appropriated by the capitalist. Thus, the process of performing and appropriating surplus labor in the form of surplus value defines two class positions: creators of surplus value ("productive laborers," in Marx's terms) and initial appropriators of that surplus value (what Marx called the "functioning" or "industrial" capitalists). This process of performance and appropriation of surplus value can be called the capitalist *fundamental* class process.

It is also possible to extend the analysis of class to consider the distribution of surplus labor. In the case of capitalism, once surplus value is appropriated, it is distributed to finance some of those social processes necessary for the reproduction of the capitalist fundamental class process. For example, portions of the appropriated surplus value may be distributed to such individuals as merchants, money-lenders, stock owners, and state officials, all of whom participate in processes that secure some of the "conditions of existence" of the original appropriation of surplus value. The surplus value may be distributed directly by the industrial capitalist, as in the case of interest payments to money-lenders, or indirectly, the case where merchants realize part of the surplus value through the differential between wholesale and retail prices. Whatever the mechanism, this process of distributing and receiving distributed surplus value, as distinct from the process of performing surplus labor and appropriating surplus value, can be called the capitalist *subsumed* class process (see Resnick and Wolff 1987 and this volume, ch. 1).

Finally, individuals may earn income or receive revenue in activities entirely separate from fundamental and subsumed class processes. Such flows of value, which represent neither the sale of productive labor-power, the direct appropriation of surplus value, nor the initial distribution of surplus value, are termed *non-class* payments.

To illustrate, consider a typical industrial capitalist enterprise, that is, one in which means of production (with value c) and labor power (of value v) are combined to produce capitalist commodities.[18] Surplus value (SV), once appropriated from productive laborers, is distributed in the form of subsumed class payments (ΣSC). One of the particular conditions of existence of this enterprise, especially in the context of domestic and international competition, may be the accumulation of additional means of production (Δc) and labor power (Δv). Thus, one of the specific subsumed class distributions will be outlays for this accumulation of "productive capital." Therefore, the class revenues and expenditures of the industrial capitalist enterprise may be written as

$$SV = \Sigma SC = \Delta c + \Delta v + \Sigma \overline{SC} \tag{1}$$

where $\Sigma \overline{SC}$ represents all other subsumed class distributions of appropriated surplus value beyond those devoted to capital accumulation.

In general, the class structure of capitalism includes the fundamental class positions of productive laborer and industrial capitalist, but also numerous other subsumed class positions. Individual human beings may occupy one or more of these fundamental and subsumed class positions during the course of a day, a year, or a lifetime. Thus, the class analysis of a particular capitalist society must be capable of distinguishing positions in fundamental and subsumed class processes, as well as non-class processes, in order to comprehend their constitutive effects. And since each of these processes and positions is conceived to interact with and "overdetermine" all of the others, the goal of a class analysis is to construct an understanding of just this complex interaction.

The remainder of this section elaborates these basic concepts in application to the specific development problems associated with external debt. The case of loans to industrial capitalists is the first step in the presentation; other borrowers are then considered.

The Industrial Capitalist. We begin with the analysis of financial or interest-bearing capital in *Capital*. According to Marx, lender/borrower relations involve an unequal exchange of value in the form of money, M-M′. In the particular case of finance capital highlighted by Marx (1976, 566–652), an initial sum of money (M) is lent to an industrial capitalist who is obliged to repay a larger sum (M′) in the form of amortization and interest payments. The original loan is itself a non-class revenue to the industrial capitalist, but it alters the restrictions imposed by the strict equality between surplus value and subsumed class payments assumed in equation (1). The subsequent flow of interest to the creditor represents a transfer of currently extracted surplus value, funds lost to the industrial capitalist in return for the use of the money as capital. As receivers and payers of interest respectively, financial and industrial capitalists occupy what we have termed above subsumed class positions: a portion of surplus value is distributed by the industrial capitalist to the money-lender to secure access to credit, one of the conditions of existence of the extraction of surplus value. Therefore, following Marx's reconceptualization of the "Trinity Formula" (1981, 953–70), the flow of interest payments from industrial to financial capitalists involves not a fundamental class process of extracting surplus value but a subsumed class process of distributing a portion of surplus value already appropriated from productive laborers.

A class analysis of the interest payments on loans to an industrial capitalist in another country makes use of these distinctions. The unequal exchange of value in the form of money between, say, Citicorp and an Argentine industrial firm establishes an international lender/ borrower relation in which surplus value is first extracted from Argentine productive laborers and then distributed as subsumed class revenue to the U.S. bank. Therefore, the foreign profits, P_f, of the U.S. (or German, British, etc.) lending agency represent subsumed class interest revenue, *SCR*, in return for providing an economic condition of existence of the exploitation of Argentine (or Mexican, Brazilian, etc.) workers; that is

$$P_f = SCR \qquad (2)$$

Such flows of subsumed class revenue may be received by any of several sorts of lending institutions: private bank consortia, state-owned bilateral lending agencies such as central banks, and multilateral lending agencies like the World Bank. As long as the loan is made to an industrial capitalist for use in securing one or another of the conditions of existence of the extraction of surplus value, the interest payments represent a subsumed class revenue to the lending institution.

In the case where borrowed money capital is used for commodity purchases of means of production and labor power, that is, where productive capital is accumulated, if all other subsumed class distributions of surplus value are constant, then the upper bound on the amount of interest payable is the extra surplus value (ΔSV) extracted in production. Therefore, the rate of interest paid to the lender (i) cannot be greater than the rate of self-expansion of value based on this new debt (ΔD):

$$i \leq \Delta SV/\Delta D \tag{3}$$

Any deviation of i from $\Delta SV/\Delta D$ implies an increase or decrease in the other subsumed class distributions of surplus value: for example, a lower interest rate on concessional borrowing will allow other subsumed class payments to increase. Alternatively, a rise in the rate of interest on variable-rate loans requires a decrease in other subsumed class payments, which include the enterprise's retained earnings. Therefore, even in the case where private external borrowing leads to increased extraction of surplus value, the industrial capitalist enterprise may not be able to make the subsumed class payments necessary to secure the other conditions of existence of extracting surplus value from Third World workers.

We can explore the further effects of such foreign borrowing on domestic capital accumulation in the following manner.[19] Assuming the industrial capitalist borrower uses foreign loans to expand capital accumulation, equation (1) is rewritten to include, on the left-hand side, the newly created debt (ΔD) and, on the right-hand side, the subsumed class distribution of interest payments on total debt (iD) such that:

$$SV + \Delta D = \Delta c + \Delta v + iD + \Sigma \overline{SC} \tag{1'}$$

It can be shown (see Appendix) that a decision to increase the role of foreign debt in financing productive capital outlays can positively affect the long-run rate of capital accumulation if the interest rate is less than the net rate of return (net of other subsumed class distributions $\Sigma \overline{SC}$) on productive capital. It is also clear that, everything else held constant, an increased interest rate will lower the rate of accumulation.

Balance of Payments. This initial instance of external borrowing to finance productive capital accumulation requires, in addition, a reconceptualization of the traditional balance of payments statements. Based on the analysis above, the interest payment component of "services" on the current account includes subsumed class flows of value from Third World industrial capitalist enterprises to foreign creditors. This point has many important implications, three of which are noted here. First, debt service payments, because they do not involve the direct extraction of surplus value, should not be seen as a form of "foreign exploitation." Rather, international money-lending secures a condition of existence of the exploitation of Third World productive laborers by *domestic* (Third World) capitalists; a portion of the surplus value extracted from those workers is, in turn, distributed to *foreign* creditors for securing this particular condition of existence. Thus we should distinguish the "cost" to the "nation," based on the flow of interest payments out of the country, from the "cost" imposed by the extraction of surplus value. The different social tensions and conflicts set in motion by these two costs will have fundamentally different implications for such diverse phenomena as the process of democratization and the success of policies designed to solve the debt crisis (see Ruccio, Resnick and Wolff 1991).

Second, since these foreign interest payments are predicated on prior extraction of surplus value from Third World workers, a surplus in the remainder of the current and capital accounts will not, in general, solve the payments imbalance from such interest payments. Only in the case where merchandise exports realize surplus value pumped out of the direct producers (and/or new borrowing directly finances debt service payments) can entries on the credit side of the balance of payments ledger be said to "solve" a balance of payments problem created by debt service payments.[20] External debt servicing is obviously not independent of net export performance; foreign interest payments must, in the end, be made in the form of foreign currency earnings.[21] However, an exclusive focus on net export performance and, hence, on *non-class* balance of payments entries means that the performance, appropriation, and distribution of surplus value—and therefore the *class* nature and effects of the debt service—are hidden from view. To "forget about" these class aspects of debt servicing is to miss the struggles generated by attempts to increase the extraction of surplus value and/or modify its distribution among different subsumed classes. Such struggles may undermine the best laid plans to service the debt.

Finally, even though debt service payments do not in themselves represent foreign exploitation, the rise in subsumed class interest payments may create the conditions for an eventual rise in the exploitation of domestic workers by foreigners. For example, domestic and/or international decision-makers may react to a balance of payments "crisis" by requiring additional external payments entries on the credit side. As stressed by the orthodox approach surveyed above, foreign capital inflows in the form of foreign direct private investment represent such a credit entry. Therefore, attempts to solve an imbalance of external payments may take the form of policies to promote foreign direct investment, thereby increasing the extraction of surplus value by foreign citizens (as in the case of Mexico, which relaxed restrictions on foreign investment as part of the "adjustment" policy package).

Other Borrowers. The preceding analysis focused only on private industrial capitalists' borrowing of external funds, for the purpose of expanding the accumulation of productive capital. However, the current external debt of most developing countries has arisen with the participation of borrowers other than industrial capitalist enterprises and for purposes other than the accumulation of productive capital.

There are at least three other major categories of borrowers that must be considered in analyzing the class structure of external debt: state-owned industrial enterprises, government administration (government agencies and enterprises other than industrial capitalist enterprises), and private non-industrial enterprises (including commercial banks and other financial enterprises, merchant companies, etc.). Each of these other borrowers must be analyzed in turn to determine the class nature of the revenue flows from interest payments to foreign lending institutions.

Following the logic of the analysis above, loans to state industrial capitalist enterprises generate subsumed class interest payments to foreign creditors in a way analogous to that of loans to private industrial capitalist enterprises. The provision of money capital in the form of loans provides a condition of existence of the extraction of surplus value, now from state employees, and generates a direct distribution of surplus value—a subsumed class flow of revenue—to the lending institution. Certainly, other conditions of existence of the exploitation of productive laborers differ in this case, for example, state ownership of the means of production, but the "unequal exchange" of value in the form of money with state industrial capitalist enterprises continues to generate foreign interest payments that represent subsumed class revenue. Again, the international lender/borrower relation involves a foreign distribution of surplus value and not foreign exploitation.

So far in our analysis, the foreign profits of lending agencies have been classified as a subsumed class income because those lenders occupy a class position subsumed to the capitalist fundamental class process in another country. More generally, though, the class nature of interest payments, foreign or domestic, depends on the class position of the *borrower* of money. This is, of course, largely irrelevant to the lender, for whom a successful loan is simply one which performs; the apparent irrelevance of the identity of the borrower is precisely why money-lending appears to be an independent form of capital. However, from a class-analytic standpoint, interest is a subsumed class distribution of surplus value only when the borrower occupies the position of industrial capitalist, either in state or private enterprise. Foreign profits on loans to government agencies and private non-industrial enterprises have a different class content, since in these cases neither the extraction of surplus value nor its direct distribution as subsumed class revenue takes place. Because the borrowed funds are not deployed by the borrower to secure a condition of existence of the extraction of surplus value, then, whether these funds are later lent to industrial capitalists or deployed for some other purpose, the lending agency occupies a non-class position and the interest received represents a non-class flow of revenue from borrower to lender. When neither the extraction nor the initial distribution of surplus value is involved, the foreign profits of the lending institution must be categorized as non-class flows of revenue (*NCR*); the expanded foreign profit equation for the creditor is then

$$P_f = SCR + NCR \tag{4}$$

An international lender/borrower relation continues to exist and interest payments across national boundaries continue to form part of the debits on the current account, but the class nature of those debt service payments depends on the class status of the borrower; the existence of external debt does not by itself indicate the class-structural form of that debt.

Typically, then, interest payments on the external debt of a capitalist developing country will involve both subsumed class and non-class flows of value to foreign lenders. Similarly, the non-merchandise "service" export revenue of the country in which the lending agency is located includes both subsumed class and non-class revenues. Therefore, typical balance of payments data need to be further reconceptualized to distinguish these different flows of value. In particular, the non-class division of external debt and debt service payments into "official" and "private" accounts can be reinterpreted by means of this distinction between subsumed class (ΣSC) and non-class (ΣNC) payments. Figure 1 represents a first approximation to this end: official debtors are broken down into state industrial capitalist enterprises (K^s) and other government agencies (G), while private debtors include non-industrial (B) and industrial capitalist (K^p) enterprises.

Borrower		Class Nature of Interest Payments	
Official	G	ΣNC	
	K^s		ΣSC
Private	B	ΣNC	
	K^p		ΣSC

Figure 1: Class Structure of External Debt and Debt Service

It is worth stressing that the non-class nature of certain debt service payments does not imply that these flows are any less important for the general course of development of the country concerned or, in particular, for the reproduction over time of the capitalist fundamental class process. It is, in fact, the task of class analysis not only to distinguish the fundamental, subsumed, and non-class aspects of social reality but also to analyze their complex mutual interactions. For example, the non-class status of interest paid on government agency borrowing (G) leaves open the question of the uses of the borrowed funds, any of which may have various important effects on the class (and non-class) processes of the country in question. The government, among other possibilities, may lend the borrowed money or sell foreign exchange to industrial capitalists, or create infrastructure (roads, dams, etc.) that positively affects the extraction of surplus value. These government money-lending, money-dealing, and infrastructure-building activities may secure conditions of existence of the capitalist fundamental class process and, therefore, create the basis for a governmental claim on appropriated surplus value. These subsumed class payments to the government may take the form of interest payments, fees on sales of foreign exchange, or taxes on industrial capitalist income. Thus, even when governmental interest payments to foreign creditors represent non-class payments, the source of revenue for those payments may be a subsumed class position established by government expenditures financed by foreign borrowing.

As another example of the different class structural forms of debt, consider a government guarantee of the private debt of industrial capitalists. Such official guarantees are often important conditions for international borrowing by residents of developing countries. So long as the industrial capitalist borrowers meet their debt obligations, the interest payments remain subsumed class distributions of appropriated surplus value. Only in the event of a perceived failure by private borrowers to maintain debt service payments, when the government itself is forced to assume the servicing obligation,[22] do the interest payments become non-class flows of value. Such a government "bailout" thus implies that one claim on appropriated surplus value, that of foreign creditors, has been eliminated. Unless the debt service is financed by taxes on industrial capitalist firms, the debt burden will tend to fall on individuals occupying other class positions in the country. Other subsumed class claimants on distributions of surplus value (merchants, domestic money-lenders, corporate managers, etc.) may in turn support such a class transfer of the debt burden, a possibility suggestive of the complex tensions created by government guarantees.

A similar example involves the case of non-government enterprises such as commercial banks whose foreign interest payments on debt also represent non-class flows of value. Their borrowing activity in international money markets may be motivated by the opportunity to capture a differential between the foreign interest rate at which they borrow and the domestic rate at which they can lend. They may expand their lending to domestic industrial capitalist enterprises unable to participate directly in international money markets, thereby providing access to foreign exchange and/or lowering the domestic interest rate to industrial capitalist borrowers through an increase in the supply of loanable funds. Here, the domestic commercial bank creates a subsumed class claim on domestically appropriated surplus value as the means to finance its own international obligation to make non-class payments.

Class and Debt. The important point here is that "non-class debt" may have significant class effects. In the recent literature, the examples most discussed (though not in the terms elaborated here) concern the conditions for debt rescheduling (e.g., Feinberg and Ffrench-Davis 1988). Foreign recipients of non-class interest payments often form alliances with government officials, central bank officers and industrial capitalists within their own country, with international multilateral lending agencies, and with capitalists, officials, and other groups within the debtor country to demand that the government of the latter country enact an "adjustment" policy as the condition for receiving "bridging" loans and a new debt repayment schedule. Immediate policy goals often include raising domestic interest rates, decreasing the government deficit, lowering the exchange-rate (devaluation), forcing down real wages in order to lower inflation and promote exports, and encouraging foreign investment. The most common measures advocated involve some combination of restrictive fiscal and monetary policies. But such policies may have contradictory effects, undermining certain conditions of existence of industrial capitalist enterprises while making possible increased extraction of surplus value.

A typical policy package will include, for example, higher real interest rates and lower import tariffs (see Canitrot 1980 and Ffrench-Davis 1983). Such measures may force industrial capitalist enterprises to distribute an increased share of their surplus value in the form of subsumed class payments to domestic banks, even as heightened import competition undermines their domestic sales. The realized surplus value of domestic capitalists may decline as a result. The combined effects of these conditions thus threatens the continuation of the subsumed class payments needed to secure the various conditions of existence of those in the class position of industrial capitalist. In particular, less surplus value may be available in the form of retained earnings to distribute to managers of those enterprises for the purpose of accumulating capital. Ironically, then, policies enacted to maintain access to foreign credit lines—in the form of non-class debt to the government and financial enterprises —may threaten the very existence of the industrial capitalists. Nowhere is the contradictory situation of the state in a typical developing country more evident.

Of course, other factors can, in part, offset this threat to industrial capitalists. If the wages (and, in time, the value of labor power) of productive laborers can be lowered enough, then the additional surplus value extracted will enable industrial capitalists to continue their subsumed class distributions of surplus value, including interest payments to domestic and foreign creditors. Various policies of Third World governments appear to have had just this effect. For example, restrictions on forms of labor association have contributed to reduced absenteeism and weakened trade union bargaining power. In addition, absolute decreases in the employment of both government and industrial workers have lessened pressures for nominal wage increases. In this sense, it is the increased exploitation of domestic workers, and not stand-by credits from the IMF, loans from private banks, or agricultural exports, that has "financed" the foreign debt problem.

Thus, the non-class process of debt servicing produces a complex set of political and economic interactions that may lead to increased domestic exploitation and, with a rise in foreign investment, to foreign exploitation as well.[23] But there is another dimension of debt that deserves at least brief mention as a further demonstration of the class complexity of development problems in debtor countries.

Capital flight is frequently a major concern in attempting to manage a debt crisis. Cumby and Levich (1987), for example, used the World Bank method to estimate capital flight ranging from 24 percent of Brazil's total external borrowing (during the period 1976–84) to 66 percent for Argentina (during 1979–82) and 68 percent for Mexico (1976–84). Interpretation of these data requires an extension of the analysis to allow for the use of external funds for purposes other than capital accumulation by industrial capitalist enterprises, domestic lending by financial enterprises, and the purchase of equity in other domestic enterprises by both industrial and non-industrial firms. Consider once again the example of industrial capitalist enterprises. If capital outflows are directed into purchases of stocks and bonds of foreign industrial capitalist enterprises, Third World residents in effect use their own foreign borrowing to create or extend subsumed class claims on surplus value generated in other countries. In this case, foreign funds are used not to secure a condition of existence of any domestic fundamental class position; instead, the non-class revenues from external borrowing flow out of the country to secure a condition of existence of the extraction of surplus value by industrial capitalists in the United States and other countries. In return, the Third World investor receives a subsumed class distribution of surplus value appropriated elsewhere.[24] The original foreign lenders—in all likelihood the same financial institutions that facilitated the capital flight—now receive non-class interest payments from the developing country's industrial capitalist borrowers. Only in the case where debt is used to secure a condition of existence of the *fundamental* class position of the borrower do the interest payments themselves represent a subsumed class claim on surplus value extracted from Third World workers.[25]

We can extend our previous analysis of the effects of external debt on the domestic accumulation of capital by including, on the right-hand side of equation (1′), the foreign portfolio investments made by the industrial capitalist enterprise (ΔA) and, on the left-hand side, the subsumed class revenue derived from such investments (SCR):

$$SV + SCR + \Delta D = \Delta c + \Delta v + \Delta A + iD + \Sigma\overline{SC} \qquad (1'')$$

Again, it can be shown (see Appendix) that, all other variables held constant, an increase in the interest rate on outstanding debt will reduce the rate of domestic capital accumulation. An increase in the ratio of external debt to the firm's productive capital can increase the long-run rate of domestic capital accumulation, if the interest rate on foreign debt is less than the overall rate of return (net of other subsumed class distributions $\Sigma\overline{SC}$) on total assets. Finally, an increase in foreign portfolio investment may itself have a *positive* effect on long-run domestic accumulation of productive capital if the rate of return on such foreign assets exceeds the net rate of return (net of interest payments and other subsumed class distributions) on the portion of domestic capital owned free of debt ($c + v - D$). That is, domestic productive capital accumulation may actually *increase* as a result of foreign unproductive capital accumulation if the rate of return to the latter is high enough and, of course, if the returns are repatriated. Otherwise, such capital flight will leave the domestic accumulation of capital unaffected or actually lower it.

An additional issue that arises here concerns the use of foreign subsumed class revenues to make expenditures, such as those sustaining capital accumulation, which reproduce a capitalist's domestic fundamental class position. Such a transfer of funds within the enterprise will lower the expenditures that secure the foreign subsumed class position of the capitalist and thus may jeopardize that position and the future receipt of subsumed class revenues.

It is also clearly possible for subsumed class revenues to be redirected to processes other than the accumulation of productive capital. The revenues from foreign portfolio investment may, for example, be distributed to internal managers, interest payments, dividends or taxes. However, if the rate of return on foreign investment is less than the "internal" rate of profit derived from exploitation of domestic productive laborers, increased foreign investment may lead to a decrease in domestic subsumed class payments.[26] Such a situation may generate alliances among various domestic classes to restrict the capital outflow. Alternatively, domestic industrial capitalists may seek to ally with other domestic classes to resist interest payments to foreign banks and to support a new government capable of rescheduling the existing debt burden.

CONCLUSIONS

The class analysis of external debt focuses on exactly those class processes left out of other accounts of international lender/borrower relations, both orthodox and radical. It provides a framework for analyzing interactions, since class processes are both shaped by and participate in shaping the other class and non-class processes of the various socially diverse Third World nations. Such an approach allows us to reconceptualize the problem of external debt by investigating the class and non-class processes operating, as it were, "behind" the official balance of payments statements.

As in the examples considered, domestic borrowers can use non-class revenues in the form of foreign loans to create or extend domestic and foreign fundamental, subsumed and non-class positions. For industrial capitalist enterprises, such non-class revenues allow them to evade the restrictions imposed by the originally assumed equality between fundamental and subsumed class revenues and the expenditures made to secure those revenues. The class nature of the interest payments to creditors varies, though, depending on the specific class position(s) of the borrowers. Thus, for example, interest payments to private banks in New York by Third World industrial capitalist enterprises may represent subsumed class distributions of surplus value or non-class expenditures, depending on whether the debt is used to secure the fundamental class position of capitalist appropriator of surplus value or a class position subsumed to other industrial capitalists. A similar class-analytic study can be made of other borrowers.

Distinguishing these various class-structural forms of debt is a necessary step in exploring the contradictory effects on class and non-class processes typically experienced by capitalist developing countries. For example, "adjustment" policies, those designed to correct the external imbalance created in part by previous external borrowing, come into focus as a source of new contradictions within industrial capitalist enterprises and the state. One response by Third World industrial capitalists has been to engage in new foreign borrowing and capital export to create or extend their foreign subsumed class positions.

Debt Crises. To take this analysis a step further, consider the conditions under which a debt crisis might arise. To begin with, a domestic borrower can increase expenditures through external indebtedness only on condition that, first, the money returns to its original owner after a definite time interval and, second, it returns as a sum greater than the original loan. Leaving aside, for simplicity's sake, repayment of the principal, the borrower can avoid constraints on other expenditures only if expectations prove correct and the loan is used to generate additional revenue at least equal to the interest payments due. A payments crisis would emerge, then, if actual revenues fell short of those expected. For a typical industrial capitalist borrower, servicing external debt requires that the additional domestically appropriated surplus value (ΔSV) and foreign subsumed class revenues (ΔSCR), free of all other claims, are not less than the subsumed class and non-class interest payments on outstanding debt (iD). Success thus depends on avoiding unexpected depletions of either surplus value appropriated at home or subsumed class payments from abroad. Should either circumstance occur, interest payments to foreign creditors would be threatened and a debt crisis would emerge.

There are, of course, numerous ways of attempting to overcome such a crisis, each with its own different class effects. Creditors might be induced to extend additional non-class revenues by creating new loans. The industrial capitalist borrowers might attempt to decrease other subsumed class and non-class payments, both inside and outside the enterprise. However, such cutbacks—a drop in the accumulation of productive capital, for example—would jeopardize their fundamental and subsumed class positions. Finally, borrowers might attempt to find other means of increasing their appropriation of surplus value and subsumed class income receipts. Any of these changes could alter the conditions of struggle over production and distribution of domestic surplus value. Thus, the debt crisis is likely to produce qualitative change in the form of fundamental and subsumed class struggles.

Class and Capitalist Development. This class-theoretic analysis of external debt is one example of an emerging "new direction" in the radical analysis of international capitalist development. At the general level of theory construction, it shares the aims of recent efforts to rethink the central role of concepts of power in radical political economy (e.g., Amariglio 1988; Norton 1988).

More specifically, reaffirming the centrality of class recasts a significant number of issues within radical development theory. Among its other effects is a different concept of development itself. Rather than defining development as the accumulation and distribution of wealth in the form of use-values—whether equal, as in orthodox theory, or unequal, as in existing radical accounts—development is reconceptualized in terms of class, as a matter of the differential effects produced by the various forms and types of class and non-class processes which jointly make up both "developed" and "developing" nations and the international relations among and between them. The accent of this alternative approach, then, is not on "more" or "less" development —whether measured by the amount of use-values produced (Richards 1986), the level of development of the productive forces (Warren 1980; Bardhan 1986), or an understanding of wealth as power (Chakravarty 1987)—but on the various class-specific forms of development. From the perspective of this approach, the analysis of development according to wealth is more appropriate for an approach based on Smith and Samuelson than for the tradition of radical development theory initiated by Lenin and Baran.

Still, the class-theoretic approach to debt outlined here is only a first step in rethinking some of the well-known arguments and conclusions of radical development thought. Brewer (1980) and Willoughby (1986), for example, have initiated the process of critically examining and, in some cases, rejecting the results of previous radical approaches to imperialism.

> Imperialism does not represent a special stage in the development of capitalism; uneven development does not always culminate in the breakdown of capitalist order; there is no necessity for the super-exploitation of the periphery by metropolitan capital; and consequently, it is possible for some Third World economies to develop sophisticated industrial capitalist structures. (Willoughby 1986, 80)

The political economy of the peasantry has been subject to similar critical scrutiny through a clarification of the class concepts that inform radical approaches to "peasant studies" (Deere 1986).

Finally, the collapse of existing socialist regimes in Eastern Europe and the ongoing turmoil of the Soviet Union and China have created a thoroughly spurious sense of the "correctness" of the orthodox approach celebrating capitalism. It is therefore even more urgent to criticize the effects of orthodox development theories and strategies; as a result, the issues raised by class-analytic approaches to the state (Thomas 1984; Bryan 1987) and socialism (Fagen et al. 1986; Ruccio 1987) will likely be at the forefront of radical debates over the next few years. At least one orthodox development economist has recognized the need to develop a "theory of class formation and class conflict" (Lewis 1984, 8). Radical political economists have the opportunity to respond to this need and, even more important, to elaborate a class-analytic framework that builds on and extends their own approach to development.

APPENDIX

To explore the effects of external debt on domestic capital accumulation, rewrite equation (1′) in the text as:

$$\Delta c + \Delta v = SV + \Delta D - iD - \Sigma\overline{SC}$$

The rate of productive capital accumulation can be obtained by dividing through by the flow of value $(c + v)$:

$$\frac{\Delta c + \Delta v}{c+v} = \frac{SV}{c+v} + \frac{\Delta D}{c+v} - \frac{iD}{c+v} - \frac{\Sigma\overline{SC}}{c+v} \qquad \text{(A-1)}$$

Assume a given long-run ratio of debt to productive capital, $\alpha = D/(c+v)$. Given α, $\Delta D = \alpha(\Delta c + \Delta v)$. Define $K^* = (\Delta c + \Delta v)/(c+v)$, $p' = SV/(c+v)$, and $\mu = \Sigma\overline{SC}/(c+v)$. Substituting these expressions into (A-1) yields

$$K^* = p' + \alpha K^* - \alpha i - \mu$$

which can be solved for K^*:

$$K^* = \frac{p' - \alpha i - \mu}{1 - \alpha} \qquad \text{(A-2)}$$

The sustainable long-run rate of capital accumulation (K^*) thus depends on the rate of surplus value appropriation (p'), the "gearing ratio" for debt (α), the rate of interest on foreign borrowing (i), and the ratio of other subsumed class distributions of surplus value to productive capital (μ). Assuming that p', i, and μ are determined independently of α, the results referred to in the text can be derived by partially differentiating (A-2) with respect to α and i:

$$\frac{\partial K^*}{\partial \alpha} = \frac{(-i + p' - \mu)}{(1-\alpha)^2} \gtreqless 0 \;\text{ iff }\; i \lesseqgtr p' - \mu, \quad \alpha \neq 1$$

$$\frac{\partial K^*}{\partial i} = \frac{-\alpha}{(1-\alpha)} > 0, \quad 0 < \alpha < 1$$

To examine the additional effects of foreign portfolio investments, assume that the enterprise earns a rate of return r on its foreign portfolio investments A; then $SCR = rA$. Assume further a given long-run ratio of foreign portfolio investment to domestic productive capital, $\beta = A/(c+v)$. Substituting into equation (1″) in the text and solving for K^* yields:

$$K^* = \frac{p' + \beta r - \alpha i - \mu}{1 - \alpha + \beta} \qquad \text{(A-3)}$$

The sustainable long-run rate of capital accumulation thus depends additionally on the given "foreign portfolio weight" (β) and the subsumed class rate of return on foreign portfolio investment (r). Again assuming that p', i, r, and μ are determined independently of the enterprise's choices for α and β, the results in the text follow from partial differentiation of (A-3) with respect to i, α, and β:

$$\frac{\partial K^*}{\partial i} = \frac{-\alpha}{(1-\alpha+\beta)} < 0, \quad \alpha - \beta \neq 1$$

$$\frac{\partial K^*}{\partial \alpha} = \frac{-i(1+\beta) + p' + \beta r - \mu}{(1-\alpha+\beta)^2} \gtreqless 0 \text{ iff } i \lesseqgtr \frac{p' + \beta r - \mu}{1+\beta}, \quad \alpha - \beta \neq 1$$

$$\text{where } \frac{p' + \beta r - \mu}{1+\beta} = \frac{SV + SCR - \Sigma \overline{SC}}{c + v + A}$$

$$\frac{\partial K^*}{\partial \beta} = \frac{r(1-\alpha) - p' + \alpha i + \mu}{(1-\alpha+\beta)^2} \gtreqless 0 \text{ iff } r \gtreqless \frac{p' - \alpha i - \mu}{1-\alpha}, \quad \alpha - \beta \neq 1$$

$$\text{where } \frac{p' - \alpha i - \mu}{1-\alpha} = \frac{SV - iD - \Sigma \overline{SC}}{c + v - D}$$

NOTES

1. The estimates in this paragraph come from the International Monetary Fund (1990); they apply to the total of developing countries and include short-term debt.

2. On orthodox development theory and its differences from radical approaches, see Resnick, Sinisi and Wolff (1985).

3. In fact, one longstanding critic of the benefits of foreign aid for developing country growth continues to plead his case; see Bauer (1984).

4. See, e.g., Fishlow's critique of Cline (1983) in Ruccio and Kim (1986).

5. This summary of the orthodox approach is not meant to imply that the differences among and between mainstream economists—in their explanations of the debt crisis and in their proposed solutions—are unimportant. The various strategies advocated by orthodox economists for overcoming the debt crisis, e.g., export promotion, currency devaluation, seizing foreign assets, and/or capping interest payments, would, if implemented, have radically different implications for the development of both advanced capitalist and Third World countries. The point here is that orthodox ecomomists are biased toward considering some kinds of development policies to the exclusion of others—toward which radical economists would be equally but differently biased—because of their framework of analysis.

6. See the review by de Janvry (1981, 50–55). The unequal exchange debate began with Emmanuel (1972); critics of Emmanuel include Bettelheim (in Emmanuel 1972, 271–322), de Janvry and Kramer (1979), Evans (1984), and Szentes (1985).

7. The notion that capital-importing countries are "exploited" by capital-exporting countries has been developed most recently by Roemer (1988, 105).

8. Elsewhere, MacEwan (1987) has analyzed the external debt crisis as part of a more general "crisis of imperial decline."

9. There are, however, neoclassical models in which countries may not always gain from

trade, as when "distortions" are present, e.g., if there are non-economic objectives or if "largeness" distorts product or factor markets; see Bhagwati and Srinivasan (1983).

10. Palma (1978) observes that radical development economists have been more successful in inverting the neoclassical paradigm—for example, in arguing that foreign trade, instead of promoting economic development, actually creates obstacles to development—than in formulating an alternative position.

11. Frank has elaborated his theory of dependency in numerous texts (1967; 1969; 1972; 1978; 1979; 1984). Another version of dependency theory, originally published in Spanish in 1971, was presented by Cardoso and Faletto (1979); Cardoso (1977), in fact, challenged the originality of Frank's approach.

12. See the surveys by Foster-Carter (1978) and Ruccio and Simon (1987, 142–56).

13. For a more extended discussion of Brenner's further criticisms, see Ruccio and Simon (1987, 137–42).

14. For a discussion of both the positive contributions and limitations of Lipietz's "regulation theory" approach, see Ruccio (1989).

15. Wright (1985) and Resnick and Wolff (1987) discuss the diverse interpretations of Marx's concept of class. Richards (1986) chooses to employ the property relations/individual choice approach to class; Ruccio (1988), in turn, has criticized that approach, associated with the "rational choice" school of radical economics.

16. Marx explicitly refers to class as a process in the *Grundrisse* (1973, 258): "Capital is not a simple relation, but a *process*, in whose various moments it is always capital." The stress here on class as a process is based on an interpretation of Marxian theory in which class refers to one particular social process aming the many that comprise social life.

17. The feudal class process, in contrast, involves appropriation of surplus labor in the form of feudal rent (in kind, in labor, or in money). Different class processes are defined by the different ways in which surplus labor is pumped out of the direct producers; see Resnick and Wolff (1987, ch. 3).

18. Here and throughout I will assume, with Marx in *Capital*, vol. 1, that commodities exchange at their values and that circulating capital alone (with yearly value $c+v$) is advanced in the production sphere. Consideration of the issues involved in transformation to prices of production, fixed capital, etc. would modify but not fundamentally change the thrust of the analysis. See Wolff, Callari and Roberts (1984) and Roberts (1987) for a treatment of value-theoretic issues in line with the approach taken here.

19. The choice here to focus on the process of accumulating productive capital should not be interpreted to mean that capital accumulation is the only or most important process involved in reproducing the fundamental class position of the industrial capitalist. It is only one of many conditions financed by subsumed class distributions of surplus value; others include managerial supervision, access to the means of production, sales, and the adjudication of contract disputes. The focus on capital accumulation is for illustrative purposes only.

20. In the former case, the prior exploitation of developing country workers must have occurred before the commodity is exported; export allows the enterprise to realize the surplus value necessary to make the subsumed class payment of interest. In the case of new debts, extraction of surplus value is merely postponed until a later date.

21. Thus, for example, changes in the external terms of trade will affect export earnings and, therefore, the foreign exchange available for debt service payments. Debt service may also depend on export earnings, as in the case where the borrower is also a producer of exports. In this case, the ability to realize the surplus value contained in the exported commodities, and not

the hard currency earnings per se, is a necessary condition for making interest payments.

22. As, for example, in Chile during 1983–84; see Ffrench-Davis and de Gregorio (1985).

23. For a fuller discusion of the class effects of orthodox (neoclassical and structuralist) stabilization and adjustment policies, see Ruccio (1991).

24. Of course, such capital outflows may also be used to secure foreign *non-class* positions, by purchasing the bonds and securities of institutions other than industrial capitalists, e.g., foreign governments and financial enterprises.

25. Equation (3) would be rewritten as $i \leq (\Delta SV + \Delta SCR)/\Delta D$. In addition, the term iD in equation (1″) below now includes both subsumed class and non-class interest payments to foreign creditors.

26. Third World capitalists may engage in foreign investment even when the rate of return is less than the "internal" rate of profit, if there is uncertainty concerning future exchange rates or their control over domestic bank accounts, and foreign investments are considered more secure.

REFERENCES

Amariglio, J. 1988. "The Body, Economic Discourse, and Power: An Economist's Introduction to Foucault." *History of Political Economy* 20 (4): 583–613.

Amin, S. 1974. "Accumulation and Development: A Theoretical Model." *Review of African Political Economy*, no. 1: 9–26.

——. 1988. "*Accumulation on a World Scale*: Thirty Years Later." *Rethinking Marxism* 1 (Summer): 54–75.

Bacha, E. L., and Diaz Alejandro, C. F. 1982. "International Financial Intermediation: A Long and Tropical View." Essays in International Finance No. 127. International Finance Section, Department of Economics, Princeton University. May.

Bagchi, A. K. 1982. *The Political Economy of Underdevelopment*. Cambridge: Cambridge University Press.

Bardhan, P. 1986. "Marxist Ideas in Development Economics: An Evaluation." In *Analytical Marxism*, ed. J. Roemer, 64–77. Cambridge: Cambridge University and Paris: Edition de la Maison des Sciences de l'Homme.

Barone, C. 1983. "Dependency, Marxist Theory and Salvaging the Idea of Capitalism in South Korea." *Review of Radical Political Economics* 15 (Spring): 43–67.

——. 1984. "Reply to Martin Hart-Landsberg." *Review of Radical Political Economics* 16 (Summer-Fall): 195–97.

Bauer, P. T. 1984. *Reality and Rhetoric: Studies in the Economics of Development*. Cambridge: Harvard University Press.

Becker, D. G. et al. 1987. *Postimperialism: International Capitalism and Development in the Late Twentieth Century*. Boulder, CO: Lynne Rienner Publishers.

Bell, D. E., and Reich, M. R., eds. 1988. *Health, Nutrition, and Economic Crises: Approaches to Policy in the Third World*. Dover, MA: Auburn House Publishing Company.

Bhagwati, J. N., and Srinivasan, T. N. 1983. *Lectures on International Trade*. Cambridge: M.I.T. Press.

Brenner, R. 1977. "The Origins of Capitalist Development: A Critique of Neo-Smithian Marxism." *New Left Review*, no. 104 (July-August): 25–90.

Brewer, A. 1980. *Marxist Theories of Imperialism: A Critical Survey*. London: Routledge & Kegan Paul.

Bryan, R. 1987. "The State and the Internationalisation of Capital: An Approach to Analysis." *Journal of Contemporary Asia* 17 (3): 253–75.

Canitrot, A. 1980. "Discipline as the Central Economic Objective of Economic Policy: An Essay on the Economic Programme of the Argentine Government Since 1976." *World Development* 8 (11): 913–28.

Cardoso, F. H. 1977. "The Consumption of Dependency Theory in the United States." *Latin American Research Review* 12 (3): 7–24.

Cardoso, F. H., and Faletto, E. 1979. *Dependency and Development in Latin America*. Trans. M. M. Urquidi. Berkeley: University of California Press.

Chakravarty, S. 1987. "Marxist Economics and Contemporary Developing Economies." *Cambridge Journal of Economics* 11 (March): 3–22.

Chenery, H. B., and Strout, A. M. 1966. "Foreign Assistance and Economic Development." *American Economic Review* 56 (September): 679–733.

Cline, W. R. 1983. *International Debt and the Stability of the World Economy*. Washington, D.C.: Institute for International Economics.

Cornia, G. A.; Jolly, R.; and Stewart, F., eds. 1988. *Adjustment with a Human Face*. 2 vols. Oxford: Oxford University Press.

Cumby, R., and Levich, R. 1987. "On the Definition and Magnitude of Recent Capital Flight." In *Capital Flight and Third World Debt*, ed. D. R. Lessard and J. Williamson, 27–67. Washington, D.C.: Institute for International Economics.

Deere, C. D. 1986. "The Peasantry in Political Economy: Trends of the 1980s." Paper presented at session, "Peasant Studies: Obstacles to Theoretical Advances." Latin American Studies Association Meetings, 23–25 October, Boston, MA.

de Janvry, A. 1981. *The Agrarian Question and Reformism in Latin America*. Baltimore: Johns Hopkins University Press.

de Janvry, A., and Kramer, F. 1979. "The Limits of Unequal Exchange." *Review of Radical Poltical Economics* 11 (Winter): 3–15.

DeWitt, R. P., and Petras, J. F. 1979. "Political Economy of International Debt: The Dynamics of Financial Capital." In *Debt and the Less Developed Countries*, ed. J. D. Aronson, 191–215. Boulder, CO: Westview Press.

Emmanuel, A. 1972. *Unequal Exchange: A Study of the Imperialism of Trade*. New York: Monthly Review Press.

Evans, D. 1984. "A Critical Assessment of Some Neo-Marxian Trade Theories." *Journal of Development Studies* 20 (January): 202–26.

Evans, P. 1985. "After Democracy: Recent Studies of Class, State, and Industrialization." *Latin American Research Review* 20 (2): 149–60.

Fagen, R. R.; Deere, C. D.; and Coraggio, J. L., eds. 1986. *Transition and Development: Problems of Third World Socialism*. New York: Monthly Review Press.

Feinberg, R. E., and Ffrench-Davis, R., eds. 1988. *Development and External Debt in Latin America: Bases for a New Consensus*. Notre Dame, IN: University of Notre Dame Press.

Ffrench-Davis, R., ed. 1983. *Relaciones Financieras Externas y su Efecto en la Economia Latinoamericana*. Mexico: Fondo de Cultura Económica.

Ffrench-Davis, R., and de Gregorio, J. 1985. "La renegociación de la deuda externa de Chile: Antecedentes y comentarios." *Colección estudios CIEPLAN*, no. 17 (September): 9–32.

Foster-Carter, A. 1978. "The Modes of Production Controversy." *New Left Review*, no. 107 (January/February): 47–77.

Frank, A. G. 1967. *Capitalism and Underdevelopment in Latin America*. New York: Monthly Review Press.

———. 1969. *Latin America: Underdevelopment or Revolution*. New York: Monthly Review Press.

———. 1972. *Lumpenbourgeoisie, Lumpendevelopment: Dependence, Class, and Politics in Latin America*. New York: Monthly Review Press.

———. 1978. *World Accumulation 1492-1978*. New York: Monthly Review Press.

———. 1979. *Dependent Accumulation and Underdevelopment*. New York: Monthly Review Press.

———. 1984. *Critique and Anti-Critique: Essays on Dependence and Reformism*. New York: Monthly Review Press.

Gourevitch, P. A. 1978. "The International System and Regime Formation: A Critical Review of Anderson and Wallerstein." *Comparative Politics* 10 (April): 419–38.

Gunnarsson, C. 1985. "Development Theory and Third World Industrialisation: A Comparison of Patterns of Industrialisation in 19th Century Europe and the Third World." *Journal of Contemporary Asia* 15 (2): 183–206.

Hart-Landsberg, M. 1984. "Capitalism and Third World Economic Development: A Critical Look at the South Korean 'Miracle.'" *Review of Radical Political Economics* 16 (Summer-Fall): 181–93.

Hawley, J. 1979. "The Internationalization of Capital: Banks, Eurocurrency, and the Instability of the World Monetary System." *Review of Radical Political Economics* 11 (Winter): 78–90.

Hopkins, T. K., and Wallerstein, I. et al. 1982. *World-Systems Analysis: Theory and Methodology*. Beverly Hills: Sage Publications.

International Monetary Fund. 1990. *World Economic Outlook*. Washington, D.C.: International Monetary Fund.

Jenkins, R. 1984. "Divisions Over the International Division of Labour." *Capital and Class*, no. 22 (Spring): 28–57.

Laclau, E. 1971. "Feudalism and Capitalism in Latin America." *New Left Review*, no. 67 (May/June): 19–38.

Landsberg, M. 1979. "Export-led Industrialization in the Third World: Manufacturing Imperialism." *Review of Radical Political Economics* 11 (Winter): 50–63.

Lewis, W. A. 1984. "The State of Development Theory." *American Economic Review* 74 (March): 1–10.

Lipietz, A. 1987. *Mirages and Miracles: The Crises of Global Fordism.* Trans. D. Macey. London: Verso.

MacEwan, A. 1985. "The Current Crisis in Latin America." *Monthly Review* 36 (February): 1–18.

———. 1987. "Imperial Decline and International Disorder: An Illustration from the Debt Crisis." In *The Imperiled Economy, Book 1: Macroeconomics from a Left Perspective*, ed. R. Cherry et al., 205–14. New York: Union for Radical Political Economics.

Marx, Karl. 1973. *Grundrisse.* Trans. M. Nicolaus. New York: Vintage Books.

———. 1977. *Capital.* Vol. 1. Trans. B. Fowkes. London: Vintage Books.

———. 1981. *Capital.* Vol. 3. Trans. D. Fernbach. London: Vintage Books.

Norton, B. 1988. "The Power Axis: Bowles, Gordon, and Weisskopf's Theory of Postwar U.S. Accumulation." *Rethinking Marxism* 1 (Fall): 6–43.

Palma, G. 1978. "Dependency Theory: A Formal Theory of Underdevelopment or a Methodology for the Analysis of Concrete Situations of Underdevelopment." *World Development* 6 (July-August): 881–924.

Payer, C. 1974. *The Debt Trap: The International Monetary Fund and the Third World.* New York: Monthly Review Press.

———. 1982. *The World Bank: A Critical Analysis.* New York: Monthly Review Press.

Resnick, S. A., and Wolff, R. D. 1987. *Knowledge and Class: A Marxian Critique of Political Economy.* Chicago: University of Chicago.

Resnick, S.; Sinisi, J.; and Wolff, R. 1985. "Class Analysis of International Economic Relations." In *An International Political Economy*, ed. W. L. Hollist and F. L. Tullis, 87–123. Boulder, CO: Westview Press.

Richards, A. 1986. *Development and Modes of Production in Marxian Economics: A Critical Evaluation.* Fundamentals of Pure and Applied Economics 12. New York: Harwood Academic Publishers.

Richards, L. 1977. "The Context of Foreign Aid: Modern Imperialism." *Review of Radical Political Economics* 9 (Winter): 43–75.

Roberts, B. 1987. "Marx After Steedman: Separating Marxism From 'Surplus Theory'." *Capital and Class*, no. 32 (Fall): 84–103.

Roemer, J. 1988. *Free to Lose: An Introduction to Marxist Economic Philosophy.* Cambridge: Harvard University Press.

Ruccio, D. F. 1987. "State, Class, and Transition in Nicaragua." *Latin American Perspectives* 15 (Spring): 50–91.

———. 1988. "The Merchant of Venice, or Marxism in the Mathematical Mode." *Rethinking Marxism* 1 (Winter): 36–68.

———. 1989. "Fordism on a World Scale: International Dimensions of Regulation." *Review of Radical Political Economics* 21 (4): 33–53

——. 1991. "When Failure Becomes Success: Class and the Debate Over Stabilization and Adjustment." *World Development* (forthcoming).

Ruccio, D. F., and Kim, K. S., eds. 1986. *Debt and Development in Latin America.* Notre Dame: University of Notre Dame Press.

Ruccio, D. F.; Resnick, S.; and Wolff, R. 1991. "Class Beyond the Nation-State." *Review of Radical Political Economics/Capital and Class* (forthcoming).

Ruccio, D. F., and Simon, L. H. 1987. "Radical Theories of Development: Dependency, the Modes of Production School, and Amin." In *The Political Economy of Development and Underdevelopment*, ed. C. K. Wilber, 121–73. New York: Random House.

Singh, A. 1986. "The Great Continental Divide: Asian and Latin American Countries in the World Economic Crisis." *Labour and Society* 11 (September): 415–32.

Skocpol, T. 1977. "Wallerstein's World Capitalism: A Theoretical and Historical Criticism." *American Journal of Sociology* 82 (March): 1075–89.

Szentes, T. 1985. *Theories of World Capitalist Economy: A Critical Survey of Conventional, Reformist and Radical Views*. Budapest: Akademai Kiado.

Taylor, J. G. 1979. *From Modernization to Modes of Production: A Critique of the Sociologies of Development and Underdevelopment.* London: Macmillan.

Taylor, L. 1988. "Macro Effects of Myriad Shocks: Developing Countries in the World Economy." In *Health, Nutrition, and Economic Crises: Approaches to Policy in the Third World*, ed. D. E. Bell and M. R. Reich, 17–37. Dover, MA: Auburn House Publishing.

Thomas, C. Y. 1984. *The Rise of the Authoritarian State in Peripheral Societies*. New York: Monthly Review Press.

Wallerstein, I. 1974. *The Modern World-System I: Capitalist Agriculture and the Origins of the European World-Economy in the Sixteenth Century.* New York: Academic Press.

——. 1980. *The Modern World-Sytem II: Mercantilism and the Consolidation of the European World-Economy, 1600–1750.* New York: Acadmic Press.

Warren, B. 1973. "Imperialism and Capitalist Industrialization." *New Left Review*, no. 81 (September/ October): 3–44.

——. 1980. *Imperialism: Pioneer of Capitalism.* Ed. J. Sender. London: Verso.

Willoughby, J. 1986. *Capitalist Imperialism, Crisis and the State.* Fundamentals of Pure and Applied Economics 7. New York: Harwood.

Wolff, R.; Callari, A.; and Roberts, B. 1984. "A Marxian Alternative to the Traditional 'Transformation Problem.'" *Review of Radical Political Economics* 16 (Summer/ Fall): 115–35.

Wolpe, H., ed. 1980. *The Articulation of Modes of Production: Essays from "Economy and Society."* London: Routledge & Kegan Paul.

World Bank. 1980. *World Tables.* 2d ed. Baltimore: Johns Hopkins University Press.

——. 1988. *World Development Report, 1988.* Washington, D.C.: World Bank.

Wright, E. O. 1985. *Classes.* London: Verso.

POWER, CLASS AND ECONOMIC DEVELOPMENT: A COMMENT ON RUCCIO

Anthony Brewer

THE CONTEXT

The main facts of economic growth in less developed countries (LDCs) are now well known.[1] From 1950 to 1980, total output grew considerably faster in LDCs, taken together, than in more developed countries (MDCs). Population grew faster in LDCs (though it is now slowing down), so the record is less impressive in terms of per-capita income, but the LDCs at least held their own in comparison with MDCs.[2] Industrial output and employment grew faster than other sectors, while agriculture declined in relative importance and shed labor. Industrial exports expanded rapidly, and savings and investments as a share of GNP increased from rather low levels (typically around or below 10 percent) to levels of 20–30 percent, close to those in developed capitalist countries. Social indicators, such as life expectancy and literacy, show even more dramatic gains. Capitalist development in LDCs has been a striking success, one that hardly anyone predicted, and one that has not been as widely recognized as it should be.[3]

Growth has, however, been very uneven. Some countries have developed very rapidly, while at the other end of the scale per-capita incomes have actually fallen in a few. Within each country, development has typically been uneven between regions and sectors, and the benefits have not been equally shared. Growth of industrial exports has been concentrated in relatively few countries (notably the four "little tigers" of East Asia). There is, of course, nothing very surprising in this; it is the normal pattern of capitalist growth, but the reasons why some countries have been so much more successful than others are still not well understood.

Panos Tsakloglou and the editors of this volume made helpful comments on an earlier draft, but should not be blamed for the result.

As Ruccio above stresses, the early 1980s were much less happy. Growth rates overall fell, though some growth continued. It is too early for a final judgment, but it seems more likely that this setback was a (moderately severe) cyclical downturn, with all the misery that downturns always bring, rather than a real change in the trend. Capitalist growth has, after all, always been cyclical as well as uneven. The debt crisis may be a more serious matter. It is not difficult to see why debt became a problem for some (not all) LDCs in the 1980s; the low or negative real interest rates of the 1970s tempted governments and other bodies to borrow on a very large scale, and they were caught out by the combination of a large, unexpected increase in real interest rates and falling export revenues. The crucial question is whether growth in production and exports can resume, at rates comparable to those of the earlier period, and whether real interest rates will soon return to more normal levels. It is safe to predict that debt will remain a serious problem for some countries and regions, and not for others; where the dividing the line will be drawn remains to be seen.

Radical (and orthodox) theories of development have been rather slow in coming to terms with the changing world scene; indeed, the "dependency" theories which dominated radical development economics for a time were based on a flat denial of the obvious facts of capitalist development summarized above. Since the 1970s, however, radical writers have broken away from the dependency approach and started to explore in new directions, as Ruccio explains above. After a few comments on orthodox theories and dependency theory, I will explain why I regard the analysis of political power and of state policy as the most urgent tasks for radical development economics. Ruccio's emphasis on class rather than national interests fits in well with this view, but he chooses to emphasize transfers of surplus value and the formal classification of different types of payments.

"ORTHODOX" DEVELOPMENT ECONOMICS

A natural way to introduce a discussion of radical economics is to compare it with "orthodox" theories, but in development economics, it is not clear quite what the orthodoxy is, or where the dividing line between orthodox and radical views should be drawn. A useful, if rather crude, distinction can be drawn between "structuralist" and "neoclassical" theories (e.g., Little 1982, 19). Structuralists see the world as inflexible, because of a variety of bottlenecks and constraints. Supplies and demands are typically inelastic, at least in important sectors, so the price mechanism is relatively ineffective, and growth is only possible with widespread government intervention and planning. By contrast, neoclassical economics is "a paradigm that tells one to investigate markets and prices, perhaps expecting them to work well, but also to be on the watch for aberrations and ways of correcting them" (Little 1982, 25). Structuralists and neoclassicists have at least one thing in common. They treat state policy as exogenous, not as something to be explained (except in a rather casual sense: "mistaken" policies may be attributed to the in-fluence of mistaken theories). Radicals, by contrast, typically treat state policies as things to be explained, along with the actions of other agents.

Structuralism was once the orthodoxy in development economics, but since the 1960s it has come under sustained attack from neoclassical writers. Structuralist concerns appeared increasingly irrelevant, and some structuralist models, at least, were too crude to stand up to further examination. It is, however, still much too early to speak of a new, neoclassical orthodoxy; the fact is that there is now no well-defined orthodoxy. The neoclassical revival has had very little influence on government policy in most LDCs, which remains unrepentantly structuralist.[4]

The term "neoclassical" is sometimes used (by radicals) as if it were a term of abuse. Neoclassical analysis, at its best, consists of a close examination of the rational behaviour of individuals, and of the constraints they are subject to. No radical should object to this. It is true that neoclassicals often give the market the benefit of any doubt, where many radicals do just the opposite, but it is entirely possible to learn from neoclassical writings without being compelled to accept laissez-faire policy conclusions (cf. Bardhan 1985).

DEPENDENCY THEORY

The unexpected success of capitalism in the Third World has precipitated a crisis in radical development economics, as "dependency" theory collapsed and left something of a vacuum. In its simplest form, dependency theory makes the claim that capitalism cannot generate development, so Third World countries face a stark choice between socialist transformation or continued stagnation and poverty. The world system, in this view, is divided into the "center" and the "periphery"; the relations between them are such that the center develops while the periphery experiences, in Ruccio's words, "either underdevelopment or distorted and dependent development."

With hindsight, it is fairly clear why this account proved false. The simple division of the world into center and periphery does not adequately capture the variety of conditions in the Third World. Where do the oil-rich countries (major ultimate creditors in the system of international indebtedness) or the newly industrializing countries fit in? It is possible to force awkward cases like these into the center-periphery framework, but why would anyone want to? Better to abandon the attempt, and concentrate on the reasons why some LDCs have grown so much faster than others. The idea that the periphery was doomed to stagnate was simply an act of political faith, while the attempt to dismiss observed growth as "distorted and dependent" was a transparent attempt to preserve the theory from the verdict of recent experience. What, after all, would undistorted and independent growth be? Merely to pose the question reveals its utopian character.

Challenged to explain why capitalism in the periphery should stagnate, contrary to all previous experience of capitalism in MDCs, dependency theorists pointed to the exploitation of the periphery by the center, through a variety of mechanisms including debt interest. This argument directs attention away from the real issues. In a Marxist sense, the workers in every capitalist country are exploited. What passport the exploiters carry, or where they live, is not important in itself; what matters is the use that is made of the surplus, and the rate and composition of investment. Investment has increased massively in LDCs, but the increase, like everything else, has been very unequal; some LDCs now invest a larger fraction of GNP than most MDCs; others have a long way to go. Countries with low investment rates are not, in general, the most indebted or those with the largest outflows of surplus. Large parts of Africa have grown very slowly, not because they were exploited by world capitalism, but because they were neglected by it. I suggest that attention should be switched to the determinants of profitability, and hence of the incentive to invest.[5]

In addition, some dependency theorists argued that state policy has been actively hostile to development. Thus, Frank claimed that there is no hope of a progressive national bourgeoisie taking control of the state and "leading the economy and people out of underdevelopment" (1969, 118), because the the state is dominated by export-import traders and agricultural export interests who support a "policy of underdevelopment" (1972, 13). This claim may have some merits when applied to Latin America in the nineteenth century, but for the modern period it is simply ludicrous; virtually every LDC has adopted policies of import substitution which discriminate very heavily against importers and exporters. Capitalist states have not adopted socialist policies, of course, nor have they done as much as they might for the poorest of their citizens. However disappointing this may be to radicals, it does not justify the quite different claim that they have neglected (capitalist) development. The interesting question is the very opposite of the one proposed by dependency theorists: how was it that so many LDCs adopted policies of industrialization at a time when domestic industrial capital, the ultimate beneficiary of such policies, was still very weak, or virtually nonexistent?

CLASSES AND CLASS STRUCTURES

The main strength of radical analyses, in my view, is not in the theory of value, surplus value and exploitation (cf. Brewer 1986), but in the analysis of classes, class structures, and the state. Radicals, unlike structuralists or neoclassicals, treat the state as an integral part of the system and try to explain state policies in terms of the interests of the dominant classes and the alliances between them.

Industrial capitalism, once it is fully developed, tends to produce very similar results everywhere; "the country that is more developed industrially only shows, to the less developed, the image of its own future" (Marx 1976, 91). The process by which it establishes itself, however, is very different in different countries and regions, depending on their starting point, on whether the country is early or late in developing, and so on. Class structures and class alliances are particularly complex during the transition, which has reached different stages in different parts of the Third World. Analysis of the relation between class structures and state policies offers a real hope of understanding the different paths of development in different LDCs. As yet, there is no satisfactory general theory of the transition to capitalism and the process of industrialization, so I will point to three examples which I think show something of the potential of class analysis. All of them trace important aspects of the movement towards a fully capitalist economy, in specific cases, and all owe much to Marx's account of primitive accumulation.

First, consider Giovanni Arrighi's (1970) study of the proletarianisation of the African peasantry in Rhodesia.[6] Mine owners initially found it difficult to recruit a sufficient labor force, not because peasants were immune to market stimuli (as structuralists would have it), but because they responded quite rationally; working their own farms gave a better return. The settlers, however, controlled the state, and were able to seize ownership of the land and impose a combination of rent and taxes which induced the peasants to supply both food and labor at prices favorable to capitalist mining. Arrighi's analysis of the behaviour of peasants is entirely consistent with neoclassical theories of labor supply; state action simply shifted the "initial endowments," in the standard terminology of economic theory.

Another example is Alain de Janvry's (1981) study of the relative stagnation of agricultural production in Latin America. There is only space here to sketch some of the main points of a complex and important piece of work.[7] De Janvry argues that Latin American countries are dominated by an alliance between urban capitalists and rural landed interests; in some countries urban capital rules alone, in others it is the senior partner. Import-substituting industrialization serves the interests of urban industrial capital, but potentially threatens the interests of landowners; agricultural policies are the result of a difficult compromise between them. Low wages are good for profits and for accumulation, and low food prices help to keep wages down; conversely, low wages keep the demand for food down, and hence help to keep food prices low.[8] Agricultural exports, however, are still needed. De Janvry describes a set of policies designed to square this circle. Food prices are held down by food imports and price controls. Food production is therefore relatively unprofitable and is left by default to the peasant sector, while capitalist farms concentrate on export crops and are given much more favorable treatment. Peasants are squeezed onto marginal plots, and have to supply some labor to make a living (this is like the African case discussed above), so they constitute a cheap labor force for capitalist farms. Input prices are distorted by tariffs to favor mechanization (which is labor saving) but discourage the use of fertilizers (land saving), to depress wages but keep up rents.

Neoclassical writers have argued that agricultural stagnation is caused by distorted prices; de Janvry agrees, but argues that the distortions must themselves be explained as the consequence of class interests acting through the political system. Similarly, what he calls "technological determinists" blame backward technology, while "neo-Malthusians" concentrate on the way population growth has kept pace with agricultural output; both lines of argument rephrase the question rather than providing a solution. Population growth is the result of rational behaviour by peasants, while technological backwardness is the result of state policy and market distortions. Like Arrighi, de Janvry insists that peasant behaviour is entirely rational, given the circumstances they find themselves in; instead of rejecting standard economic models, he adds something to them.

A final example is Colin Leys' (1978) examination of Kenya. In pre-colonial and colonial Kenya, he argues, an indigenous class of "accumulators" (predecessors of an indigenous bourgeoisie) had emerged. In the colonial phase, their progress was blocked by the effective monopoly of opportunities held by settlers, but they were able to dominate indigenous politics, invest in education, and then move into positions in the state apparatus. After independence was achieved, "the state apparatus superintended a series of measures which rapidly enlarged the sphere and the rate of indigenous capital accumulation" (Leys 1978, 250), through licensing, state enterprises, direction of credit, and so on. The nascent national bourgeoisie displaced settlers (using the capitalist structures created by imperialism), moving first into commercial agriculture, then into trade, and finally into manufacturing. The state sponsored the formation of a national bourgeoisie because it was controlled by those who were becoming the national bourgeoisie.

CONCLUSION

The rate and pattern of economic development are shaped by the conflicts of classes and other interest groups in the political arena, as well as by individual choices in markets. Individual choices can be analyzed using standard neoclassical methods; the great strength of radical economics is that it can combine the analysis of individual choices with an account of the control and use of political power.

My approach has much in common with that taken by Ruccio above. I have, however, a number of doubts about his strategy of examining flows of payments and relating them to surplus value.[9] Ruccio's models of capital accumulation take little account of the incentive to invest; they implicitly assume that outflows of interest are automatically deducted from investment, and borrowing automatically added to it. I would argue that investment opportunities are the primary factor, and that flows of borrowing and of interest payments follow. The stress should be on the determinants of profitability, and hence on production relations and the framework set by state policy. In addition, Ruccio's classification of different types of revenue is derived by a priori deduction from the basic concepts of capital, surplus value, and so on. It could equally well be used to analyze the indebtedness of LDCs or of the U.S.A. (which became one of the largest debtors during the 1980s). There is, of course, nothing wrong with this, but it needs to be complemented by historical analysis of class formation and transformation in specific stages in the process of development, if it is to avoid falling into ahistorical formalism.

NOTES

1. As Ruccio above says, all "facts" are, in a sense, theoretical; different theories may conceptualize the facts summarized here differently, but they must still account for them.

2. In many sources (e.g., World Bank 1988), middle income countries seem to have done particularly well, and the poorest seem to have fallen behind. This is an optical illusion; countries which grow fast soon lift themselves into the middle income category, leaving the slower growing in the low income group.

3. Among radical writers, Warren (1973; 1980) deserves special credit for pointing this out more forcefully than most.

4. That is, given to high levels of protection, quantitative restrictions, exchange controls, overvalued exchange rates, and so on.

5. In the words of John Rae (1965, 29): "It can only be . . . from the effects of some great inherent vice, that, in any community, a very profitable investment for capital can be held out, and yet capital not accumulate with great rapidity." As Ruccio's analysis shows, if profit rates are high, domestic capitalists can accelerate capital accumulation by borrowing, despite the interest cost.

6. For more detail, and for discussion of Arrighi's writings on tropical Africa, which have more in common with dependency theory, see Brewer (1980, 202–6).

7. The analysis is set in a wider framework which owes a lot to Samir Amin, and is thus a modified version of dependency theory (on Amin, see Brewer 1980). The contrast between "articulated" and "disarticulated" accumulation used by Amin and de Janvry is a variant of the center-periphery distinction, and there are also elements of underconsumptionism in de Janvry's model. These could be removed without damaging the main lines of the argument.

8. This is reminiscent of Ricardo, of course, but also of the Soviet industrialization debate: can peasants be exploited to finance industrialization? On the latter, see Sah and Stiglitz (1984).

9. The notion of surplus value is itself a source of problems, since it depends on the labor theory of value, which has well-known, and in my view fatal, shortcomings. The difficulties with the concept of surplus value are severe enough in the context of a closed economy; to discuss international economic relations involves studying open economies, and the problems become insuperable.

REFERENCES

Arrighi, G. 1970. "Labour Supplies in Historical Perspective: A Study of the Proletarianisation of the African Peasantry in Rhodesia." *Journal of Development Studies* 3 (April): 197–234. Reprinted in G. Arrighi and J. S. Saul. 1973. *Essays on the Political Economy of Africa*. New York: Monthly Review Press, 180–234.

Bardhan, B. 1985. "Marxist Ideas in Development Economics: A Brief Evaluation." *Economic and Political Weekly*, Bombay, 30 March, 550-5.

Brewer, A. 1980. *Marxist Theories of Imperialism: A Critical Survey*. London: Routledge and Kegan Paul.

——. 1986. "Marx's *Capital* Today." In *Ideas in Economics*, ed. R. D. Collison Black, 160–75. London: Macmillan.

De Janvry, A. 1981. *The Agrarian Question and Reformism in Latin America*. Baltimore: John Hopkins University Press.

Frank, A. G. 1969. *Capitalism and Underdevelopment in Latin America*. New York: Modern Reader.

——. 1972. *Lumpenbourgeoisie: Lumpendevelopment*. New York: Monthly Review Press.

Leys, C. 1978. "Capital Accumulation, Class Formation and Dependency—The Significance of the Kenyan Case." *Socialist Register 1978*: 241–66.

Little, I. M. D. 1982. *Economic Development: Theory, Policy, and International Relations*. New York: Basic Books.

Marx, K. 1976. *Capital*. Vol. 1. Harmondsworth: Penguin.

Rae, J. 1965. *Statement of Some New Principles on the Subject of Political Economy*. In R. W. James, *John Rae, Political Economist*. Vol. 2. Toronto: University of Toronto Press.

Sah, R. J., and Stiglitz, J. E. 1984. "The Economics of Price Scissors." *American Economic Review* 74 (March): 125–38.

Warren, B. 1973. "Imperialism and Capitalist Industrialization." *New Left Review*, no. 81: 3–44.

——. 1980. *Imperialism, Pioneer of Capitalism*. London: New Left Books.

World Bank. 1988. *World Development Report*. Washington D.C.: World Bank.

CONTRIBUTING AUTHORS

Anthony Brewer is Reader in Economics at the University of Bristol. His work has covered theories of imperialism, Marxism, and the history of economics. His *Marxist Theories of Imperialism: A Critical Survey* recently appeared in a second edition. He is working on *Richard Cantillon: Pioneer of Economic Theory*.

Susan F. Feiner is Associate Professor of Economics at Hampton University. Her publications cover economic history, particularly the political economy of American slavery, the history of economic thought, and economic education. She is current chair of The Commitee for Race and Gender Balance in the Economics Curriculum.

Herbert Gintis is Professor of Economics at the University of Massachusetts, Amherst. He is co-author, with Samuel Bowles, of *Democracy and Capitalism: Property, Community, and the Contradictions of Modern Social Thought*. They are working on a book entitled *Contested Exchange* and, in addition, he is currently editing volumes on the microfoundations of political economy and progressive macroeconomic policy for the 1990s.

Jane Humphries teaches economics at Cambridge University. She has published many articles on the political economy of women's work and the family, and is currently working on a book which integrates women's and children's experiences into an evaluation of British industrialization. Her recent article "Enclosures, Common Rights and Women: The Proletarianization of Families in Late Eighteenth and Early Nineteenth Century Britain," which appeared in *Journal of Economic History*, vol. L, no. 1, was awarded the Arthur H. Cole prize for the outstanding article published in that journal in 1990.

E. K. Hunt is Professor of Economics at the University of Utah. His publications have covered the history of economic thought, Marxism, and critiques of neoclassical theory. Recent books include the second edition of his *History of Economic Thought* and a co-edited volume, *Critical Political Economy*.

Makoto Itoh is Professor of Economics at the University of Tokyo. He has taught at the New School for Social Research, New York University, Thammasat University in Bangkok, Cambridge University, and the Universities of London and Manitoba. He is the author of *The Basic Theory of Capitalism*, *Value and Crisis*, and *The World Economic Crisis and Japanese Capitalism*, co-author of *The Value Controversy*, and author, in Japanese, of *The Theory of Value and Capital* and *Credit and Crisis*, among other books.

David P. Levine is Professor of Economics in the Graduate School of International Studies, University of Denver. He has also held visiting appointments at Stanford University, Université Catholique de Louvain, and Flinders University of South Australia. He is author of *Economic Studies* (1977), *Economic Theory* (two volumes, 1978–81), *Needs, Rights, and the Market* (1988), and, with James Caporaso, of *Theories of Political Economy* (1992). He was a founding editor and continues as a member of the Editorial Board of *Social Concept*.

Julie Matthaei is Professor of Economics at Wellesley College, where she teaches courses on gender and race, radical political economy, and the history of economic thought. She is the author of *An Economic History of Women in America: Women's Work, the Sexual Division of Labor, and the Development of Capitalism* (1982), and *Race, Gender, and Work: A Multicultural Economic History of Women in the United States* (1991), written with Teresa Amott. She is on the Editorial Board of *Social Concept*, and is a member of the Economic Literacy Project of Women for Economic Justice of Boston, and of the Marxist-Feminist 1 Study Group.

Bruce Norton teaches economics at the University of Hartford. His research and publications have focused on contemporary accumulation and crisis theories, especially monopoly capital theory and the "social structures of accumulation approach," as well as economic history and methodology.

Stephen Resnick is Professor of Economics at the University of Massachusetts, Amherst, and a member of the Editorial Board of *Rethinking Marxism*. With Richard Wolff, he is co-author of *Knowledge and Class: A Marxian Critique of Political Economy* and *Economics: Marxian Versus Neoclassical*. They are currently working on a class analysis of the Soviet Union.

Bruce Roberts is Associate Professor of Economics at The College of William and Mary. His published articles cover the history of economic thought, the Marxian theory of value and price, race and gender in economic theory, and economic methodology. He is a member of the Editorial Board of *Rethinking Marxism*.

David F. Ruccio teaches economics and is a Faculty Fellow in the Helen Kellogg Institute for International Studies at the University of Notre Dame. A member of the Editorial Board of *Rethinking Marxism*, he has published numerous journal articles and book chapters on the state and planning in transitional economies, development in Latin America, and methodology in economics. He is currently working with Stephen Resnick and Richard Wolff on *Crisis and Transitions: A Critique of the International Economic Order*, to be published by Westview Press.

Howard J. Sherman is Professor of Economics at the University of California, Riverside. In political economy, his most recent book is *Foundations of Radical Political Economy* (1988); in business cycle analysis, *The Business Cycle: Growth and Crisis Under Capitalism* (1991); in the comparative analysis of economic systems, he has recently co-authored *Comparative Economic Analysis* (1989).

Anwar Shaikh is Professor of Economics at the Graduate Faculty of the New School for Social Research in New York. He was educated at Princeton University (B.Sc.) and Columbia University (Ph.D.). His research and publications cover Marxian economics, international trade theory, non-linear macrodynamics, the welfare state and the social wage, and long-term growth and technical change.

Richard D. Wolff is Professor of Economics at the University of Massachusetts, Amherst. He is co-author, with Stephen Resnick, of *Knowledge and Class: A Marxian Critique of Political Economy* and *Economics: Marxian Versus Neoclassical.* A member of the Editorial Board of *Rethinking Marxism,* he has been active in labor and political movements in New Haven, Connecticut.

AUTHOR INDEX

SUBJECT INDEX